THE BLACK MESSIAH

THE
BLACK
MESSIAH

Albert B. Cleage, Jr.

Africa World Press, Inc.

P.O. Box 1892
Trenton, New Jersey 08607

Africa World Press, Inc.
P.O. Box 1892
Trenton, NJ 08607

©Sheed and Ward Inc.

First AWP edition 1989

Cover design by Ife Nii-Owoo

Library of Congress Catalog Card Number: 88-70198

ISBN: 0-86543-078-0   Paper

Contents

THE BLACK MESSIAH

Introduction

For nearly 500 years the illusion that Jesus was white dominated the world only because white Europeans dominated the world. Now, with the emergence of the nationalist movements of the world's colored majority, the historic truth is finally beginning to emerge— that Jesus was the non-white leader of a non-white people struggling for national liberation against the rule of a white nation, Rome. The intermingling of the races in Africa and the Mediterranean area is an established fact. The Nation Israel was a mixture of Chaldeans, Egyptians, Midianites, Ethiopians, Kushites, Babylonians and other dark peoples, all of whom were already mixed with the black people of Central Africa.

That white Americans continue to insist upon a white Christ in the face of all historical evidence to the contrary and despite the hundreds of shrines to Black Madonnas all over the world, is the crowning demonstration of their white supremacist conviction that all things good and valuable must be white. On the other hand, until black Christians are ready to challenge this lie, they have not freed themselves from their spiritual bondage to the white man nor established in their own minds their right to first-class citizenship in Christ's kingdom on earth. Black people cannot build dignity on their knees worshipping a white Christ. We must put down this white Jesus which the white man gave us in slavery and which has been tearing us to pieces.

Black Americans need to know that the historic Jesus was a leader who went about among the people of Israel, seeking to root out the individualism and the identification with their oppressor which had corrupted them, and to give them faith in their own

3

power to rebuild the Nation. This was the real Jesus whose life is most accurately reported in the first three Gospels of the New Testament. On the other hand, there is the spiritualized Jesus, reconstructed many years later by the Apostle Paul who never knew Jesus and who modified his teachings to conform to the pagan philosophies of the white gentiles. Considering himself an apostle to the gentiles, Paul preached individual salvation and life after death. We, as black Christians suffering oppression in a white man's land, do not need the individualistic and otherworldly doctrines of Paul and the white man. We need to recapture the faith in our power as a *people* and the concept of Nation, which are the foundation of the Old Testament and the prophets, and upon which Jesus built all of his teachings 2,000 years ago.

Jesus was a revolutionary black leader, a Zealot, seeking to lead a Black Nation to freedom, so the Black Church must carefully define the nature of the revolution.

What do we mean when we speak of the Black Revolution? I can remember an incident at the beginning of the Harlem Rebellion only a few short years ago when a news reporter snapped an unforgettable picture of a black girl who was present when a black boy was brutally killed by a white apartment house caretaker. She stood there on the sidewalk, her face contorted with anger and frustration, tears streaming down her cheeks, and she screamed at the cops who had rushed to the scene to keep their kind of law and order, "Kill me too! Kill me too!"

This was the absolute in frustration. "The problem of being black in a white man's world is just too big. I don't know what to do with it. So just kill me too and get it over with." That was what she was saying.

Black brothers and sisters all over the country felt a spontaneous identification with that girl because every black person has felt just this kind of frustration. We feel it every day. At every meeting some young black man jumps to his feet screaming, "I can't stand it any longer. Let's take to the streets and get it over with!" We all know how he feels and why he feels that way. Sometimes we go home and say it was a very "nervous" meeting, and everyone knows what we are talking about because each of us has felt that same sense of powerlessness that makes us ache with helplessness and hopelessness and drives us to seek death as an easy way out. Those of us who cry out think of ourselves as revolutionists and participants in the Black Revolution. But a revolution seeks to change conditions. So each day we must decide. Either we are trying to achieve the power to change conditions or we have turned from the struggle and are seeking an heroic moment when we can die in the streets.

As black people, we have entered a revolution rather than the evolution or gradual change which white folks would like us to accept. We want to move fast enough to be able to see that we are moving. And four hundred years of standing still is a long time. We are trying to make the world over so that our children and our children's children can have power and live like human beings. We look at the world in which we live today and we are determined to turn the world upside down.

But when I hear cries of "Kill me too!" I know that that individual no longer has any hope. When he screams, "Let's get together and die in the streets," I know that in his desperate hopelessness this individual has put aside the revolution. Dying in the streets is not revolution. This is escapism. This is suicide. But it is *not* revolution. As long as there is the slightest possibility of victory, we are still engaged in a revolution. But when an individual sees no way to achieve power to change conditions, then the revolution is over. It doesn't make any difference how he spends his remaining time, singing hymns, getting drunk or buying guns. For him the revolution is over.

The Black Church has not always been revolutionary, but it has always been relevant to the everyday needs of black people. The old down-home black preacher who "shouted" his congregation on Sunday morning was realistically ministering to the needs of a black people who could not yet conceive of changing the conditions which oppressed them. If you can't solve your problems, you can at least escape from them! So we had Saturday night to escape in one way, and Sunday morning to pray for repentance and to escape in another way. The Church was performing a valuable and real function. However uneducated the old-time preacher was, he was relevant and significant. What he offered was an ingenious interpretation of a slave Christianity to meet the needs of an oppressed and suffering people. He took it and used it so that black people could go to church on Sunday morning and find the strength to endure white folks for another six days. You could go to church and "shout" and feel that God was just, even though the world in which you lived was unjust. Implicit in every ignorant black preacher's sermon was the faith that God must eventually shake white people over hell-fire, and that after death black people were going to heaven. White people were the oppressors. They were the sinners, they were guilty. Black people were innocent and suffered oppression through no fault of their own. Therefore, they were going to heaven and walk on golden streets, and white people were going to hell. There is still profound truth in this simple message of the primitive Black Church.

But today the Church must reinterpret its message in terms of the needs of a Black Revolution. We no longer feel helpless as black people. We do not feel that we must sit and wait for God to intervene and settle our problems for us. We waited for four hundred years and he didn't do much of anything, so for the next four hundred years we're going to be fighting to change conditions for ourselves. This is merely a new theological position. We have come to understand how God works in the world. Now we know that God is going to give us strength for our struggle. As black preachers we must tell our people that we are God's chosen people and that God is fighting with us as we fight. When we march, when we take it to the streets in open conflict, we must understand that in the stamping feet and the thunder of violence we can hear the voice of God. When the Black Church accepts its role in the Black Revolution, it is able to understand and interpret revolutionary Christianity, and the revolution becomes a part of our Christian faith. Every Sunday morning when we preach from the Old Testament, or when we preach about Jesus, we seek to help black people understand that the struggle in which we are engaged is a cosmic struggle, that the very universe struggles with us when we fight to throw off the oppression of white people. We want black people to understand that they are coming to church to get the strength and direction to go out and fight oppression all week. We don't pray for the strength to endure any more. We pray for the strength to fight heroically.

Basic to our struggle and the revitalization of the Black Church is the simple fact that we are building a totally new self-image. Our rediscovery of the Black Messiah is a part of our rediscovery of ourselves. We could not worship a Black Jesus until we had thrown off the shackles of self-hate. We could not follow a Black Messiah in the tasks of building a Black Nation until we had found the courage to look back beyond the slave block and the slave ship without shame.

In recent years the contradiction inherent in the worship of a white Christ by black people oppressed by whites has become increasingly acute. In the Negro Renaissance after World War I the anguish of this contradiction was voiced by poet Countee Cullen in his famous lines:

> . . . *My conversion came high-priced;*
> *I belong to Jesus Christ, . . .*
> *Lamb of God, although I speak*
> *With my mouth thus, in my heart*
> *Do I play a double part . . . .*
> *Wishing he I served were black . . . ?* *

The widespread repudiation by many black Americans of a white Christ has added to the attractiveness of the Black Muslim movement. But many more black Americans, race conscious enough to

* Abridgement from fifth and sixth stanzas of "Heritage" in *On These I Stand* by Countee Cullen, Copyright 1925 by Harper & Brothers; Renewed 1953 by Ida M. Cullen. By permission of Harper & Row Publishers.

reject a white Christ, have been reluctant to embrace Islam in view of the role played by the Arabs in fostering and carrying on the slave trade in Africa. The result has been the self-exclusion of most black militants from any religious affiliations whatsoever.

The only black leader in this country to meet this problem head-on was Marcus Garvey who organized the African Orthodox Church with a black hierarchy, including a Black God, a Black Jesus, a Black Madonna, and black angels. Forty years ago black Americans apparently were not yet ready for Garvey's religious ideas, although to this day, in every major city, individual Garvey-ites continue to circulate portraits of a Black Jesus. In Africa, however, Garvey's religious ideas played a key role in founding the African Independent Churches which in many countries acted as the center of the liberation movement. As Roosevelt University professor and writer, St. Clair Drake, has pointed out, the Kenya Africans invited one of Garvey's bishops to train and ordain their preachers and to help form the African independent schools and churches out of which the Mau Mau eventually grew.

The Black Church in America has served as the heart and center of the life of black communities everywhere, but, for the most part, without a consciousness of its responsibility and potential power to give a lost people a sense of earthly purpose and direction. During the Black Revolt following the 1954 Supreme Court desegregation decision, the Southern Black Church found that involvement in the struggle of black people for freedom was inescapable. Without a theology to support its actions (actions almost in contradiction to its otherworldly preachings, it provided spokesmen and served as a meeting place and source of emotional inspiration. In the North, where the black man's problems at one time seemed less pressing, the Black Church has failed miserably to relate itself to the seething ghetto rebellions and therefore has practically cut itself off from vast segments of the black community. The Northern Church has been black on the outside only, borrowing its theology, its orientation and its social ideology largely from the white Church and the white power structure.

The present crisis, involving as it does the black man's struggle for survival in America, demands the resurrection of a Black Church with its own Black Messiah. Only this kind of a Black Christian Church can serve as the unifying center for the totality of the black man's life and struggle. Only this kind of a Black Christian Church can force each individual black man to decide where he will stand—united with his own people and laboring and sacrificing in the spirit of the Black Messiah, or individualistically seeking his own advancement and maintaining his slave identification with the white oppressor.

The sermons included in this volume were preached to black people. They are published in the hope that they may help other black people find their way back to the historic Black Messiah, and at the request of many black preachers who are earnestly seeking ways to make their preaching relevant to the complex and urgent needs of the black community. White people who read these pages are permitted to listen to a black man talking to black people.

1/Fear Is Gone

"So God created man in his own image . . ."
(*Genesis* 1:27).

"So God created man in his own image." (Genesis 1:27) This is the essential Christian message which gets so mixed up in the minds of people. God created us in his own image. We intend to live as beings created in the image of God, and everything we do in the church should be designed to help us live that way.

Something has happened to black people in these United States. We are not as we were a few years ago, a few months ago, a few weeks ago. Something has happened to *us*: not to America but to *us*, to the way we think, the way we fight, the way we work together. This is the most important thing that has ever happened in America.

What is that something? It is that fear is gone. Just a few weeks ago we were so different. Down South we were afraid; up North we were afraid. The fear was a very elementary fear. It was not the fear of being brutalized, of being humiliated. Essentially, it was the fear of dying. When the white man in the South said, "Get off the sidewalk," why did we get off? Because we were afraid of dying. We are not afraid any more. So the white man has stopped saying it. Now he is afraid. Now *he* must redefine his relationship with *us*.

Why is fear gone? Fear is gone essentially because we are in the process of becoming a Black Nation, a nation that is as real as if it had a capital, a Congress and a president. We as a people are now dedicated to one purpose, freedom for black people. It is this which makes the difference. We didn't understand what this was before because each of us functioned as an individual. We were afraid to fight because we felt that if we fought we would fight alone and we would die alone. It is hard to stand up and be a man when you are all by yourself. That is the way we were. The difference now is that we are coming together. We are no longer just individuals. We are becoming a Nation. You know that the rest of us are going to support you in every way we can. If you fight back against oppression, we are not going to turn our backs and run away. When you know that, you feel different no matter how much Uncle Tom still remains in you. Now you are part of a Nation, so fear is gone. Everything that is going on in America today stems from this basic fact. Once we were alone. Now we are together. *We* have changed.

We are a Black Nation in a white man's world. Increasingly the white man's world has become an enemy world, recognized as such, an enemy world from which we have been systematically excluded and which we now despise and reject. They can't exclude us any more because we don't want to be in their world. Now we are in our own world, our own Nation, so much so that sometimes we feel uncomfortable because we have to go out into their enemy world to work and to shop. We wish that we could stay with our own people all the time. When you get on the bus and you have an "Afro" or a "Natural" hair-do and the man stares, you think to yourself, "I don't like the way he looks any more than he likes the way I look, and the way I look is just as beautiful to me as the way he looks is beautiful to him."

You can't exclude a man when he doesn't want to come in. You can't tell a man that he can't marry your daughter when he doesn't even want to spit in your face. It is a strange new world that we have created. It keeps the white man confused. He doesn't know what to make of it so he tries to concentrate upon the tangible, a burned-out building, for example. He figures that if he can do something about this physical blight, other things will go back to normal. But there is nothing he can do with bricks and steel and stone that can make us act like he wants us to act because bricks and steel and stone have nothing to do with it. It is not something physical. We are different; unless they deal with us as we are now, they can put up all the bricks and steel and stone that they want to and it won't stay too long.

We have become a Black Nation. You can see it everywhere. The white press doesn't know what to make of it. White journalists are the most confused people in the world. Sometimes when you read the things they write you think you are reading a fairy tale. Hans Christian Anderson is much closer to reality than they are because they don't have any key to understand what's happening. That is because in their minds we are inferior. We can't hate like they hate. We can't believe like they believe. We can't fight like they fight. So they have to make up some kind of story to explain why we do the things we do. Yet the answer is so simple. All they have to accept is the simple fact black people are black but in every other way there is no difference. If they could just accept this simple fact, they would realize why we cannot accept any more than they could the brutalization, the degradation, the indignities, and the criminalities to which we have been subjected. But they can't see that, and so they can't understand our Black Revolution. So they write fairy tales to amuse themselves.

When you look at what is happening, you see how we have changed. The National Student Association recently held a national convention, the same student organization that the CIA financed for years. Some black students went to that convention and said, "We don't care who is paying your bills, if you want us in the student movement you are going to endorse Black Power here and now." And the National Student Association voted to endorse Black Power.

Then the teachers. We have been looking down on black teachers for a long time. We have said that all they cared about was their own individual selves, their clothes, their cars, their social life. But a few weeks ago the American Federation of Teachers had a convention, and the black teachers got together and said what amounted to, "We don't like anything that is going on, and if you don't endorse Black Power we are walking out." You see how a Nation comes into being. A year ago they wouldn't have even opened their mouths at the Convention. The white folks would have picked one of them to speak for the Negroes and that would have been that. But now at every convention black folks put up a sign saying, "Black Caucus. Whitey, stay out!"

This is the beginning of a Black Nation. There was a time when we didn't even want to sit together. If we came into a room and saw a Negro there, we would walk over to the other side of the room and sit down. We didn't want to "segregate" ourselves. But now the first thing we do is "separate" ourselves and get together with all the brothers and sisters to find out what it is that we all want to do. That has been the pattern at every convention that has been held this summer and the white man doesn't know what to do.

The Left had a convention in Chicago, New Left, Old Left, all kinds of Lefts. Black folks went to that convention. The white folks had set up a convention just like white people always set up a convention with a separate Ghetto Day for Black folks. Buses from Detroit, Newark and Cleveland would bring in black folks to put on a show for the white folks. But black folks would have nothing to do with the planning, nothing to do with the organization of convention procedure, nothing to do with the assessment of political realities. White folks have been having Ghetto Days like this for more than 100 years. Only this year black folks weren't interested in any Ghetto Day. So they got together and they drew up a beautiful statement. Even when the newspapers got through with the statement, it was still a beautiful thing. Listen to the Preamble: "We as black people, believe that a United States system that is committed to the practice of genocide, social degradation, the denial of political and cultural self-determination of black people, cannot reform itself. There must be revolutionary change." Then they made thirteen specific Black Power demands. And there wasn't anything that those white leftists could do but accept those demands because without black people there isn't any revolutionary movement in America.

We are the revolution. There are some white people who are poor, who are exploited but they are white. There are some white people who are liberal, but they are white. There are some white people who are radical, but they are white. And in the final analysis all these white people stand together. We know this to be true. So we black people are now demanding the things that we want for ourselves. No white man, whatever he represents himself to be, is going to tell us what to do. This is the message of the conventions, of all the rebellions. It is the message from coast to coast of the burned-out buildings. Black people are going to be free, and we are going to do it ourselves.

What is fear? When I was going to school I remember studying the psychology of fear and the debate over whether the emotional reaction preceded or followed the visceral reaction. Even then I knew it to be nonsense. What does it mean when we say, "Fear is gone"? It doesn't mean that when you get into a situation you don't have an emotional or a visceral reaction. But that is not fear. The emotion, the adrenalin that is pumped into your body can lead you to either *fight* or *flight*. The body is ready for either one. Fear is determined by what you do with that energy. Don't be ashamed if you react, if your pressure goes up, if your heart starts pumping. Just be sure you do the right thing. At work, when they begin to talk about "niggers" and you are supposed to be invisible, don't worry if your heart begins to pump. What matters is, do you speak up, or do you just sit there and pretend not to hear?

We had a Peoples Tribunal to try the officers charged with the massacre of three black youths in the Algiers Motel during the July Rebellion. Right here, beneath the beautiful Black Madonna, witnesses testified. Everything possible had been done by the police to intimidate these black people, and yet they testified and told the truth. Does that mean that as they sat here, their hearts were not pounding? Of course not. They knew that the man was going to brutalize them at the first opportunity, but that wasn't fear because they did what had to be done. A whole lot of you have guilty feelings about being afraid. You needn't have. It is not fear as long as you do what has to be done.

America is set on a disaster course of conflict and violence. The black man cannot accept America as it is. The white man refuses to make the changes necessary for the black man to live in America with dignity and justice. These are two facts. We will not accept conditions as they are, and the white man will not accept the changes which we demand. There is no solution except open conflict and violence. You don't have to feel guilty about that, either. It is his fault, not ours. We say that we are created in the image of God. He refuses to accept that. It is his fault, not ours.

When there is justice there can be love, peace and brotherhood. Only the oppressor can afford to talk about the preservation of law and order without justice. For the oppressed, that is for us, for all black people, to talk about law and order, peace and brotherhood, is either insanity or it is craven cowardice. We have no choice to make. We can't be concerned with law and order, peace and brotherhood, until we first get justice. Securing justice is our basic concern.

There are black people who don't understand that we don't have justice, but they are becoming fewer and fewer. Everything about the elections in Mississippi was crooked. There wasn't any law and order there because there was injustice. They were determined that black people would not be elected. In American cities during the recent rebellion every constitutional right guaranteed citizens was denied to black people. The courts became kangaroo courts. The judges functioned as though they were part of the police department. The newspapers were part of the police department. All the white community came together to protect order, that is, to protect white supremacy, to protect and to preserve injustice. Even as they talked about law and order, they were the perpetrators of injustice and the destroyers of law and order. The police talked about looters in the street, and they themselves were doing more looting every day than the looters in the street.

But injustice had to be preserved. White supremacy had to be maintained. The white man was willing to sacrifice the Constitution, the courts and the law, to preserve what he held sacred, the status quo. To preserve his injustice he was willing to go to any lengths, and he did. Some of you were arrested. You know what they did in the jails, the prisons and the concentration camps. You remember the wanton brutality against men, women and children. And all the time they were talking about law and order.

America is headed for increased racial conflict and violence. There is no escape because the white man is determined to preserve injustice and we are determined that justice is ours by right and that we shall have it. We have decided that we are willing to die rather than continue to suffer the injustice that we have suffered for four hundred years. We have the strength necessary for this kind of struggle because we have come together and we are a Black Nation. But it is going to take every bit of our united strength to withstand the kind of persecution that is being prepared for us.

I don't care how nice you feel inside, how much you would like to go along, how much you wish you could live out your life-time without so much conflict and violence. I am sorry. You were just born at the wrong time. There is no way that that kind of injustice can be preserved. Even when you long for the good old days when you could be a comfortable Uncle Tom, you realize that the good old days are gone forever.

We are living in the midst of a revolution, and in a time of revolution the old values are no longer valid. When they draft you into the army, they take you to camp and teach you how to kill. That is against the values of society but the society has declared that in this emergency it is necessary that you forget what you have been taught. So you learn how to kill and how to kill well. The old values are no longer valid. We have got to understand this. We have got to understand that in a time of revolution the old values must also be rescinded. When America revolted against England, they looted a ship in Boston Harbor. They took the cargo of tea and threw it overboard. They burned everything that they needed to burn because they said, "We are engaged in a revolution, and in revolution the old values must be cast aside." They knew it then because they were engaged in a revolution. They were fighting against injustice and oppression. Now *we* know it.

An old lady called me up the other day. She said that she lived on West Warren Avenue, and she talked about the way "those people" were acting during the Rebellion, how they ran up and down the streets with the things they had taken and told her to get off her front porch or they would burn down her house. (They probably saw her writing down license numbers to give the police.) She said that everything we black people do is wrong and that I should stop fussing with white people and start fussing with black people to get them to do right. She said that she had tried so hard to keep her little house neat and clean, to plant a little grass, to organize a block club. But the black people in her block wouldn't cooperate. They said, "This ain't our community, the man owns it"; and she was hurt because she had wanted to make her block a little Grosse Pointe. She was so happy because a white lady she worked for called her up during the Rebellion and asked her how she was doing and sent her some canned food.

I tried to explain to her that in a time of revolution the old values are no longer valid. The old virtues she had cherished so long, of saving up to buy a little house and putting a fence around it, won't work. It is time for all of us to build a community together, and if you are still thinking of protecting your little thing, trying to make your fence high enough to keep us out, you are wrong. You ought to love the looters because they are part of the Black Nation. If you were too old to participate, then the least you could do was not talk about those who did. It is one struggle and we are in it together. We have got to love one another. We have got to remember that even if at the end of the struggle, down the road a piece, we end up in concentration camps together, we are still brothers and sisters and we must love one another.

White people in America don't understand this. A white daily had an editorial the other day. The U.S. dailies are undoubtedly among the most biased newspapers in the world, but this was a new low even for an Establishment newspaper. The editorial said that H. Rap Brown and the Ku Kluxers who voted twenty times in Mississippi are equally wrong, and if it is accepted that Brown is privileged to foment violence, then the KKK is also so privileged. This is the Hitler technique. Tell a big lie and tell it over and over until the whole world believes it to be true. The press knows that there is a basic difference between H. Rap Brown and the KKK. Brown says one simple thing: that black people must fight for justice by all means necessary, while the KKK says that white people have got to preserve injustice by all means necessary. Do you see the difference? It doesn't become the same thing because the white man's press pretends to believe that it is the same.

We have got to fight injustice by all means necessary. If that is sedition, then we are all guilty. White people in organizations all over the country are joining together in support of one basic philosophic position: we have got to use all means necessary to preserve injustice against black people. That is why conflict and violence are inevitable. The white man could change his position but he is not changing it. The sale of guns to white people has increased by leaps and bounds. Even as they write long articles in newspapers and magazines against black violence in the streets, they have special flights bringing in guns every day to white people in Detroit. They are dedicated to the preservation of injustice. Without injustice they wouldn't need guns. We don't even want to live in their communities or go to their schools. All we want is control over our own communities.

They would have nothing to fear except for the simple fact that they are unwilling to give up their control over our community. They want to live in Dearborn and Grosse Pointe and still control our schools and teach our children, and they are not going to do it. That is why they are buying guns, because we are demanding change. That is why there is going to be conflict and violence. Conflict is inevitable unless the white man agrees to transfer power. We say that to him and he looks the other way. He sets up a New

Detroit Committee to rebuild Detroit. He gives it all kinds of money, but the Committee refuses to realize that its one function is to preside at the transference of power. It could say, "Black people won't accept injustice any longer, let's make some changes." But it won't do that. Instead, it reassembles the same old hackneyed Negro leadership, gives it a new name and tries to deal with it as though it speaks for the black community in order to preserve the same old injustice. But it won't work. Conflict is inevitable, because the white man won't face reality.

Oppression does not destroy a people. It is the acceptance of oppression that destroys. That is why we were sick until we started fighting. Just trying to hold in our indignation made us sick, messed up our minds. That is why a girl who gets a "Natural" feels like a whole new world has opened up to her. We have begun to throw off oppression. We don't know whether we are going to win or lose. All black people in America could be killed within the next five years. But we would be better off dead than accepting oppression. Fear is gone. The white man has got to understand that.

In this period of becoming a Nation the Black Church, conscious of its African roots, becomes increasingly significant. Many black people have given up the church, but the church can become the basis for a new unity in the black community. We ask people to join the church so that they will know that they are brothers and sisters, that they belong to a Black Nation. This church is dedicated to a Black Messiah. This church believes that the purpose of Christianity is to free black people, to rid black people of injustice. This is what we believe. This is why we are so important to the Black Revolution. This is why we need more churches like ours from coast to coast. The church must free our minds, strengthen our bodies and unite our people. This is the task of the church because God created us in his own image and as children of God we must walk with pride and dignity. We are going to be free by any means necessary.

Brothers and sisters, remember that we have agents every Sunday. If someone comes up to you talking about firebombs and guerilla warfare, don't let him make a fool out of you. One group of private investigators is in the city trying to earn a purse of $50,000 by proving a conspiracy. There was no conspiracy except the conspiracy to maintain injustice perpetrated by the white man for the past four hundred years. Let them expose that conspiracy!

Heavenly Father, we thank thee for the opportunity of worshipping in this house. We thank thee that we have this house to come together in. Be with us and help us to do those things that must be done. Let your spirit be in our midst and lead our brothers and sisters to feel the call to join together with us in this task of uniting our people. This we ask in the name of the Black Messiah, Jesus Christ. Amen.

2/A Sense of Urgency

"Behold, the hour is at hand . . ." (*Matthew* 26:45).

This morning's paper has an article listing all the Black Nationalist groups in the city, saying that for all or most of them the Shrine of the Black Madonna is their spiritual home.

There are a lot of different attitudes, different ideas, and different programs, it says, but all of them feel at home here. I think that is one of the reasons why, in Detroit, we move faster and farther and know where we're going in a more complete sense, because we do have this unity. We can come together here, knowing we're all for the Nation, and if we disagree on details, we still are brothers and we love one another.

As time passes, as the revolution in which we are all engaged develops, we have more and more a sense of tremendous urgency about the whole thing. If we look back to last year, there is in each of us a sense of urgency which we did not have then. We are much more impatient. We are much more given to being irritated at the man, at his efforts to sidetrack us and to talk us away from our objectives. We have a sense of urgency. We do want freedom, and we want it now.

This sense of urgency permeates everything that we do. We may not realize it, but it permeates every group that we're participating in. On the job you feel different than you used to feel. You are conscious of things that you never used to feel. You didn't used to mind so much when the man called you "boy." Now, if he calls you "boy," he's going to have to fight. He comes up just trying to be friendly, and he's made five mistakes before he's gotten through the first two sentences. And you don't say, "Well, that's just the way white folks talk." You say, "That's the way white folks got to *stop* talking."

That's our tremendous sense of urgency. The way you feel is the way millions of black people are feeling from coast to coast. That's why things bubble up every once in a while. Then everybody runs around trying to explain why it happened. We're just on the verge all the time. It doesn't take anything special because we don't like it any time of day or night. So anything can cause us to do something because we don't like it, never did like it, and are never going to like it. We have a sense of urgency. We're irritated; we're aching to do something.

Even the policemen realize it. They know that when they start something now they're going to have to shoot somebody. They don't just stop you and say, "Come here, nigger, where are you going?" and think nothing's going to happen. Some of them still do it, but they know it's a different kind of situation.

It is this terrible sense of urgency that grips us all, gives a different direction to everything we do, the things we say, to our organizations, to our working together, to our programs. A terrible sense of urgency.

For some this sense of urgency is a sense of hope. There are black people who believe that this whole thing is going to be settled in just a little while. Not too many, but there are some. And they work with this terrible sense of urgency thinking that they're going to do what has to be done and get it over with. "Somehow, we're going to build a new world, and the white man's going to change." There is urgency and hope there.

For others there is the urgency of despair. They have a profound conviction that nothing really can be done, that we have come to the end of a long journey, and there is no hope at all.

So there is urgency and despair on the one hand and urgency and hope upon the other.

So even in this great moment of rebellion, of revolution, of change, we are a confused people because we have not yet decided what it is that is really important as we move forward. Most of us want to do those things that must be done. Most of us want freedom and we're willing to use any means necessary to get it. We agree on these things, but when is this new world coming? When are we to be free? When are we to have the things that belong to us? If we're to have them, then we want a timetable. If we're not to have them, then we want to get about the task of tearing up everything there is in sight.

We have tremendous decisions to make, and that is a part of our inner feeling of urgency and frustration. We're not quite sure.

I am reminded of the last days of Jesus, the Black Messiah who came to a Black Nation of people who were divided and didn't know which way to turn, just as we don't. He came to bring them together and to teach them that unity, love for each other, sacrifice, commitment and discipline were essential if they were to be free. His whole ministry was going about among a Black Nation preaching to them about the things that had to be done if they were to find freedom from oppression by a white nation, Rome. Everything he did was trying to bring a people together.

Remember it says he turned his face steadfastly toward Jerusalem. This was as his ministry reached its climax. It seemed that everything was going his way. Crowds of people gathered when he passed through villages because people wanted to hear what he was saying. He talked to them about the possibility of building a Nation. And they came out and gathered around. They climbed up on trees and buildings that they might hear him. They wanted to hear. But they were not yet ready for the sacrifice, the unity and the discipline necessary to build a Nation. They came together and screamed and cried out "Hosannah! Hallelujah," and then they went home. The Nation had not yet been built because you don't build a Nation at a mass meeting. You may get the idea. You may get inspiration. You may get a feeling of strength from the brothers and sisters who are there. But you don't build a Nation at a mass meeting.

So Jesus, as he passed from town to town, from city to city, knew that these people who came together and shouted and screamed did not yet constitute a Nation. They were still divided; they were still individuals, each fighting for his own little prestige, for the things he wanted for himself. Listening to Jesus he might say to himself, "It's a wonderful dream, this dream of the Black Nation. But I don't want to get out on a limb and do the wrong thing and hurt myself." And he would drift away and go home.

So Jesus knew that a Nation had not come into being. And he said, "I will turn my face toward Jerusalem, because I must bring to a climax all these efforts, all these ideas, all these conflicting opinions, all of this individualism. I must find a way to dramatize what it means to build a Nation. I must make black people understand what it means to build a Nation." That is why he turned his face steadfastly toward Jerusalem.

When he came to Jerusalem, he had one simple task. He had twelve disciples who would follow him. He wanted them to understand what was happening and to be able to carry on after his crucifixion because for Jesus the crucifixion was not the end. For Jesus the Black Nation must last for a thousand years, for ten thousand years, for a million years. A man might die for the Nation, but the Nation must live.

Sometimes we forget that. You know, it takes courage to say, "I am willing to die," but you must then be able to say, "What am I willing to die for?" Jesus knew. He said, "I am willing to die. As an individual, I am willing to make this kind of a sacrifice that the Nation may live." We have to remember that today. You know all he went through. He brought the disciples together in the upper room, and they had the Last Supper. But we could just as easily call it the "First Supper" because it wasn't the end, it was the beginning. He brought them together, knowing that the end was at hand and that even there among their number were those who would betray him.

Always, in any movement, when any people undertake to build a Nation, there are betrayers in the midst of the closely-knit group that stands at the heart and center. Jesus knew it, and he turned to the twelve and said, "You've walked with me, talked with me. You've eaten with me. I've given you everything I've got. And yet one of you will betray me." And they said, "Who is it; is it I, Lord?" And he looked at them, and he knew, "It's all of you. In one way or another, you will all betray me." He knew it, but he didn't hate them. They would betray him out of their human weakness.

He said, "Behold the hour is at hand." The disciples could easily have said, "Our leader is about to be destroyed. We should all die with him. We must make this the greatest destruction of people in the history of the world." Wouldn't that have been ridiculous? Then what would his death have meant? Jesus said, "The hour is at hand for *my* sacrifice." And he talked to the disciples in the Upper Room that they might understand and carry on the work of building the Nation. He talked to them at great length. He had a sense of the urgency of the moment. He knew how upset they were that things were not going as they wanted them to go, how they wanted to take power, how they wanted to strike out against Rome. He knew all of their feelings. But he talked to them. He tried to get them to understand the meaning of the simple little things. He broke the bread and said, "This is my body which is broken for *you*." He poured the wine and said, "This is my blood, which is shed for you." The willingness of the individual to sacrifice himself for the Nation.

And then he washed their feet. You may have laughed at footwashing Baptists, but there is as much validity in washing the feet as there is in drinking the wine and eating the bread. Jesus did it. He washed their feet to symbolize that if you want to build a Nation, you've got to be willing to serve. He said, "I came forth to serve." Leadership is a kind of service. And you have to be humble to get down on your knees and wash your brother's feet. They said, "Oh, no, Lord. Don't do that; you're our leader." And he said, "If I can't wash your feet, get up and go because you don't belong to me." He was trying to give them a last message about what it means to build a Nation: a group of people so bound together in love that they are willing to accept menial, subservient positions because in this way they serve the Nation. A people so bound together in love that they are willing to die that the Nation may not die.

He said, "The hour is at hand." And he was right. They betrayed him. Judas did it for money. We see that every day. Thousands of such betrayers are in our own city, paid by Congressional committees, paid by other agencies, paid by one force or another to destroy us. Black brothers betraying for thirty pieces of silver.

Then he asked Peter, James and John, "Come out and pray with me a while; I know that the end is at hand." They went out, and he was wrestling with himself to keep his sense of conviction, his willingness to die that the Nation might live. He prayed, and when he looked around they had gone to sleep. Betrayers just out of natural, human weakness. They couldn't stay awake, they were tired. You know how often you betray the Nation just because you're tired. Not because you're evil or vicious, not because the man got to you. You're just tired. You just don't have the energy, that's all. That's all Jesus was telling them, "I know how it is. You're tired." He didn't say they weren't tired. He was tired too. Try a little harder, then. If he's willing to die, you can at least try a little harder to stay awake.

Then a little later on, you remember Peter's denial. After Jesus had been arrested, Peter kind of followed along, and when the guards said, "I believe he's with him," Peter said, "I don't know him; never *saw* him." The same Peter who had said, "I'll die before I'll betray you, Lord. Maybe the rest of them, but not me!" And Jesus looked at him with compassion and said, "Before the cock crows, you will betray me three times." Just a human betrayal. What was Peter afraid of? If you'd come up to fight him, he would have fought. But they weren't fighting. It was just the situation. Maybe they would laugh at him, talk about him, "Oh, you're one of his followers!" You know how they do when you go some place and they ask, "What church do you belong to?" And you try to look the other way. They say, "You belong to Rev. Cleage's church?" You know what I'm talking about—*that* kind of betrayal. That is betrayal because if you stand for something, you stand for it any time, any place, with anybody. When they say, "Do you belong to Rev. Cleage's church," say, "No, I belong to *my* church— the Nation. Rev. Cleage just happens to belong to it, too."

We have a task with our sense of urgency. We have to get a long view. Now Rap Brown is doing a tremendous thing. I think we have to keep him alive just as long as we can. He is doing the same kind of thing Jesus did. He is making himself a symbol, and the man is going to have to destroy him. There's no question about it. We've got to give him all the support and help and protection we can. Not because we all have to believe that guerilla warfare in the street is the way, but because he keeps us conscious of one thing: the seriousness of the rebellion in which we are now engaged. We can easily forget it if he doesn't keep screaming. We can easily act like this rebellion is some kind of little plaything. But he keeps reminding us, "This is a fight for survival."

So God help H. Rap Brown! We need him. I don't care what he does to the white folks, whether they're scared, whether they like it or don't like it. *We* need him because he keeps us conscious of the seriousness of the rebellion that we're in. But we don't need *just* H. Rap Brown. The revolution is not *just* getting ready for guerilla warfare. This whole thing that we are engaged in, building a Nation, is not just preparing to all die in the streets. We have to be ready to die in the street if that becomes necessary. But until it does become necessary, there's a whole lot else that we've got to be doing.

There is a whole lot of foolish talk going on among Black Nationalists these days. So many college students come to me and say, "They're telling me that I ought to drop out of college, that college is the man's bag, that I don't need education. I'm losing touch with the people." I ask, "Who's been telling you this?" And they say, "Well, the fellas out there." I say, "Where are they, in some place drinking some beer? What are *they* doing?" They say, "Well, they're staying in touch with the masses." I say, "That's good. You let them stay in touch with the masses, and you stay in school and learn something." Because we need people who are ready to *do* something. We're getting ready right now to organize the community, but you know what we black people have to do? We have to call in Saul Alinsky for $100,000 to tell us how to organize. We need some boys in school learning something. We need people learning everything because we're not living for today. We're not revolting for today. We're not revolting just so we can be free, but so that our children, and our great-grandchildren can be free. And that's not done in a day.

If we end up fighting in the streets, there has to be a remnant that remains because we're fighting for a Nation. We've got to preserve some part of the Black Nation. We have to see that a remnant remains because the Nation must go on. We are not fighting just for the happiness and satisfaction of struggle. I know you've held it all in for a long time. You've taken a whole lot of abuse. You can remember when the first little white kid called you "nigger," and you're still mad about it. But that does *not* mean that you can't use some kind of common sense when you fight. We're *not* going to all die in the street; we must have some who are left. And we've got to start preparing them.

We're building a Nation. And when you come forward here to join this church, you're coming into a Nation. And I don't think only about the next two or three years. We had a meeting the other night, and Brother Dowdell warned, "You know, Rev. Cleage can't live forever." I'm very conscious of that. We must start getting young men ready now. We are not like some other church that can pick up any rabble rouser and call him to come here, because he wouldn't know what to rabble rouse about. We have to train our own young men. We have to take some young Black Nationalists and militants and send them to school to learn how to pastor this church when I get too old to stand up here. We have to train people. That's a part of being a Nation: thinking about tomorrow and the day after tomorrow. We must plan for a thousand years.

We start out buying property right here in this neighborhood where we are. The Black Star Co-op is talking about buying a building in the next block to open a supermarket. It may be a little one to start, but a pretty good little one, though. And we'll buy other things as we go. We'll buy and we'll never sell. And in five hundred years, you can't come anywhere west of Woodward Avenue but we'll own it! That's a Nation. A Nation doesn't exist for today. The white man is building for a thousand years from now and we've been talking about satisfaction for today. We need businessmen. We need people who know what they're doing in all areas. We need to be putting something together that's going to last. We need to be bringing people together who are going to stay, who are not going to be split up by a little difference of opinion. We're building a Nation.

When you begin to think that every little child sitting here is an heir to what we're doing today, your perspective becomes different. You know you're going to do what's necessary to preserve him. He has to be preserved. You have to get all the freedom you can for him. You know, any fifty of us could be sacrificed today if by dying we could advance the Nation. But we have to keep constantly in mind that the *Nation* is the important thing. The little children yet unborn; the little children sitting here who will have children. We are concerned about *their* children. That's building a Nation. That's a perspective. That's why men are willing to die. No one would die willingly if his death was meaningless. He'd turn back, find a way out. But when you're building a Nation, your whole conception is different. And that's what we're trying to do.

We are going to have a lot of differences of opinion. It is not going to be easy. And we're growing so fast. We just don't know each other with so many people coming in so fast. But we're going to get acquainted if some Sunday morning we have to lock the door till we all get to know one another. You can't work in the Nation if you don't know each other. We've got to know whose child is running around so that we can talk to him. Our young people have to feel that this is their Nation because we're building for them.

The hour is at hand. And the hour is the hour of building a Black Nation. Some of us, if need be, must die. Anytime we forget that we must be willing to die, the Nation is through. Because anybody can oppress us if we're afraid to die. We have to have a basic commitment to build a Black Nation. And this we will build on the teachings of Jesus Christ, the Black Messiah.

That's why the black Madonna is so important to us. The Black Madonna is a black woman standing there with a little black child in her arms. And in every generation, that's what we are fighting for—that little black child. We don't care whose child it is. He's *our* child, and that's what we're fighting for. Because he has to carry on the Nation, because you are not going to be here forever either! And we have to leave this nation in the hands of people who understand it and who are willing to die for it as we are willing to die for it. That little black baby is the whole thing we're fighting for, and we need so many things to make that fight meaningful in today's world.

We need to understand ways of fighting. We don't fully understand that yet. I was talking about this to one of our members, and she suggested the idea in the Old Testament of a wheel within a wheel. The Nation is the big wheel, and inside there has to be a whole lot of little wheels always turning. Wherever you are, you've got to be a Black Caucus. Do you understand that? If you're in a school and there are only four black teachers there, you four have got to get together. If the principal is no good, then you have to dedicate yourselves as a Black Caucus to getting rid of that principal. What I mean by no good is no good as far as black children are concerned. Our black lawyers have to become a Black Caucus to clean out Recorder's Court. They don't yet understand what their function is. It's not enough for them to earn a living. They have to become a Black Caucus. All the black lawyers have to stand together. They have to point out every bit of discrimination. They know what's happening in Recorder's Court, they know what the judges are doing. They have to put pressure on them so that they know what they have to do.

That's a wheel within a wheel. If you're in a factory, you have to get your brothers together in your department. When they have you training a white person to take your position and to promote over you, you have to stop it. But it takes a caucus to do that. You can't do it by yourself. We have to have a caucus everywhere. When they see three black folks anywhere, they have to know that there is a Black Caucus.

Some of you send your children away to college. You sweat, you want them to go to a good college, you want them to learn something. Well, the best way to make them learn something is to tell them when they go, "Find the Black Power Caucus on your campus and get in it right away. Make your college meaningful in the black revolution." Then they are not getting away from the struggle when they go to college. They are a part of it because they're bringing the college into the mainstream of our black revolution. Everywhere we are we have to be a Black Caucus. If you belong to some little inane social club, and they sit around and do nothing, you've got to be a Black Caucus in that club. Change it or tear it up!

The unemployed out in the street, each one feels by himself— put upon, miserable. We have to organize a caucus of unemployed to strike at the system that's oppressing them and keeping them down, that keeps them out in the street. You read the miserable statistics in the papers where the man has to admit that our unemployment is terrible. They need organization to be a Black Caucus of unemployed. We've got to do it. We need a Black Caucus of mothers receiving Aid to Dependent Children, of welfare people. All wheels within a wheel. Our Nation, and groups functioning everywhere, disciplined, organized, together because we love one another.

The church is the soul of the Nation. It has to be. All these little wheels are whirling within the Nation, all stemming from one common faith and commitment. We buy property, train leadership, build for our great-great-great-grandchildren. And our unity, our commitment, our dedication to the Black Nation are all symbolized in the sacrament of Holy Communion.

Maybe you have taken communion lightly. But the broken bread is the symbol that we are willing as individuals to sacrifice ourselves for the Nation. The wine is the symbol that we're willing to shed our blood for the Nation. So when we come together, it's as though we were around a table united, a people, a Nation. And we are saying in our participation, in the sacrament of Holy Communion, "I am a part of the Nation. I accept this sacrifice which the Black Messiah made as the symbolic sacrifice which I'm willing to make that the Nation may be built, that it may grow, that it may have power. I'm willing." This is why we come together with the sacrament of Holy Communion.

And this is what baptism is. When members come into the church, we baptize members who have not been baptized, as well as those who would like to be baptized again because they want to be baptized into the Nation. We baptize into the Nation in the Name of the Father, the Son and the Holy Spirit. This baptism is meaningful because you die to all your old Uncle Tom ways, the slave ways you used to have. And you are born again, you are resurrected in the newness of life into the Black Nation. And then you come and take the sacrament of Holy Communion. You are in the Nation. We are building it; some of us may die, but the remnant must live. And it is a wonderful thing to be a part of the struggle and know that no matter what happens anywhere in the world, this Black Nation will go on. We are committed to it. We believe in it.

Heavenly Father, we thank thee for the opportunity which is ours to come into thy house, to participate in this service of worship and this rededication of ourselves to thee and thy service. We believe that it is thy will and thy teaching that we undertake to build on earth thy kingdom. And that thy kingdom on earth is the Black Nation which we are building. We feel that we have thy support, thy strength, thy guidance in this task which we have accepted for ourselves. Be with us to give us strength when we are weak, to give us guidance when we are lost. Be with us to give us a sense of brotherhood when we feel torn apart by feelings of individualism. Bind us together. Make us brothers and sisters in this Nation. Unite us in love. This we ask in the name of the Black Messiah. Amen.

3/An Epistle to Stokely

"But no one can enter a strong man's house
and plunder his goods, unless he first binds
the strong man; then indeed he may plunder
his house" (*Mark* 3:27).

I'd like to call your attention to the hymn we often sing:

> Fairest Lord Jesus
> Ruler of all nature!
> Fair are the meadows
> Fairer still the woodlands
> Robed in the blooming garb of spring,
> Jesus is fairer, Jesus is purer,
> He makes the willful heart to sing!

I only mention it to point out the very simple, but very obvious fact that black Christians have a whole lot to do to rewrite much of the ritual and songs that are used by Christian churches. It's kind of ridiculous for us to be sitting here singing about "Fairest Lord Jesus." We might sing about "Darkest Lord Jesus" or something else. We might rewrite the song. I'd just like you to bear this in mind as we go through the sermon.

I have suggested that it would be possible for us as an independent Congregational Church to ordain workers in the Student Non-Violent Co-Ordinating Committee for the civil rights work which they are now doing and, in that way, protect them against the conspiracy to either kill them in Vietnam or take them out of active work by putting them in a penitentiary. In either case, certainly the Movement would be renderered virtually helpless. The

35

suggestion was practical. It could be done and there is no real reason why it should not be done.

The contention has been advanced for many years that civil rights workers should be exempted from the draft because of the significance of the work they are doing. Actually, new legislation is not necessary because they are already exempt in terms of the religious nature of what they are doing, except for one very simple but inescapable fact. Most of them do not realize that what they are doing is religious, and most of them, like most young people in the 20th Century, have rejected the Christian Church, as they know it.

They have rejected it as it has been presented to them, as they see it in action in the world, as they note its influence, as they try to understand it. This is the inescapable fact which makes it very difficult for a Church to offer ordination to these young people, even as a method of continuing their work during this period of crisis. Most of you who are over thirty may find this difficult to understand, and I think that that is why young people in today's world say that anyone over thirty can't hope to understand them or their outlook on life.

Many young people would rather die in Vietnam or rot in prison than get caught up in what they term "whitey's religious bag." It may be difficult to understand why many of them would be willing to let the Movement which is so important a part of their lives grind slowly to a standstill, as one by one its leaders are immoblized by the draft, rather than sacrifice their principles and cynically embrace a lie, or perhaps even worse from their point of view, rather than hypocritically, or for reasons of expediency, permit themselves to be embraced by a lie. I realize that I am not attributing to these gallant young men who make up the front line of leadership of the Movement either sophistication or the selfishness necessary to pretend to be Christian to serve the Movement or even to save the Movement from the cold-blooded and ruthless extermination which it now faces at the hands of the Federal Government, and I say candidly that those I know personally are neither sophisticated nor selfish. They would not use the Church to escape the draft unless they honestly believed in the Church and its teachings.

So I address my remarks this morning to you and also to Stokely Carmichael, and to the young men who make up SNICK'S organization throughout the country, and to other young men who work in the Movement in other organizations. I address my remarks to those who believe in the Movement but who do not believe in the Christian Church because they do not understand that the Movement is the Christian Church in the 20th Century and that the Christian Church cannot truly be the church until it also becomes the Movement. So then, I would say to you, you are Christian, and the things you believe are the teachings of a Black Messiah named Jesus, and the things you do are the will of a black God called Jehovah; and almost everything you have heard about Christianity is essentially a lie.

You have been misled. Christianity for you has been misinterpreted. That which you believe to be Christianity, the theology and philosophy of history which you reject, is not Christianity. The Christianity which we see in the world today was not shaped by Jesus. It was put together by the Apostle Paul who never saw Jesus, and given form and shape during the Middle Ages when most of the hymns were written, the hymns which for the most part enunciate white supremacy. "Fairest Lord Jesus." Most of the famous religious pictures that you see were painted between the fourteenth and the seventeenth centuries by white artists. When Dutch artists painted religious pictures, everything looks just like it all happened in Holland. When French artists painted religious pictures, the biblical characters look French.

But we didn't realize this when we looked at our Sunday School literature as children. When we turned the pages and always saw a white Jesus, when we saw pictures of a white God pointing down at creation, we didn't realize that these were not statements of fact but statements by white men depicting what they wanted to believe was true. I say, what they wanted to believe was true, because essentially they knew that white men did not create Christianity. They borrowed it, more bluntly, they stole it. In fact, of all the peoples on earth, the one people who have never created a religion worthy of the name religion are white people.

All religions stem from black people. Think of them for a moment. The Muslim religion, the Buddhist religion, the Jewish religion, the Christian religion, they all come from parts of the world dominated by non-white peoples. The white man's religion was the primitive religion of the pagans with a pantheon of gods throwing thunderbolts and cavorting about heaven and earth, filled with lust and violence. To the Romans, religion was the deification of the Emperor. They had no God. They believed that whoever could take power must be God, and they worshipped him. The white man has never created a genuine religion. He has only borrowed religions from non-white peoples.

It's important for us to understand this because the civilization around us is not ours. We are sojourners in a strange land, and we have been taught what someone else wanted us to know. So what we have been taught about Christianity is not what Christianity is, but what white people wanted us to believe. The white man captured the religion of a Black Nation, the revelations of a Black God, the teachings of a Black Messiah, and he has used them to keep black men enslaved. We are the chosen people in a religious sense, in a historic sense, and this I will try to develop for you. The time has come for us to reclaim our God, our prophet, and our power.

I would like to outline a few basic facts and you may find it difficult to accept them because essentially they run counter to the things you have been taught. But if you will for a moment realize that many of the things you have been taught have not been for your best interest, and that you have been deliberately taught things which were intended to enslave you, then perhaps you may for a moment try to rethink these basic ideas which you have accepted as unconsciously as the air you breathe. We talk much today about air pollution, but we breathe as if we had no consciousness of the pollution in the air we breathe. We breathe without thinking. The pollution in the air is a part of that which we breathe and from it there is no escape.

And so it has been for us. We have accepted the white man's interpretation of our Christian faith because we had no alternative. I ask you to rethink a few of these basic facts. Christianity is essentially and historically a black man's religion. I ask you to go back to the beginning, to where our Christian Bible begins, back to the history of Israel, back to Abraham, the father of Israel.

Abraham, the father of Israel was a Chaldean. Look at your map of this part of the world, and you will find that there was very little likelihood that the Chaldeans were white. Abraham went out from Chaldea to build for himself and for his family a new way of life. In going out, he declared that he had received a revelation from God, and had made a covenant with God, and that God had selected him to build a Nation. This was the beginning of Israel. He went out from the Chaldean city of Ur into Africa. He went down into Egypt and dwelt in Egypt among the Egyptians. Now if there is any question in your mind about whether or not the Egyptians were black you have only to look at the Sphinx, the drawings and the inscriptions from Egypt. Recent studies prove that many of the Pharaohs were black or Negroid. Only the American white man tries to pretend that the Egyptians were white.

Abraham went into Egypt and he lived with the Egyptians and because his wife was beautiful he was afraid to admit she was his wife for fear that someone might want her and kill him. So he said, "She is my sister." And so while he lived in Egypt, his wife was taken by the Egyptian King and he made no protest. Obviously, the relationship between the Egyptians and Abraham and his clan was a very close one. We are at the beginning. There is no question about Abraham and the beginning of the Nation Israel being very closely related to Africa, to the Egyptians and to black people. This is the beginning of the Nation Israel.

The Egyptians were very good to Abraham. They gave him cattle and wealth. He came out of Egypt a wealthy man with many black Egyptian servants with him. The Nation Israel is beginning to develop now as a combination of Abraham, his family and the Egyptians who have been adopted while Abraham was in Egypt. The nature of the relationship can be deduced from the fact that he himself married Hagar, his Egyptian servant, and had a child by her named Ishmael. We still use the word Hagar. We speak of Hagar's children and you know what that means.

Then Sara, his wife, had her own child and got mad and didn't want her son to have to split the inheritance. So she told Abraham to get rid of the child Ishmael. So Hagar and Ishmael were driven out into the desert and God looked down on Hagar and Ishmael and said, "I will protect them and save them because you, Ishmael, will become the father of a great people." Ishmael is traditionally reputed to be the father of the Arabic Nation. Abraham was very closely identified with the black people of Africa.

Later on, there was Moses, born during Israel's Egyptian bondage. Moses is quite obviously, by the biblical story, part Egyptian. His adoption by Pharaoh's daughter does not ring true. Moses is at least half-Egyptian and half-Jewish, and to say that he's half-Egyptian and half-Jewish makes him unquestionably all non-white. This is Moses. We're still dealing with the Nation Israel which is always depicted as a white nation. The Nation Israel was not at any time a white nation. Where could they have picked up any white blood, wandering around Africa? They hadn't even had any contact with white people. Moses married a Midianite, a black woman, and had children.

Israel finally fought its way into Canaan and mixed with the people of Canaan. Those weren't white people either. "People of the land" they called them. The Israelites looked down on them, after a fashion, but that didn't stop them from sleeping with them. And all through the Old Testament you notice every once in a while a prophet rares up and says, "We have got to maintain our purity." And you know what that means. That means that the purity is already gone. There's nothing to maintain. Just as in the

South when the white man stands up and talks about maintaining white purity. He wouldn't be talking about it if there was any purity to maintain, and it was exactly the same with the prophets. They looked about and saw that Israel had mixed with the people wherever they went.

When Israel was taken captive into Babylon, they mixed with the people of Babylon, and Babylon was no white nation. They lived with them, intermarried with them, and then the prophets began to write down rules about how God's Chosen People should not mix with other people. At this late date, they were trying to build a sense of identity. They petitioned the king to be permitted to return to Israel. But when they finally received permission to go back, most of the Jews wouldn't go. They were happy and content. They were in business. They had friends, relatives, everything. They didn't want to go back. Only a little handful returned, and when they went back, they looked around and saw the Jews who had remained and said, "These Jews have become people of the land. They're like all of the other people. They've intermarried." And then the prophet stood up and said, "You've got to separate from the people of the land. We must keep the Jews pure."

Now how could you keep them pure? They had mixed in Babylon, they had mixed in Egypt, they had mixed in Canaan. What was there to keep pure? And yet they tried to issue a pronouncement, "You've got to separate." But it was ridiculous and impossible. It was as impossible to separate the Jews from the people of the land as it was to maintain segregation in the South after nightfall. It could not be done. Israel was a mixed-blood, non-white nation. What usually confuses you is the fact that the Jews you see today in America are white. Most of them are the descendants of white Europeans and Asiatics who were converted to Judaism about one thousand years ago. The Jews were scattered all over the world. In Europe and Russia, they converted white people to Judaism. The Jews who stayed in that part of the world where black people are predominant, remained black. The conflict between black Jews and white Jews is a problem in Israel today.

Jesus came to the Black Nation Israel. We are not talking now about "God the Father." We are concerned here with the actual blood line. Jesus was born to Mary, a Jew of the tribe of Judah, a non-white people; black people in the same sense that the Arabs were black people, in the same sense that the Egyptians were black people. Jesus was a Black Messiah born to a black woman.

The pictures of the Black Madonna which are all over the world did not all turn black through some mysterious accident. Portraits of the Black Madonna are historic, and today in many countries they are afraid to take the ancient pictures of the Black Madonna out of storage so that people can see them. Only this year in Spain they were afraid to parade with the Black Madonna because they feared that it might have political implications. But the Black Madonna is an historic fact, and Jesus as a Black Messiah is an historic fact.

We might ask why did God choose to send his son (or to come himself) to the nation Israel? It is a question you should have asked yourself. Why, of all the peoples on earth did he come to these people? Why not to some little group of white people in Europe who were living in caves and eating raw meat? Why did he pick these people? Why? Go back for a moment to the Biblical account of creation, "God created man in his own image." We say that all the time, but what does it mean? If God created man in his own image, what must God look like? I know that if you close your eyes, you see a white God. But if God created man in his own image, then we must look at man to see what God looks like. There are black men, there are yellow men, there are red men, and there are a few, a mighty few, white men in the world. If God created man in his own image, then God must be some combination of this black, red, yellow and white. In no other way could God have created man in his own image.

So if we think of God as a person (and we are taught in the Christian religion to think of God as a person, as a personality capable of love, capable of concern, capable of purpose and of action) then God must be a combination of black, yellow and red with just a little touch of white, and we must think of God as a black God. So all those prayers you've been sending up to a white God have been wasted. In America, one drop of black makes you black. So by American law, God is black, and by any practical interpretation, why would God have made seven-eighths of the world non-white and yet he himself be white? That is not reasonable. If God were white, he'd have made everybody white. And if he decided to send his son to earth, he would have sent a white son down to some nice white people. He certainly would not have sent him down to a black people like Israel.

So we have been misled. We received Christianity as we know it from our slave masters. Most of us didn't have it when we got here. We had lost it. We learned it from our slave masters. The Christianity given to the slaves and used to enslave the continent of Africa, when the white man sent missionaries back over there with guns and with Bibles, is the white man's distortion and corruption of the black man's historic faith. It is this corruption of Christianity which the black man, and especially black young people, is rejecting today.

Let me point out three things which are a part of this rejection. Christianity is essentially and historically concerned with a group, with society, with the community. In the Old Testament and in the Synoptic Gospels, God is concerned with a people, not with individuals. Yet, the slave Christianity that we were taught told us that God is concerned with each individual. And the master told each slave, "If you are a good slave, God is going to take care of you and you will be saved." He didn't tell them that if all you black people love God and fight together, God is going to help you get free from slavery. The group concept is historic Christianity. Individualism is slave Christianity.

The petty personal morality emphasized in the slave Church comes from slave Christianity. God is concerned in the Old Testament and Jesus is concerned in the New Testament with social morality, with how a group of people act, how they take care of each other, whether they're concerned about poverty, whether they're concerned about each other. Whence comes, then, this emphasis upon petty personal morality? Do you smoke? Then you're a sinner. Do you drink? Then you're a sinner. This is slave Christianity. Because this was the emphasis that the slave master wanted to make so that he could use religion to control his slaves.

The other worldly emphasis, where did that come from? That's not in the Old Testament nor in the teachings of Jesus, either. Jesus talked of the kingdom of God on earth. He talked to his followers about building a certain kind of world *here*. In the Old Testament the prophets were concerned with building God's kingdom out of the Nation Israel. Then whence comes this other worldly emphasis? This is slave Christianity. Slave Christianity deliberately emphasized the other world so that we would not be concerned about the everyday problems of this world.

The tremendous confusion in Christianity grows out of the fact that after the death of Jesus, the Apostle Paul began to corrupt his teachings with concepts which were essentially the pagan concepts of the Gentile oppressors. From the Greek and Roman world he borrowed philosophical ideas that had nothing to do with anything that Israel had ever believed or anything that Jesus had ever taught. The Apostle Paul attempted to break the covenant which the Black Nation Israel had with God. He said, "Circumcision is unimportant, all these little rules and laws are unimportant. We must accept everybody." That is why Paul was in conflict with the real disciples who had walked with Jesus and were still in Jerusalem. They said, "We are a people. We have a covenant with God. We believe in certain things, and when you go out and you try to convert the barbarians you are corrupting our faith." History has proven that they were correct. The Epistles of Paul are in direct contradiction to the teachings of the Old Testament. Slave Christianity emphasizes these distortions of the Apostle Paul and denies and repudiates the basic teachings of Jesus Christ and the Black Nation Israel.

The Black Messiah Jesus did not build a Church, but a Movement. He gathered together people to follow him and he sent them out to change the world. He sent out the seventy two-by-two, and he himself went from place to place. He built a Movement, not a Church. Like today's young black prophets, he rejected the institutionalization of religion. He rejected the Church deliberately because he said, "It's wrong, it's hypocritical, and it's opposed to the will of God." He rejected the morality of his time. He rejected the Church of his time. He was a prophet.

He was in the same frame of mind as the young black prophets today who reject Christianity as they see it institutionalized in the slave Church. Jesus tried to minister to the every-day needs of his days and he did this within the loose organizational structure of a Movement. He was a dangerous revolutionary.

In our Scripture lesson this morning we read, first, the account of Jesus' first sermon in Nazareth where he described the things that he had come to do. To give sight to the blind, to give food to the hungry, to take the chains off those who were in bondage. These things he had come to do. To minister to the everyday needs of people. In another scriptural passage we had the account of Jesus going into the Temple. A man whose arm was withered went up to Jesus, and the Scribes and the Pharisees waited to see whether or not Jesus would help the man on the Sabbath Day. Jesus looked angrily at the Pharisees and the Scribes, and he healed the man right there in the Temple because it was more important to help the man than it was to observe the laws of the Sabbath. At another time he said, "The Sabbath was made for man, not man for the Sabbath."

It's peculiar how we could misread the Bible for so long. How could we just keep on singing the same old wrong songs and keep on going through the same old wrong motions when the truth was right there in the Book. People don't really read the Bible. They listen to what somebody tells them. Now, let me tell you, your grandmother and that country preacher down home didn't know all there is to know about Christianity. And if you're going to depend on what they told you, then you're just going to be wrong about almost everything. You've got to go back and look at the

Bible itself, read some history books and find out what this Christianity is that you either believe or don't believe. Find out who this Jesus is that you either follow or reject!

In closing, I take a text from Matthew 7:21, where Jesus says "Not everyone that says to me Lord, Lord, shall enter the kingdom of Heaven, but he who does the will of my father, who is in Heaven." Let us try to free ourselves from this "Lord, Lord" business and try to join those few people in the world today who are trying to do the will of God.

To Stokely and the young men in SNICK, I would just say briefly that the Christian religion you are rejecting, that you are so opposed to, is a slave Christianity that has no roots in the teachings of the Black Messiah. You could be ordained in *this* Church as civil rights workers if we could somehow do away with the distinctions which exist in people's minds between what's religious and what's not religious. To ordain civil rights workers for civil rights work would declare that the Chrstian Church believes that this is what Christianity is all about, that individuals who give their lives in the struggle for human freedom are Christian and that the Movement is not only Christian, but that the Movement is the Church.

The Black Church must recapture the loyalty of black youth if it is to be significant in the black revolution, and it must find a way to save its brave young men from death on some distant battlefield. I read from the Gospel of Mark 3:27. "But no one can enter a strong man's house and plunder his goods unless he first binds the strong man. Then indeed he may plunder his house." When they draft all of the cream of our young men, whether they kill them in Vietnam or put them in the penitentiary, they have bound our strong men. Then indeed they may at their will and at their pleasure plunder our house.

Heavenly Father, we come into thy house seeking to understand thee, and the Black Messiah, Jesus Christ, thy son. We come as a people with a history. Certainly thou must understand that as black people, it would be impossible for us to kneel before thee, believing thee to be a white God. Be with us here and now. Give us the courage to cast aside the illusions and hypocrisies which have bound us in the past, that we may go down from this place, rededicated to thee, seeking to understand the full meaning of the faith which we have so easily and perhaps so lightly professed. We ask thy blessings upon young men and young women throughout this country who in this hour of crisis dedicate their lives that men may find freedom, that men might learn how to live, that men may stand up and say with all sincerity, "We have been created in the image of God." This we ask in the name of the Black Messiah, Jesus Christ. Amen.

4/"We Are God's Chosen People"

"How long will you set upon a man to shatter him, like a leaning wall, a tottering fence? They only plan to tear him down from his dignity" (*Psalms* 62:3).*

Speaking about the enemies of Israel, the Psalmist says: "How long will you set upon a man to shatter him, like a leaning wall, a tottering fence? They only plan to tear him down from his dignity" (Ps.62:3,4).

Forget for a moment that this is from the Bible and was written a long time ago. Just think about the simple words themselves. It is as if we were talking about the enemies of the Black Nation today. How long will they continue to oppress and to exploit and to do all the things they have been doing? How long will they continue to use violence in an effort to destroy us? As we see the plight of black people in this white man's world, we echo the words of the Psalmist, "How long will you set upon a man to shatter him like a leaning wall?" That is a beautiful figure of speech because if a wall is leaning, it isn't going to stand long. Certainly we can say, "You only plan to tear us down from our dignity."

Often we don't think of our dignity as something of great value. We even laugh at it, as when someone is said to be putting on airs. But then we are only thinking of dignity in a superficial way. Take from you your dignity and you have nothing left. Take from you

* Many scholars translate "excellency" as "dignity."

48

the right to hold up your head, to feel that you are a man, the right to think, to be—take away that dignity and there is nothing left but a groveling animal, a slave.

Let us look for a moment at the Psalm from which our text is taken. It begins with a statement of faith in God, "For God alone my soul waits in silence." The Psalmist is leading up to the description of what the enemy is trying to do, but he begins with this plaintive, and yet, heroic statement. "From him comes my salvation. He only is my rock and my salvation, my fortress. I shall not be moved." It may seem strange to us in the 20th Century that the Psalmist should move from this simple primitive statement of faith, through a description of what the enemies of Israel are trying to do, and then at the close of the Psalm, re-affirm his faith by repeating, "From him comes my salvation."

I think that it is well in this day for black militants, black nationalists, and those who believe that we must rebuild the Black Nation as Jesus tried to rebuild it two thousand years ago, to remember the Psalmist's simple words. "From him comes my salvation." We have a great tendency, as we become emancipated from slave religion, from slave thinking and from a desire to identify with the enemy, to reject God altogether. We begin to say to ourselves that we never did need God. He was only a stumbling block to our people.

Young people find this an almost irresistible temptation as they become involved in the black revolution and committed to struggle and sacrifice. The Movement exists today because black young people have been willing to make tremendous sacrifices to bring it into being and to maintain its momentum. I think of the young people at Texas Christian University who fought to protect their campus from police invasion. But more and more as they struggle they are beginning to say, "what do we need God for? We can do it ourselves. All we really need is the courage to get out there and fight."

You hear this everywhere and perhaps there are echoes in your own mind. "If only we could have gotten together a long time ago and stopped talking about God, we would be farther along." That is why in most cities those who are actively engaged in the Freedom Struggle are not a part of the Church. They look with contempt and scorn upon the Church and in many instances, rightly so, because the Church has not lived up to its obligations. It does not represent God. It does not fulfill the revelation of God which we have in Jesus Christ. It is important for us who have come into the Black Nation as disciples of the Black Messiah to remember these simple words. "For God only is my rock, and my salvation, my fortress, and I shall not be moved.'

You may think that it is unnecessary, that we don't need this. Why should we clutter up our thinking with a God who is off somewhere, who may or may not have created the universe, who may or may not have spoken through the prophets?

You need it for the same reason the Psalmist needed it, that Israel needed it. Because a man cannot maintain dignity in a world of exploitation, suffering, and oppression all by himself. If you are going to believe that you are somebody, that you have worth and value, then you must know that that worth and value was built into you. You were created with worth and value. You didn't make it by yourself. You were created by God with certain inalienable rights.

This is why you need God. It is not enough to just look at the world in which you live, to look at the people, to understand what suffering and systematic exploitation have done to you, and say that despite all of this, I am going to maintain my dignity. You can't do it by yourself. The Psalmist was not talking about his little individual dignity. He wasn't sitting off some place talking about a God who was going to do something for him. The Psalmist was talking about a God who was concerned with the Nation Israel, a God who was concerned with the destiny and the problems of the Nation Israel. This we must remember today if we are to maintain our dignity. In the greatest adversity, Israel depended upon God.

We can say that in today's world, with our knowledge of science, atomic energy and many mysterious things which we do not understand even as we use them, we don't need God any more. But we do. In the greatest adversity, the Nation Israel depended upon God. No matter what the enemy did, the Gentiles, the white people, no matter what they did to Israel, Israel was still confident.

As we look back at the history of Israel, we can ask, "How did this little handful of people, at the crossroads of the world, hemmed in by great nations on every side, maintain its identity and its confidence, even as it was conquered by first one enemy and then another? How could this little handful of people still believe that somehow they would emerge triumphant? In every adversity they believed that God was concerned about them. They believed it. They believed that their strength was a strength that their enemies could neither conquer nor destroy because it came from their unique relationship with God.

During the Egyptian bondage, it would have been easy for Israel to have given up. The conditions of their slavery were very much like our own. But they continued to believe that somehow freedom would come, somehow conditions would be changed. The enemy found it impossible to destroy them because their dignity could not be affected by anything men could do to them. Men could not destroy a dignity which had been given to them by God. So, efforts to destroy their dignity failed. No matter what the enemy did, Israel knew that it was special. When they were taken into Babylon, it was not into a harsh kind of captivity. The Babylonians had no need to destroy them. They were not that important. Only the leaders were taken to Babylon. This seemed sufficient to destroy their institutions and their identity. The Babylonians didn't beat them or use cattle prods or fire hoses on them. They just took the cream of the nation to Babylon. The Psalmist says, "Our captors required of us mirth, saying, 'Sing us the songs of Zion.' " The Babylonians weren't vicious men. They weren't beating or whipping them. They just laughed at them. "They required of us mirth," just as today in the Gentile nightclubs they say, "You black people have such a talent for singing. Sing us your spirituals."

The other night I saw the Clara Ward Gospel Singers on TV,

entertaining in a Las Vagas nightclub. They were singing the very songs which our people sang in their suffering and misery, while the white folks laughed. When the Babylonians said to the Jews in captivity (these biblical Jews were the Black Nation Israel), "Sing us the songs of Zion, laugh and make merry for us, we like your songs," what did the Jews reply? "How can we sing the Lord's songs in a strange land?" They said, "The Nation is shattered. We aren't going to sing the Lord's songs for these Gentiles." It wasn't a place that they remembered. It was a Nation, a people. They wept because they were God's people. They were not going to make light of God so white folks could laugh and make merry.

Do you know what the difference was? The ancient Jews had dignity. You may not think that dignity is important. But you know that when the Ward Singers jazzed up our spirituals, those white folks in Las Vagas had less respect for all of us. They knew that those songs were religious songs. They knew that when those songs were first sung, black women were being raped, their children were being snatched from them and sold into slavery, and their men were being whipped and killed. When they heard the Ward Singers singing those songs for entertainment, they said, "These people have no dignity"; and they thought less of all of us.

"How can we sing the Lord's songs in a strange land?" is a statement of dignity. Don't act a fool for white folks. You see it so often. Some black people think that they have emancipated themselves when they act a fool. You see it on the bus all the time. A black man without dignity will talk loud and act simple and think that somehow he is showing white folks that they don't frighten him any. A black man without dignity will do foolish things to make white people laugh. He'll talk to some imaginary friend at the other end of the bus. All the time he is talking for the man's entertainment, laughing for the man, performing for the man. The man sees him and thinks that we are all fools. It's no use my just sitting there and looking the other way because he is destroying me.

As black people, we don't have a lot of separate dignities. We have one dignity. If you mess it up, you mess it up for all of us. Or you see our black kids acting a fool out on the streets. They are messing up *our* dignity. You know why they are doing it? Because they don't understand. Because they are living in a world in which they have been shattered—leaning walls, tottering fences. So they are out there fighting back in their own little way, making a fool of themselves for the man.

We have got to find dignity somewhere because we will never be a Nation until we can first build a sense of dignity. That means that anywhere, on the job, on the bus, on the street, there are certain things that the man is not going to make you do. What can he give you if he takes your dignity? Nothing he has is worth it. You say, "I've got to eat." And I say, "Eating is not that important." You say, "I got a wife and children." I am not going to tell you that they are not that important. I am going to say that they *are* that important. They don't want a clown feeding them, and if you feed them, acting a clown, you are destroying them at the same time. "They only tear him down from his dignity." The Psalmist analyzed it all a long time ago, and he knew that it was possible to take a man and make a clown out of him.

John O. Killens means the same thing when he says the white folks took a black man and made a Nigger out of him. They robbed him of his dignity. The children of Israel remembered this one thing, and struggled to keep their dignity. They remembered that God had chosen Israel.

Don't laugh at that because *we* are God's chosen people. You don't fully recognize yet what that means. When we talk about the Black Nation, we have got to remember that the Black Nation, Israel, was chosen by God. Out of the whole world God chose Israel to covenant with, to say, "You will be my people and I will be your God." What else does a man need for dignity? He didn't go to the big nations with their big armies. He went to this little nation and said, "You are my chosen people." Perhaps if we could just remember that we are God's chosen people, that we have a covenant with God, then we would know that God will not forsake us. Even in the midst of violence and oppression, we would know that we are God's chosen people. We could look the white man straight in the eye and say, "There is nothing you can do to destroy us, and you cannot take from us our dignity."

The concept of the Nation must include the basic truth that the Nation consists of God's chosen people. Don't be afraid to say the word "God" because this is the 20th Century. You know what God means. It means that somebody is taking care of us. Don't try to make something selfish out of God. Don't try to use God to get something for *you* that *you* want. Understand that God is going to take care of *us,* the Black Nation, because we are God's chosen people. Because of this simple fact, the enemy is not going to destroy us. The time of our greatest strength (I am talking now about black people in this country) has not been in recent years, when we have had jobs and money and the illusion of being accepted. The time of our greatest strength was back in slavery when our slave forefathers believed that God was going to do something for them. They didn't just sit down because they believed this and wait for God to free them. The Underground Railroad was possible because black men and women were willing to take risks to get free. These black men and women were willing to go back into slave territory to bring out their people.

Nat Turner's faith in God did not stop his insurrection, nor thousands of slave insurrections all over the South. Every time a black man led an insurrection, he knew that he was doing the will of God. When you fight, you must believe that you are doing the will of God. Just being mad is not enough. That is the trouble with most of our rebellions. We get mad because somebody did something we didn't like, and we start throwing Molotov Cocktails and breaking out windows. This isn't enough. We must believe that our struggle is a revolutionary struggle designed to change the world and to establish us in our rightful position. We must have faith that we are doing the will of God who created us in his own image.

Anything that destroys a black man's dignity is bad. This is our yardstick. Just ask yourself, "Is this building a black man's dignity?" Then it is good. If it is destroying a black man's dignity, then it is bad. That is the only yardstick there is. It doesn't make any difference how much money is involved. Anything you do that makes black people proud, that is good. Anything that makes black people ashamed, that is bad. That is why so many black preachers in pulpits throughout this country are bad. They use the name of God but what they are doing is bad because they make black people ashamed. That is why Muhammad Ali is good, because what he did makes us proud. So he is good. What Muhammad Ali did and is doing is the will of God. You know how we know? Because it makes black people proud. That is God's will, but what preachers are doing in so many pulpits is bad. It doesn't make any difference how many times they say God on Sunday morning, or how big their Bible is, or how many songs they sing about what God is going to do in the great bye-and-bye. It is bad because they are destroying our dignity, and even the little children sitting in these churches are getting to the point where they are ashamed. It is bad, it is not the will of God.

Don't be afraid to try to figure it out in terms of the will of God. God wants us to be men. If he had wanted us to be something else, he would have made us something else. If he had wanted us to be snakes or bears, he would have made us snakes or bears. He made us men; he expects us to be men. We tend to forget. Back in slavery our people remembered. We look back and think that this is a time we would like to forget. But we must never forget it because back there we had men and women with dignity. In the midst of the most difficult conditions, they had dignity. There were men and women that Ole Massa couldn't break. That was what he was trying to do. The things he did were not only designed to make him money, but to break black men.

That is still what the white enemy is trying to do today, to break you. That is why he is happy to get Clara Ward and her singers to shuffle for him. That is why he is happy when he can get Roy Wilkins to issue ridiculous statements. He knows that he is making us ashamed. If he can take our little children and make them think that being a pimp is the greatest thing in the world, he is happy. He is breaking us, making us ashamed.

Everything he has done to us was intended to make us ashamed, to destroy our pride. Why do you think he gives black children second-class schools which teach white supremacy? Because he knows that this is one certain way to keep a people down, by robbing them of pride. It is a miracle that we have a Black Nation today, that so many black men and women and children believe that they are somebody, after the systematic effort that has gone into breaking us. But millions of us are bewildered and confused, not even understanding that the man is deliberately trying to break us by robbing us of our dignity.

I was talking to a friend of mine in the barber shop the other day. He means well. He bought a house out there where some of you are trying to buy or have already bought. He lived around the corner for a long time, but when he started making a little money he wanted something better for his children. He wanted good schools for them and a good neighborhood. So he took his children out of public school and put them into a Catholic school. He was getting the best for them. There were only a few black children in the school or in the neighborhood. Everything was so fine. He was telling me about his son.

I said, "You are destroying that child." He loves that boy more than anything in the world. He works 12 hours a day trying to do his best for the boy.

He said, "How am I destroying the child? Everything I do is for that boy. That's why I took him out there so he wouldn't be with these. . . ."

"That is the first wrong thing, telling him that you took him out there so that he wouldn't be with us."

"But I look out on 12th Street at night and see little children running up and down the street. I don't want that for my children." So I said, "If I had to choose, I'd choose one of those running up and down 12th Street, because if he comes out of it alive, he is going to have some sense of identity with his own people. Out there where your child is, you have destroyed that possibility. How is he going to get it in a white Catholic school, in a white neighborhood? What can you say to him?"

"I tell him to stay in school and he will get a better job. He won't be like. . . ."

"There you go again—won't be like *them*. That is what you are trying to say. You can get a better job, you can live in a white neighborhood, you can send your children to a white school, that is what you are trying to tell him. You are separating him from the Black Nation. Your whole way of life is designed to separate him from his own people."

He said, "Oh, no, he knows he's black, he has pride in being black."

"Does he know that white people are his enemy?"

"That isn't so, white people are not his enemy," he said. "Let me give you a little illustration. My little boy and another little boy play together, and there is a little white girl who lives across the street. So my little boy and the boy he plays with were talking to the little white girl, and they asked her which one she liked best. The little white girl said that she liked the other little boy best. She didn't like my boy best, yet the little boy she picked is darker than my little boy."

I said, "Now how about *that?* Do you think you have really proved your point? Don't you know that they were both little 'Niggers' to that little white girl, and don't you see what you have done? You've got your little black boy out there in a white neighborhood, begging a little white girl to say that she likes him. Now there's no hope for either one of you."

The important thing is that this black father doesn't see anything wrong with his little boy trying to get a little white girl across the street to say that she likes him.

I asked, "How many times have they called your little boy 'Nigger' in school?"

Now he was getting defensive, "Not much, just once or twice, that's all."

"Do you think that being called 'Nigger' once or twice a day is doing him a whole lot of good?" I asked. "And do you think that all these white folks teaching him all about white supremacy are really going to make him a better black man? Don't you think that all of this will ruin his mind?"

"No," he replied, "what he is learning is good. He's in the best school that I can afford."

I asked, "Don't you think that when he gets through the day with all those white teachers, priests, and nuns, he must hate you when he comes home because you are black and inferior?"

"Oh, no, you don't understand," he protested, "I am protecting him from all that. I will give you another illustration. You know all these slick-headed 'processes' that the boys wear in black neighborhoods? Well, out in our neighborhood, he never sees one. Well, the other day a teen-age black boy came to pick up a maid from across the street and he had a 'process.' He is nine years old and he had never seen a process, isn't that good?"

I said, "I'm on the verge of tears, go on with your story."

"Well, that night when I came home, he told me that he would like to have his hair fixed like that so it would be long and slick and shiny. He didn't know what to call it, but he wanted one."

I asked, "What did you think about that?"

He said, "I was glad that he won't see that kind of thing very often out where we live."

I said, "Aren't you worried about the fact that the very first time he saw a black boy with a 'process' he wanted one? Why do you think he wanted it? Can't you see that your little boy is ashamed of being black with kinky hair, and he wants to be white?"

He said, "Oh, no, it just shows what a little bad influence can do to a child."

There we have a poor little black boy being torn to pieces by white people—or as the Psalmist says, "being shattered." And his poor father, thinking that he is doing the best thing for his child, sacrificing, working himself to death, and his wife working herself to death, and this poor little black boy going straight to hell. By "hell" I mean the place where a man has no dignity and no respect for himself.

We have only one basis for judgment. If anything gives a black man a sense of pride and dignity, it is good. If it destroys his pride and dignity, it is bad. Remember this when you get ready to buy a house in a white neighborhood. Is it going to give your child a sense of pride to be out there in an all-white school where he is despised by teachers and students alike? The public schools are not good and the fight to improve them seems almost futile, so you are going to send him to some Lutheran or Catholic school and destroy him completely. Many black people see other black people only through the white man's eyes. The white man has completely destroyed their love of self. They have no sense of pride. They are actually afraid of us and of our influence upon their children.

We are not going to hurt their little children. From the front steps of the Church everyday, I see hundreds of little children who live in our neighborhood. They are all better off than this black child in his better white neighborhood. They look around and everybody is black. I may scream at them for throwing stones through the back windows, but I scream at them because I am concerned about them. I don't want them tearing up our Church building, but I don't hate them and I don't despise them. I can't call them "Nigger" because they are a part of me. And that is the way everybody else is, up and down the street. But out in my friend's better white neighborhood, his little boy isn't a part of anything, and he knows it. He can walk up and down the street and ask little white girls whether or not they like him, but every day his dignity is slipping away and self-hate is taking its place.

Those of us who are in the Black Nation realize that we are God's chosen people. No matter what the enemy does to us, we are God's chosen people and we must love each other. We fight together against a common enemy, confident of ultimate victory because we are God's chosen people. "How long will you set upon a man to shatter him, like a leaning wall, a tottering fence? They only plan to tear him down from his dignity."

5/"He Who Is Not with Me..."

"He who is not with me is against me, and
he who does not gather with me scatters"
(*Luke* 11:23).

I want to talk about the moment of decision when people are forced
to decide where they stand. Most times in life we hate to make a
decision. We hate to be forced to decide where we stand. We hate
to be forced to stand up and be counted. We try to sort of slip and
slide from day to day, hoping that no one will ever really make us
face an issue.

So I go back to an incident in the life of Jesus which is compara-
ble to the moment of decision which we face in today's world. In
his efforts to build a Nation out of the corruption and disunity of
Israel, he constantly faced the people's conviction that anything
they might do would be futile, because they felt that it was impossible for Israel to ever become a Nation again. Jesus called men to
decision saying, "He who is not with me is against me. He who does
not gather with me, scattereth." Each individual was trying to
secure his own little individual benefits from his relationship with
the Roman oppressor, some little favor, some little special privilege.
The Black Nation of Israel had degenerated into total corruption
and hopelessness. Black people no longer believed in themselves
and black people no longer loved each other. Their lives were
molded by what they thought they could get out of the Romans.
They loved their oppressors and hated their brothers because their
oppressors had power and their brothers were powerless.

The Nation Israel to which Jesus talked still remembered the

Maccabean Revolution against Rome. Israel fought for many years but was defeated, and out of this defeat had come the belief that there was now no hope for the Nation. They could stand on the hillside and look out over the plains and see the cities which had been burned to the ground. They remembered the men who had died in the struggle. They were no longer prepared to fight and die. They were willing to accept the degradation of their oppression. They were willing to go along from day to day, doing the best they could for themselves as individuals.

So no real Nation existed when Jesus began his ministry. He walked from village to village, preaching, teaching, healing, performing miracles, anything to get a group of people together so that he might give them his simple message. "It is necessary that you turn your back upon individualism and join with your brothers to again build a Black Nation of which we can be proud." Jesus called men to a real decision. In all probability his disciples were already committed to the revolutionary struggle as Zealots before they saw Jesus, but when they heard him, they accepted his leadership and followed him.

They were part of a small underground revolutionary movement which included John the Baptist, dedicated to complete separation from Rome. Some Zealots engaged in terrorism and sabotage and refused to pay taxes to Rome. The Zealots sought to punish Jews who collaborated with the white oppressors. This struggle between the revolutionary Zealots and the collaborating Scribes and Pharisees largely shaped the ministry of Jesus, and eventually all found reason to take offense at his teachings which sought to change the minds of men as a basis for a new kind of revolution.

Jesus was the leader of a revolutionary movement, some of it above ground and some of it below ground. When he went into the synagogue to preach his first sermon in Nazareth, he read from the prophet Isaiah and declared that the freeing and healing of men was the purpose of his ministry. The people resented his claim to be the fulfillment of prophecy and they tried to kill him. They would have stoned him, but he escaped. His ministry began in violence and conflict, just as it ended in violence and conflict.

Soon he heard of the arrest of John the Baptist, the accepted head of the revolutionary Zealots. The power structure was trying to destroy the movement. Jesus fled from Galilee. There was nothing cowardly about his flight, it was the only sensible thing he could do. He carried on the basic part of his ministry in Capernaum, moving by stealth and by night. With John the Baptist in prison, the movement was leaderless, and Jesus began to take control. John sent disciples to inquire as to his credentials for leadership. Jesus could only say, "Tell John the things you see. I am building the movement by freeing and healing men that the Black Nation may be reborn."

With the death of John the Baptist, Jesus moved into unquestioned leadership of Israel's revolutionary forces, making inevitable the combined opposition of the white oppressor, Rome, and of those black collaborators who feared that revolution might destroy their privileged positions. There were the revolutionary Zealots on one side and the collaborating Scribes and Pharisees on the other, but most of the people hesitated to make a decision and refused to support either side.

So Jesus dealt with a group of people who would do nothing. When he spoke to them about the Nation and its possibilities, they would listen gladly, but they refused to take a position. They wanted to stay neutral. They didn't want to make their oppressors angry. They didn't want to provoke the oppressors into taking any kind of reprisals against them. Jesus seemed foolish to his friends, talking about rebuilding a Black Nation. They looked about them and asked, "How can anyone rebuild a Nation out of this? Out of our degradation, our corruption, our fear, our inadequacy. Oh, we have a few people who are doing well, but for the most part we are poverty-stricken, we are helpless. How can anyone build a Nation out of this?"

This is what Jesus faced wherever he talked, even when multitudes gathered. The words of Jesus sounded foolish even to his mother and to his brothers. You remember how he was preaching and healing and his mother and his family came to take him home because he was making a fool out of himself. They said, "Anybody who thinks that he can make a Nation out of us must be insane." This is the self—hate that oppression creates in the oppressed and this is the advice that friends give down through the generations. A friend can always find reasons why you shouldn't do anything. Most of your friends will tell you, "That is ridiculous. You're getting yourself out on a limb and you're going to get in trouble. Why do you want to get involved in all of this? Why must you go around talking like this?" We can imagine the friends of Jesus cautioning him, "All you're doing is making everybody mad. The Romans are beginning to look at you. The Scribes and the Pharisees are watching you, pretty soon you won't even be able to hold a job or anything."

These weren't his enemies. These were his friends, his relatives, the people he knew, who were outside of the movement. The more he talked and preached, the more people began to listen, the more his friends were concerned about his welfare, because they didn't believe that anything he said was possible. They said, "You're talking like a crazy man. You can't make anything out of us. We're too far gone. All you're going to do is get yourself killed." They were trying to put into Jesus the weakness and the fear that they had in themselves. He embarrassed them.

But even if what he said seemed foolish and ridiculous, it was still something that they knew ought to be. They knew that black people ought to be free. They knew that they ought to be willing to stand up and fight against oppression, even if it was dangerous. So when they argued with him, they were arguing with themselves as well. If he could stand up and speak out, then they knew they ought to stand up and speak out. If they could sit him down, then they could go back to sleep, the nightmares would go away and they wouldn't feel guilty all day when they walked around doing nothing. If they could just shut that mouth, if they could just stop him from telling them "We can be a Nation," if he would just stop saying it, they could remain the way they were. They could go back slipping and sliding, and trying to get along. But here he was every day, in the market place, in the synagogue, in somebody's house, talking.

They convinced themselves, he's got to be insane. There's no way a sane man could look at us and decide that he could make a Nation out of us. We were a Nation once, a long time ago. It is enough to look back at our past glories. We have Moses and Abraham, isn't that enough for any people? But Jesus was talking about what could be done today, and they said, "Jesus, you're a fool." They were doing it because they loved him, they thought. Just like some of you parents when your children talk about trying to do something to change this world in which they live. You tell them, "You don't understand. I've lived in this world for fifty years, and I know you can't get away with that kind of stuff."

Your boy comes and tells you he's not going to Vietnam, and you say, "Oh, no, son, you've got to go. Just think, if you don't go, what's going to happen. When you come back from jail, you can't get a job." (You don't say anything about if he doesn't come back from Vietnam.) "It'll always be on your record. Oh, son, don't do this, it'll hurt me so. What will I tell my friends?" Just tell them that you've got a son in the penitentiary because he wouldn't go get killed in Vietnam. That's what you tell them. Or your daughter comes home and says, "I'm going down to work in Mississippi," and you say, "Girl, have you lost your mind? Now, you go down to the telephone company and take a little exam. Get a good job, work there a little while, get married and you'll be doing alright. Quit talking all this foolishness about civil rights. You must have been listening to Reverend Cleage." That's what you tell your own children, so you understand how the friends and relatives of Jesus felt and talked. They felt just like you do about involvement in the freedom struggle. It doesn't pay off like individualism.

Some girls were telling me about the office they work in. Quite a few black sisters work there. They have a black group leader who is a real Aunt Jemima. Do you know what she says when she goes home at night? She says to herself, "I don't care what they say, I'm smarter than all them Niggers, because I know how to get along." You can sit there and say she's a fool, but she's no fool. She just made a decision to betray the Nation, that's all. She's going to shuffle her way through. The white man in that office, the boss, doesn't have to do anything. He lets her hang all of the black folks for him. He tells her, "You see that girl over there, she's not doing so good, is she?" And she says, "I've been kind of dissatisfied with her myself." He says, "I think you ought to kind of watch her." Then he comes back in about a week and says, "If she gets much worse, we're going to have to let her go, don't you think?" And Aunt Jemima agrees.

Thats the way it is. When the man gets ready to hang us, he gets some Aunt Jemima or Uncle Tom to do it. What this whole situation means is that when people don't realize that they belong to anything, when they don't see any power that is theirs or can be theirs, they start looking for individual benefits. That's all this Aunt Jemima is doing. She looks at the world and says, "This white man has everything. I'm going to work with him."

It's the same way in the factory, with a whole lot of black shop stewards. They won't do a thing to help a black brother, but they will run all over the plant to take care of some little grievance that a white boy has. Finally, the union bosses notice and say, "That's a good one. He's been tested. He's hung black brothers and sisters for years. We don't have to worry about him. Take him out to Solidarity House. Put him on the payroll." Now he's on his way up. His field of operations has been broadened. Now he's a union official and he can hang brothers and sisters out in the community. He is sure that his decision to work for the white man was a good one. We can understand the decision. The only thing that tricks us is that we don't understand how many black people have made that kind of decision. We try to go along pretending that we're all brothers because we're all black, and that we're all catching hell together, but that's not the way it is.

The Nation that Jesus was talking about was to be made up of people who had made a different decision, black brothers and sisters who could say, "I'm not going to work with the man, I'm going to work for my black brother." Jesus picked twelve disciples who were no longer going to work with the man, and that was the beginning of the Nation. He preached to five thousand, and a handful would come up to follow him. That was the beginning of the Nation. Some were making one kind of decision about what's best for the Nation, while a lot of other people were making another decision about what seemed best for them as individuals. The great mass of people never really made any decision. They just drifted along, doing little selfish individualistic things, without ever realizing that not to decide for the Nation is, in fact, to decide against the Nation.

We live at a time when conscious decisions ought to be made. Applying the words of Jesus, "He who is not with the Nation is against the Nation. He who does not gather with me, scattereth." The time has come to get up off our knees and stop shuffling for petty little individual advantages from the oppressor. The decision to come into the Nation is the decision to stop being a slave and to stand up and live with pride and with dignity. Each individual must decide for himself. The friends of Jesus told him, "Forget it." Your friends will tell you to forget it, too. If you start pointing out all the things that are wrong with the way they treat black folks on your job or in your community, your friends will take you aside and tell you, "You're making a bad fellow out of yourself." They'll try to stop you, just like they did Jesus.

It wasn't only Jesus' friends, it was also the established Uncle Toms who were profiting from the system of oppression, that came to Jesus, the Scribes and the Pharisees. They weren't friends. They weren't even pretending to be friends. They said, "He's dangerous." They had to destroy him. When Jesus started talking and people started listening, they were alarmed, because if Jesus could bring together a Black Nation, their positions were in jeopardy. They said, "We've got to start something that will destroy him." So

they began a whispering campaign, "He's in league with the devil."
"He performs miracles by the power of Beelzebub." They were
frightening the people. "What he's doing is evil. He's the devil. You
good people better not get too close to him." You see the same
thing happening everywhere today. If anyone starts putting the
Black Nation back together, all kinds of systematic propaganda is
launched to destroy him and the Black Nation. "He's the devil."
That's so that the people he's working with will repudiate him.
That's what they did with Jesus. That's what they did with Marcus
Garvey. That's what they did with Malcolm X. But the Nation will
not die.

Jesus didn't spend his life waiting to be crucified. A lot of people
seem to have the impression that Jesus walked around with his
hands folded, waiting for his enemies to nail him to a cross. That's
a lie. He was fighting and twisting and turning all of his life, trying
to teach and organize, even while he knew that his enemies were
working day and night to destroy him and his influence with the
people. When Jesus finally came before Pilate and the people
screamed "crucify him, crucify him," this was the result of the
campaign of vilification that had been carried on against him by
the priests, the Scribes, the Pharisees, and the people in power who
were afraid that their power would be lost if a Black Nation came
into being. There were the friends who said that he was insane, or
he wouldn't be risking himself, and there were the enemies who
said that he was evil and in league with the devil. These were the
people who killed Jesus. Not the white Gentiles, but his own black
people.

It is the same today. The white man uses his black flunkies to destroy us. He doesn't have to do it himself. We don't realize it as we
go along from day to day. Any time he gets ready to hang us he
finds an Uncle Tom to do it for him. Whenever he comes up all
smiling and patting you on the back and saying, "I want you to do
something for me," watch it, because he's probably going to use
you to hang some black brother. That's the same kind of thing

that happened during the lifetime of Jesus. You can take a Tom and use him to hang anybody. If I were a white factory owner and wanted to keep black folks in their place, I would get a good black personnel manager. They used to do that out at Ford's a long time ago, even before black people really started to get together. They'd have their big Nigger sitting there in the personnel office and then they would hire two or three little ones that they picked up out of some college some place. They would sit there and black folks couldn't get a thing because they knew just what to do.

The Black Nation has to stop that kind of foolishness. We must find a way to do something about the Toms that are destroying us. We get a Negro in some kind of position and we see him working for the white man, day after day after day. We can't just say, "Well, after all, he's a Negro, he's got a good job, and we ought to be proud." I'm not proud when he's down there hanging me day after day. If he's on the City Council and he's not doing anything, I'm not proud that we have a Negro on the City Council. And I'm not proud of the prospect that we might soon have two of them down there doing nothing. I'm not proud when we have two Negroes on the Board of Education doing nothing either. We have to get over this plantation pride about the number of Negroes in the big house. We have to understand that the Nation exists and that either you're in it or you're out of it. And if you're a Tom, you're out of it. We have to stop talking about them being brothers, and how proud we are of them. When the time comes, and we can get rid of them, we must do it.

We must get to the place where a black politician knows that the first time he makes a really wrong step, we are going to hang him at the next election. The only way you build a Nation is to put the fear of God in the hearts of those who would betray the Nation for personal gain. They must know that when the next election rolls around, we are going to be out in the streets, working just as hard to take them out as the white folks are working to keep them in. You say, "But that's putting the Church into politics." Yes, sir, right in the middle of it! And I don't mean on the sly, either. I mean to tell them publicly, "We're out to defeat you." Let everybody know it.

Institutions that are not serving the Nation must also be destroyed. That's the way you build a Nation. You can't build a Nation just standing around talking about it. If we're going to build a Nation, then we're going to have to make people understand that if we say something, we believe it, and if we believe it, we are willing to work for it. Jesus and his followers were working together all the time, until Jesus could say, "All the friends that I have are in the Nation. My mother, father, brothers and sisters are the people who believe as I do."

We must work together and not let somebody come to us at election time, and say, "I'm black just like you are." We can't go along with him when we know that everything he has been doing has been against the Nation and for the benefit of our oppressor. That's the next big step we must make. We are so loyal that once we get a black man in any office we keep voting for him, even if he's working against us every day. We say, "It's better to have him in there." But it isn't better to have him in, it's better to take him out. The only way you build a Nation is to establish discipline. Black politicians must learn to be afraid to do anything we don't want them to do. We are the Black Nation and those who are not with us are against us. They must decide! Either they are with the Nation, or they are against the Nation.

They hate to make a decision. During the strike which we organized in support of Adam Powell, one of our outstanding local Uncle Tom politicians pleaded, "Don't make me say anything. Let me slide." A big black leader didn't want to say anything in a crisis confronting all black people! "He who is not with me is against me." And if he's against me, he is just another enemy. Let's teach this lesson to our children. "He who does not gather with me, scattereth." Think of how true that is. If he's not gathering the Nation together, he's scattering it, tearing it up, destroying it. That was Jesus' experience in Israel and we are having exactly the same experience today, in this city and in these United States.

Heavenly Father, we thank thee for the opportunity of coming into thy house. We thank thee for the sense of fellowship which we have as we gather here to rededicate ourselves to the emerging Black Nation. We thank thee for the opportunity which our worship gives us to make basic decisions. We thank thee for the opportunity to work for the gathering of the Black Nation. Help us to remember always that he who is not with us is against us and he who does not gather with us scatters. Be with us as we seek to remember and to understand the meaning of the life and the teachings of our Lord, Jesus Christ, the Black Messiah. Amen.

6/"He Stirs Up the People"

"And when he drew near and saw the city
he wept over it . . ." (*Luke* 19:41).

Palm Sunday marks the beginning of Holy Week, a most significant
period in the life of Jesus, and tremendously important for those
who would understand the message of Jesus within the framework
of the revolutionary nationalism of the Zealot Movement. From its
very beginning the Church has celebrated Palm Sunday and the
triumphant entry of Jesus into Jerusalem.

It is difficult today, almost two thousand years later, to understand what this triumphant entry really was. It is difficult for us to
understand *any* of the events in the life of Jesus because more and
more we have tended to see him as a not quite human figure who
preached and talked to people in a kind of ritualistic preparation
for a mystical act that was designed to redeem mankind. We tend
to think of Jesus and the events of his life not as real events in the
life of a real man, but as a series of ceremonial acts leading up to
the splendid ceremony of the Resurrection on Easter morning.

This is not the way it was at all. Jesus was a man engaged in
everyday revolutionary activities designed essentially to free the
Nation Israel from oppression and bondage. It is necessary that we
understand this because our interpretation of his message depends
upon what we think he was doing. If we think of Jesus as just an
individual sent by God to suffer, die and then mysteriously rise, we
will attach no importance to the events of his life. For most of the
early Christian converts, this was true. They attached no real significance to the things Jesus had done nor to the things he had said.

71

They made little real effort to preserve his words or a record of his activities, and only the fragmentary accounts, almost incidentally preserved in the Synoptic Gospels, enable us to piece together something of the meaning of his life.

The early Church remembered his death, not his life. They did not think of his death as the death of a man who was killed by enemies because of the things he taught and did, but rather as a dramatic event which God had provided for mankind's salvation. But this simply was not true. Jesus lived a very real life. The things he did were real, just as the things we do are real. The things Jesus did had meaning, just as the things we do have meaning. Jesus was pitted against forces, just as we are pitted against forces. Jesus recognized the existence of enemies, just as we must recognize the existence of enemies. Jesus spent his life trying to resurrect a Nation and he pitted himself and his Movement against enemies who were deadly serious about destroying him and the things for which he lived and for which he was willing to die.

Years later, his disciples and others looking back at his entry into Jerusalem called it a triumphant or triumphal entry. Only in a very relative sense was it a triumphant entry. When he reached Jerusalem, there were no thousands upon thousands of people waiting to greet him.

Jesus was trying to rebuild the Black Nation Israel and to free it from Rome, the white oppressor. When we say the Nation Israel, we are speaking of the Black Jews of the biblical period, many of whom still remain in Israel and the Arab world. We would misunderstand the struggle in which Jesus was engaged if we interpreted his so-called triumphant entry into Jerusalem as the acceptance of his separatist position by the vast majority of the Jewish people who were still willing to accept oppression rather than join the revolutionary movement which Jesus represented. A people demoralized by oppression does not easily rally behind a nationalist leader. They are afraid. Moses had found this to be true in Egypt.

During Lent we try to describe the various things that Jesus found it necessary to do because of the degradation of the Nation

Israel. People had come to the point of complete dejection. They no longer had any hope that they could build for themselves a Nation or a decent way of life. A people who had once been a Nation, who had been delivered from bondage in Egypt, who had wandered for forty years in the wilderness, who had fought their way into a promised land, this people had degenerated into a mass of individuals who no longer had any sense of a Nation. Each person plotted only for his own individual advancement. Each individual was willing to sell out the Nation for personal gain. The white oppressor, Rome, took advantage of this situation by pitting one individual against another, preventing the unity of the Black Nation, Israel.

Jesus had the task of trying to rebuild a Nation out of these fragmented individuals. He realized that most of the people were incapable of forming a Nation. They had been too corrupted by contact with the oppressor. They were afraid. The Uncle Toms of their day were so identified with Rome that they could not possibly have any loyalty to their own people. So Jesus was forced to go from place to place and bring together the few black nationalist revolutionaries who were willing to say, "I am willing to subordinate myself to the resurrection of a Nation." Twelve of these Zealots who made up a loosely coordinated revolutionary movement became his disciples.

It was this kind of situation that Jesus faced as he made his way steadfastly towards Jerusalem. A good part of the Gospels is devoted to this journey. Jesus was beginning to recognize the tremendous difficulties that he faced because everywhere he went there was danger of betrayal from his own people. There were always those who would run to the enemy and say, "Listen to what he's saying. He's telling us that we can be a Nation and that means rebellion. He's talking against you good white folks." So Jesus had to remain constantly on the move. He couldn't even remain in the villages overnight. You read that in the Gospels. You think he just went out to pray because it was nice and cool in the countryside? He went out into the countryside to hide and pray so that he couldn't be betrayed by his own people. He was trying to tell them that they could be free, and they weren't ready to be free. They were frightened. So they would run and tell the man, "This prophet Jesus, he's talking some mighty funny talk."

Gradually his enemies began to close in on him. It wasn't a big enough area for him to do too much hiding. So Jesus began to realize that it was only a matter of time until they caught him off some place by himself and killed him. He was dangerous because he was talking to a people who had lost the dream of being a Nation and he was rekindling that dream. He didn't want to die off someplace by himself where no one would even know that he was dead. That is what is happening all over Africa today. A leader arises, then suddenly he just disappears, because the easiest way to kill a leader is to just take him off some place by himself. Remember Lumumba? The mistake the white folks made with Malcolm X —and I'm sure it was the white folks—was that they had him killed publicly. They made him a martyr. They didn't intend to do that with Malcolm, any more than they wanted to do that with Jesus. They wanted to catch him off by himself and get rid of him. Jesus realized that it was not fitting that a prophet should die outside of Jerusalem. All the corruption, all the power, everything was centered in Jerusalem. So he decided to go right into the middle of Jerusalem and do what he had to do, and if they were going to kill him, they would have to do it there where everybody could see and understand.

This is why he turned his face steadfastly towards Jerusalem. We have made out of this some kind of myth, that Jesus just had to get to Jerusalem to fulfill prophecy and to die. He didn't want to die. He had a job he was trying to do. And Jerusalem was the place it had to be done. If he had to die, he was willing to die, but there is a tremendous difference between being willing to die and seeking death. Jesus was not looking for death. He was organizing all the way to Jerusalem. He would stop and talk to his disciples. He would tell them, "Have faith in yourselves. You don't have to believe that the Romans are entitled to hold you in subjection." He would teach in the little villages, he would talk to the children. He preached revolution and black nationalism all the way to Jerusalem.

The Romans were afraid that Jesus was going to put together a force that could disrupt the empire. They didn't worry about individuals. They didn't care how much money a Jew had. But when somebody began talking about a Nation, then they began to worry. A Black Nation would be a problem. They were very worried about him as he turned his face steadfastly towards Jerusalem. When he reached Jerusalem, he had some people with him, some disciples, and other followers. These were people who were capable of rising above individualism, people who were capable of dedication to the Nation. He had picked some here, some there. He had sent seventy of them out, two by two, to preach the message of the Black Nation. He had followers, not a multitude, but a number of people who believed in him. He was just beginning the process of building a Nation.

He had some people already in Jerusalem, but as he came to the city, he wept because he knew that most of the people there had no understanding of the possibilities. He knew that they were not a Nation and that they had no dream of ever becoming a Nation again. He knew that they were lost in corruption and selfishness. And so, he wept as he looked down at Jerusalem. That doesn't sound like a man getting ready to make a triumphant entry. He sounds like a man who understood the people he was trying to work with. He looked at them and he wept.

I know exactly how he felt because as I ride around election day and watch black folks going to the polls, it is enough to make you weep. They go to the polls to vote because they believe that it is right to vote. But they vote wrong every time. They don't have any faith in themselves so they go into the polls to do what somebody else has instructed them to do. They vote against themselves.

Then as Jesus came down to enter Jerusalem with his little band of followers, the people screamed, "Hosanna!" They put him on a little colt. He didn't try to look impressive. He knew that if he en-

tered looking too impressive, he wouldn't have time to do anything. They would kill him on the way in. He went in on his little
colt. They didn't even have a saddle on it, but they put coats on it.
A small group walked in front, another behind, all screaming
"Hosanna." It was a nationalistic demonstration. That means it was
participated in by a small group who believed that they could build
a Nation. There were no huge throngs when Jesus entered Jerusalem. Even the little group he had with him and the little group that
greeted him didn't really understand what Jesus was talking
about, but they caught a glimmer of hope and so they screamed,
"Hosanna!" Hosanna means "to save." More specifically, at that
time, it meant "God save Israel; God save the Nation." That's why
it was a nationalistic demonstration. They were calling on God to
save the Nation Israel.

And they were also attributing to Jesus, as a leader, the power
to call the Nation into being. "Blessed be the Kingdom of Our
Father, David, that is coming." Historically, the mission of David
was to re-establish the Nation. So the emphasis in the triumphant
entry was not upon Jesus as an individual who was soon to be crucified and resurrected to bring about some kind of mystical salvation;
it was upon Jesus as a prophet who had called a Nation to repentance, a nation that was coming into being. "Blessed be the Kingdom
of our Father, David, that is coming." The sense of triumph came
from the feeling that they were at the beginning of the rebuilding of
a Nation. The people wanted to be a Nation. That was evident
from the crowd which gathered to see this man who said that they
could become a Nation.

But few understood the process by which a Nation is built. Most
thought that a Nation was something that could come into being
through the efforts of somebody else, through the efforts of God,
through the efforts of a leader, or a prophet. They wanted a Nation,
but they didn't want to do the things necessary to build a Nation.
They didn't want to stop "Tomming" to get a Nation. If they could
have gotten a Nation without sacrificing anything, they would have
been happy. They didn't want to give up their individualism, and

perhaps most important, they were not willing to take a chance. Maybe it wouldn't work. They longed for the establishment of a Nation and the end of oppression, but they weren't sure that it was worth the risk.

Think back a few years to the Freedom March we had in Detroit in June of 1963. That was much more of a triumphant thing than Jesus had in Jerusalem. National television networks announced at one point that there were 300,000 people marching down Woodward Avenue. Black people as far as the eye could see. We all marched down Woodward Avenue to Cobo Hall, filled up the Arena and every Convention Room in Cobo Hall, and sat all over the lawn and the streets and everywhere. That was a triumphant entry! We were protesting against everything that was happening in Birmingham, Alabama, and all over the South. It was a nationalistic protest against an enemy who was beginning to be revealed to us. As we marched down Woodward Avenue, we didn't know exactly what we wanted to do any more than the people who entered Jerusalem with Jesus did. In a sense we wanted a Nation. We knew that we had to come together if we were going to do anything about the problems that confronted us. Somehow we understood at the moment that our individual possessions, our cars, our houses, our jobs, our college degrees, all of these things that we had as individuals didn't mean anything. Somehow only what we possessed together had real value.

That is why 300,000 people came together to walk down Woodward Avenue. We felt that somehow we had to become a Black Nation if we were to find escape from the racial oppression which we saw revealed on television every night. Just walking together seemed to be a move in that direction. And so, in a sense, the kind of nationalistic demonstration Jesus had when he entered Jerusalem was what we had walking down Woodward Avenue. Instead of Jesus, we had Dr. Martin Luther King. When you marched down Woodward Avenue, you thought Dr. King was the leader who was going to build a Black Nation and give us deliverance. In a sense we were giving him the same kind of loyalty that the people who entered into Jerusalem with Jesus gave to him. We marched down Woodward Avenue and went into Cobo Hall.

There the Mayor got up and gave his greetings, and told us what good Niggers we were. He was up there talking and black people were still marching down Woodward Avenue. He was talking and we knew that he was destroying the very thing that we had walked down there for. We had a feeling that if it was possible for 300,000 of us to come together, we certainly hadn't come together to listen to Mayor Cavanagh who was one of our oppressors. He wasn't one of us.

Then Walter Reuther got up and told us how much he believed in us and we listened to him. What was happening to our triumphant entry? It was collapsing, falling to pieces. The nationalism, the sense of Nation, was being dissipated. The platform was full of dignitaries. Every preacher in town who could get up there was up there, but the feeling of Nation wasn't there. The unity was gone and we were disappointed. During the few minutes which I was given to speak, I voiced our need for protest and struggle against the enemy, and I have never heard such a thunderous response.

Jesus had better control of his demonstration than we had of ours, because he understood what was happening. When he went into Jerusalem, he didn't just go in to meet with Pontius Pilate and Herod and let them make speeches. He went in to confront an enemy. That's the difference. He went in to do battle against an enemy. The first night he got out of sight as quickly as possible. The next day he came back into the city and went to the Temple. The Temple was the center of the corruption that was destroying the Nation. The priests, the Scribes and the Pharisees controlled the power there. But it wasn't real power. It was Uncle Tom power. They depended upon Rome for their very existence, but Rome let them carry on their little rackets. No matter where you came from, you had to change your money into Jewish money before you could buy anything to sacrifice. And the Scribes and Pharisees had made a racket out of this. They had made another racket out of selling sacrificial animals for exorbitant prices. Everything in the Temple had been reduced to a racket, and the rackets were operated by Jews with the connivance of Rome.

So Jesus went into the Temple and drove the money changers out. No matter how much we are taught about how filled with love Jesus was, we cannot forget that moment of righteous anger when he drove the money changers out of the Temple. He drove them out with a whip. He said, "Get out! You have made the House of God a den of thieves." The Scribes and the Pharisees were afraid to say anything because the crowds of people who were in Jerusalem for the religious festival knew that they were being cheated and robbed. So they went aside and they began to plot to destroy Jesus because now he was hitting at their income, the source of their privileged position. They were not concerned about the Nation.

It is the same today. Go into any city in America and if you are trying to do something to help black people, you will find one force that will be against you from beginning to end, and that's the Black Church. You can't get together a group of black preachers to fight for the benefit of black people in any city. Anytime an independent black man decides to run for political office, who will work night and day to defeat him? Black preachers. The Temple in Jerusalem had become an instrument in the hands of the enemy, and so it is today with most of our Churches. They, too, have become instruments in the hands of the enemy.

Let me tell you how it works. In the first place, they confuse our minds. They keep us mixed up. They tell us that the things on earth are unimportant. There are black Churches within walking distance of this building right now where black preachers are telling black congregations of thousands that we don't have to worry because God is going to take care of everything. "God can do anything but fail." That's just like the Temple in Jerusalem. That's corruption. That's the destruction of a Nation. When a people feels that the problems of life are not their problems to deal with and solve, they are doomed to extinction.

We have the same problem that Jesus had, but he was not afraid to attack the Scribes and the Pharisees who were in control of the black community because he knew they were being used by the enemy. Our Churches also are being used against the Nation. Our Churches are also being used to destroy our unity. Our Churches are being used to block both political and economic unity. Our black Churches are being used against us. In attacking the Temple, Jesus pitted himself against the power structure which was holding his people in bondage. You can't free a people as long as their leaders are taking orders from the enemy. You can't free a people as long as they believe that the enemy is trying to help them. That was the problem that Jesus faced in trying to talk to the Nation Israel. The people couldn't believe that they could escape from powerlessness. They would go to the Temple and let the Scribes and Pharisees brainwash them. They were afraid to take their chances in a power struggle. The followers of Jesus longed for a Nation, but they didn't know that a Nation comes into being only when a people are willing to unite and rise above their individual desires and ambitions. That is also our basic problem today. We have been oppressed so long that we have come to feel that we must have the white man's approval before we can do anything. This is the essence of powerlessness!

After the cleaning of the Temple, the Scribes and the Pharisees came back to argue and debate with Jesus. They tried to trick him. The first question they asked was the question people ask today right here in Detroit. "By what authority do you do these things? Who authorized it?" They didn't even realize that what they were saying was, "Name the white man who gave you permission to do this." That was what they really wanted to know. Then they tried to trick him again. "Are you loyal to Caesar? Should we pay taxes to Caesar? What do you have to say about our relationship with Caesar?" They were trying to identify Jesus with the separatist revolutionary black nationalist Zealots who refused to pay taxes. They wanted him to say something that they could take back to Caesar. They were trying to trick him into betraying himself so they could say that he was not loyal. Then they tried to involve him in an elaborate religious argument about the resurrection. Obviously they were trying to discredit him before the people. They failed because they were stupid. It is difficult for a fool to discredit the truth. Jesus was pitted against the power structure. They said, "He stirs up the people. He pretends to be King of the Jews." That is the tale they took back to the Romans and that is the charge that was brought against him. They weren't concerned about his religious teachings. They were concerned about the threat which his Movement presented and the fact that he was bringing a Nation into being.

Jesus went through the whole of Holy Week fighting to salvage what he could of his Movement, leaving people something that they could pass on when he was killed. Every day of this climactic week before his crucifixion he tried to do what he could to see that his teachings about the Nation were understood. On Wednesday he went to Bethany with his friends. He made almost a whole day's journey to sit down alone with the people who were to be the nucleus of the Nation. He sat down in the home of Mary and Martha with others who were committed to the revolution, and talked to them all day and far into the night. You remember the woman who came bringing the expensive ointment. "She anoints me for my burial," he said. But he was trying to tell them the things they were to remember.

Then, on Thursday, he went back for the Passover meal with his disciples. He knew that if anything was to be preserved after his death it all depended upon the understanding of these twelve men. They had heard him. They knew his message. If they couldn't carry it on, it was done, it was lost and his work was finished. So on Thursday he sat down with the twelve and talked to them. He tried to get them to understand that the Nation can come into being only when we are willing to sacrifice and be humble. That is why he got down and washed their feet. This was not an arrogant leader riding around in a Cadillac and living in a big house. He sat down with the twelve and said, "This message I give you. You must be servants to the Nation. If you are going to lead the Nation, then give more to the Nation than anyone else is willing to give."

He got down on his knees and washed their feet as a common servant. He wanted them to understand that the Nation comes into being only as we are willing to rise above our individualism, only as we are willing to sacrifice, only as we are willing to be humble, only as we are willing to put unity above our personal desires. When one of the disciples protested, he said, "If I can't wash your feet, then you are not my disciple. If you can't understand what I'm talking about, then get out."

Then he gave them a symbolic ceremony that they could remember, the Last Supper. He said, "They are going to kill me." The disciples wouldn't believe it. He said, "They are going to kill me and I'm trying to tell you what to do when I'm gone. Now here's a ceremony. Do it in remembrance of me. Don't run away and be discouraged. Remember what I have taught you.".He took the bread and broke it and said, "This is my body which is broken for you. You must also be willing to have your body broken for the Nation. If you are not willing to have your body broken for the Nation, you are not my disciple." The message Jesus gave to the disciples as he was preparing to die was so simple: "You must serve the Nation because the Nation is more important than you are. You must be willing to let your body be broken, to suffer and to shed your blood for the Nation." His disciples did not understand.

He went out into the garden, knowing that it was the end. He knew how little he had accomplished. He knew how little they understood what he had said. He asked them to pray with him for a little while: "Pray with me. Give me a sense of fellowship here in this last moment." While he prayed, they fell asleep. They didn't understand. He had asked them to be willing to die, to shed their blood, to have their bodies broken, but they couldn't even stay awake for a few moments. Here we have symbolized at the very end that individual selfishness which fills all of us and defeats our struggle against oppression. They couldn't even stay awake. Everywhere in the Church, in this Church as well as in all other

Churches, people are too busy to do the things which must be done. We can't stay awake. We have someplace else to go. It's not important enough. That's all it means. Jesus said, "Can't you just stay awake for just a few minutes?" And they answered, "I fell asleep without knowing it." We do it all the time because the Nation isn't important enough to us. They went to sleep again, and the soldiers came to arrest him.

We often get confused at this point. Judas came in, as a Tom will, and kissed Jesus. Jesus looked at him. Then one of the disciples took a sword and wanted to start fighting, and Jesus said, "Not now." What good was it standing out there in that little park trying to fight with only two swords? If they were going to fight, they should have been getting ready to fight a long time ago. That story is so much like us. We're walking up the street and we see something a white policeman does and we get so mad that we're ready to tear a police car apart by ourselves with our bare hands. At the moment we don't care if we get shot down right there in the street. But that's stupid and that's what Jesus told them. "Why are you dragging out that little piece of sword? Here these soldiers are armed to the teeth. They came out here to kill me and you are going to take one little sword and give them an excuse to do it here and now." That was it. The disciples scattered. Peter, his strongest disciple, followed after him, and then denied him. All the dreams of building a Black Nation evaporated as soon as they grabbed Jesus.

And where did they take him? To the Sanhedrin. You know, that was just like taking Stokely Carmichael before the black Ministerial Alliance to try him. Naturally they found him guilty. Then they took him to the Romans who did what the oppressor always does. They said, "Your own people have found you guilty. We wash our hands of the whole thing." It is so easy to do it that way. It is so easy when we are not a Nation and everybody is out for himself. It is so easy for the man to use you if he wants to hang me. He'll get you to say I'm guilty. If he wants to hang you, he'll get me to say you're guilty.

Jesus understood all of this. When they arrested him, that was it. From the triumphant entry, it was just a few days to the moment when Pilate could ask, "What shall I do with this man?" And many of these same people who had thrilled at his entry into Jerusalem screamed, "Crucify him! Crucify him!" He had failed as they feared he would, his very powerlessness made them angry. "Crucify him! Crucify him!" they screamed. If you can't understand that Jesus was crucified because he tried to bring a Black Nation into being and fought against white oppression, you can't understand the Resurrection, because the Resurrection is the Resurrection of a Nation.

Heavenly Father, be with us, give us a sense of thy nearness as we worship here, and give us a sense of the real meaning of the life and teachings of thy son, the Black Messiah, Jesus Christ. Help us to understand this black prophet, and what he was trying to do in working and sacrificing to build a Black Nation. Be with us here and now and give us a sense that here, in this house, we are the Nation. We have been selected and set aside. We have been committed to the task which is ours. We are the Nation, and we seek to build, to select from people everywhere those who can understand, and who can commit their lives. Amen.

7/The Resurrection of the Nation

"But we had hoped that he was the one to redeem Israel. Yes, and besides all this, it is now the third day since this happened. Moreover, some women of our company amazed us. They were at the tomb early in the morning and did not find his body; and they came back saying they had even seen a vision of angels, who said that he was alive" (*Luke* 24:21-23).

Instead of a sermon, we could just sit here and look at the chancel mural of the Black Madonna which we unveiled on Easter Sunday, and marvel that we have come so far that we can conceive of the Son of God being born of a black woman. It wasn't so long ago that such a conception would have been impossible for us. Our self-image was so distorted that we didn't believe that even the Almighty God could use us for his purpose because we were so low and despised. Now we have come to the place where we not only can conceive of the possibility, but we are convinced, upon the basis of our knowledge and historic study of all the facts that Jesus was born to a black Mary, that Jesus, the Messiah, was a black man who came to save a Black Nation.

It would have little significance if we unveiled a black Madonna and it had no more meaning than just another picture in a church. Our unveiling of the Black Madonna is a statement of faith. We will unveil other murals to illuminate our interpretation of the his-

toric truth which we have at long last uncovered. On either side of
the Black Madonna, I would like to see a picture of Jesus, done
by a black artist. I would like one to be of the Crucifixion with the
white Romans at the feet of the Black Messiah, the jeers and
mockery upon their faces and the hatred in their eyes. Only a
black artist could paint that picture. On the other side, I would like
to see a picture of Jesus driving the money changers out of the
Temple, a powerful black man supplanting the weak little mamby-
pamby white Jesus. The money changers would be depicted just as
they were, Uncle Toms, exploiting their own people with the connivance and support of the white Gentile oppressors.

It is an unfolding conception, tremendous in its meanings, as we
begin to think through this knowledge which has been kept from us
for so long, and which we are only now beginning to understand.
To reclaim our own history, our own faith, our own religion, our
own Black Messiah, and to begin to conceive again of the resurrection of a Black Nation is a wonderful thing. Do not be surprised if
you cannot comprehend the magnitude of our discovery here on
one Sunday morning. Don't be surprised if you feel uncomfortable.
Just remember that the white man has been telling you what to
think for a long, long time. You are supposed to feel uncomfortable
this morning. He intended it that way. He never dreamed that
you would unveil a Black Madonna and worship a Black Messiah.
You feel uncomfortable? That's the way you've been conditioned.
You feel that maybe there's something wrong with a Black Madonna, that if Jesus was black, maybe there was something wrong
with him!

Let's even go beyond that. Jesus was the Son of God. Do you
dare face the implication of this? Don't be frightened, God is happy
because we are beginning to understand. The way they have been
explaining it to us, we have been all mixed up. The way I read it in
the Bible, Mary was pregnant. She carried Jesus for nine months
just like any other mother. Then don't tell me God doesn't have
any color. There had to be a seed there. I don't care how he put it

there. There had to be a seed there that could grow and eventually come to birth as a child.

"Oh, I never think of God or Jesus as having any particular color." That's what you're thinking, isn't it? You deceive yourself! You think of both God and Jesus as white. What do you mean when you say "no particular color?" Only white and black are no particular color and you certainly haven't been thinking of God and Jesus as black all these years, since ole massa called us together on the plantation because he had decided that it would be better if Niggers had something to worship. Then he gave it to us. He said, "This is your Jesus, be as much like him as you can. He's white and you're black, but be as much like him as you can. And he's the Son of this white God." That's what he told us, 'way back on the plantation, and that's what we've been believing ever since. There's nothing strange about that. You believe what somebody teaches you, especially somebody who has power, when you're powerless. We would have been fools to stand up there and tell ole massa, "We don't believe that." So what did we do? We said, "That's right."

But that was *then* and this is *now*. Now we know better. But to-day, in thousands of black churches all over this land, millions of black Christians will be running up and down the aisles and shouting hallelujah, because a white Jesus saved them two thousand years ago. If that doesn't sound peculiar to you, go home and think about it. Why do you think that a white Jesus would save you from the oppression of white men? That doesn't make sense. If he's their Jesus, he's saving them. If he's our Jesus, then we have got to think this whole Christian thing through again. All that we have been taught stems from a false history, a false theology and a false interpretation of the Bible. Everything about traditional Christianity is false. Just because you have been believing it a long time does not make it true.

I want to talk to you about the Resurrection and what it really means, instead of what the white man wants you to think it means. Don't be disturbed when I say white man and black man, because that's what we are. Don't let two little words close your mind. Just think of the black people all over this world who need some kind of resurrection. Think of the young black men in Vietnam today, wading around in the mud, getting killed, and killing yellow people. For what? Because the white man says that it must be done. Today in Vietnam, they will call all the soldiers in and the chaplain will talk to them about the Resurrection. He'll say, "Two thousand years ago Jesus died upon the cross and made it possible by his resurrection for you also to be resurrected. When you die over here in Vietnam, don't take it too seriously because you're going to be resurrected. Your life on earth has been hell, but when you are dead and resurrected, you will go up into heaven and up there everything is going to be all right."

The scriptural account of the Resurrection was written many, many years after the death of Jesus. The first gospel written, the Gospel of Mark, was written at least seventy years after Jesus was dead. During that time, many things happened to the teachings of Jesus. Other gospels were written, some as much as 130 years after Jesus had died. You know how hard it is for you to remember things that happened last year. If I ask you today about something your wife said last Christmas, you would have a hard time remembering. Seventy years after Jesus died, they were trying to remember the things he said and did. A hundred and thirty years later they were still trying to remember. This means that little in the Gospel stories is accurate in a historical sense. The Gospels reflect the importance which people attached to the life of Jesus.

People realized the significance of the things Jesus said, and in a sense, people were still just talking about Jesus. Little was actually written down except for fragmentary collections of saying. During this early period when people were trying to determine the meaning of the life and death of Jesus, the Apostle Paul came on the scene with an entirely new interpretation. He had never seen Jesus in the flesh, but his interpretation dominated the early Church and greatly influenced the Gospels when they were written. So in the Book of Galatians and in the Acts of the Apostles, you have a whole lot of arguing going on between the Disciples and the Apostle Paul. Paul was out in the field moving from city to city, organizing churches. He was a great organizer in the modern sense. He did whatever was necessary to put an organization together. The Disciples and the followers of Jesus back in Jerusalem said, "This man is not organizing the right kind of churches. He has forgotten the things that were important to Jesus." But Paul wrote letters and they wrote nothing. Why were the followers of Jesus critical of the Apostle Paul? Because the Apostle Paul was leaning over backward to convert the Gentiles. "Apostle to the Gentiles" meant Apostle to the white people. Paul was taking the religion of a Black Nation to white people who had no background in religion. But to make it acceptable to them he had to change it.

I know a lot of you say, "I can get along with white people. I don't have a bit of trouble with them." But who changes? You talk like they want you to talk; don't you? That's what you mean when you say you don't have any trouble with them. You voice their ideas. You talk their talk. So you don't have any trouble with them. If something controversial comes up, you just disappear.

The Apostle Paul was a Jew. He went to the Gentiles with a religion about a Black Messiah and immediately he began to change it so that they would be able to accept it. Greece and Rome were heathen nations. They conceived of God in primitive terms as someone who went around throwing thunderbolts at his enemies. And when you got into Europe, it was even worse. Rome and Greece had at least been touched by the civilizing hand of Africa. So when the Apostle Paul tried to take the religion of Jesus to them, he distorted the Black Messiah to make him fit their primitive conceptions. To understand what paganism did to Jesus, compare the Gospel of Mark with the Gospel of John. That is because the Gospel of John has taken on the pagan, heathen philosophy of the Gentiles and tried to weave it into the life of Jesus. The historic Jesus is completely lost. Paul's distortion of Jesus could even be taken into Europe where there were nothing but heathens, pagans and barbarians who lived in caves and ate raw meat. They accepted violence as a way of life. These were the white barbaric European Gentiles who now dominate the world. The Apostle Paul kept trying to change the religion of Jesus to meet their needs and so he lost the concept of the Black Nation which gave the teachings of Jesus meaning.

Our scripture lesson is the traditional scripture for Easter. You remember how the women went to the tomb on the first day and found Jesus gone. Two men stood there and said, "Why did you come here looking for Jesus? You knew that he was going to rise." But apparently they didn't know. They hadn't even thought about it because they brought spices and everything necessary to anoint the body. Now if you believed in something and you thought that it was going to come to pass, you would show some kind of anticipation, wouldn't you? If you believed in me and I told you, "I'm going to die today, but next Saturday I'm coming back," I would be very disappointed to see you drive up next Saturday with the undertaker. But that's what the women did. They got together the spices and they went to the tomb to anoint the body and give it a decent burial. They were surprised, and they went back to the Disciples and the followers of Jesus and told them, "We had a strange experience. We went to the tomb and Jesus wasn't in it and two men said that Jesus had risen." Then Scripture says, "And to the disciples their words seemed an idle tale, and they believed them not."

These were his followers. When the women told them about the empty tomb, they did not believe them. Only gradually did the Disciples come to believe that Jesus had risen. First they separated. They went back to their fishing boats and their former occupations, but gradually they came to believe that the power which Jesus had exhibited on earth was still available to them. Then they came back together. This was the group of Disciples and followers who met together daily in the upper room. Back in Jerusalem at Pentecost, you remember, the Disciples were all together in one place and it seemed that the room was filled with the rush of a mighty wind, and flames came to rest above the heads of each of the Disciples, and they went down into the street and they began to talk and preach. Jews were there in Jerusalem from all over the world. They came back to Jerusalem for religious occasions and each heard his own tongue being spoken. This is a biblical symbol of the unity of the Black Nation, Israel, for which Jesus had labored and for which he had died. Gradually the number of those who followed in the footsteps of Jesus began to grow. People began to join and it became a movement, a revolutionary Christian movement uniting the Nation Israel in its struggle against oppression.

The Apostle Paul, on the other hand, had his little experience on the Damascus Road, and said, "This was the risen Christ and now I have that mind in me that was in Jesus Christ." He went out organizing Churches, from city to city, changing the religion *of* Jesus to a religion *about* Jesus. The Epistles of Paul are his letters to the Churches he had organized. The basic theme of all his letters is his new religion about Jesus. "Jesus rose from the dead, and in rising from the dead he made it possible for each of us to rise from the dead." Jesus never said a word about anything like that. This was a religion about Jesus which Paul created for the Gentiles.

We can go back to the charges brought against Jesus on Good Friday. When Jesus was brought to trial, they charged him like this: "We found this man perverting our Nation and forbidding us to give tribute to Caesar." "This man stirs up the people, teaching throughout all Judea, from Galilee even to this place." The charges brought against Jesus were political charges against a revolutionary who was leading a nation into conflict against an oppressor. This is the kind of life that Jesus lived. It was necessary that he be crucified because he taught revolution. He brought together a fragmented Black Nation and he pitted it against the power of Rome.

We can go forward to the early Church. Everyone lived together sharing all things in common. It was a kind of primitive socialism. All gave as they had, and all received as they had need. In a sense, a Nation had come into being at Pentecost. A people had come together. They were concerned about each other. They were sharing with each other. They waited for the transformation of the world.

Or let us go back to the Old Testament. Everything in the Old Testament upon which Jesus built his teachings, talks in terms of a Nation, not in terms of an individual seeking individual salvation. Everything that Jesus mentions has to do with the Black Nation, Israel, because it is the Nation Israel that he is building. The Nation Israel was freed from bondage in Egypt. The Nation Israel wandered in the wilderness for forty years. The Nation Israel fought its way into the Promised Land. The Nation Israel became corrupt in the Promised Land. The prophets spoke, saying, "You have departed from the teachings of God. You are corrupt. You have lost your unity. You are no longer concerned about each other. Each person is living for himself alone."

In the New Testament we find all of the contradictions which grow out of these basic differences. On the one hand we have fragments of the teachings of Jesus, in the first three gospels, Matthew, Mark, and Luke. In Nazareth where he preached his first sermon, he spoke in terms of the needs of people. "I have come forth that men might be freed from bondage, that the blind might see, that the lame might walk." To free men from bondage was Jesus' own definition of his ministry. He labored that the Nation Israel might be free. So, in the New Testament we find a revolutionary message addressed to a Black Nation by a Black Messiah.

But we also find in the Epistles of Paul, a religion addressed primarily to persons who are seeking an individual escape from death and punishment for sin. These individuals found in the Resurrection an individual assurance that after death their lives would take on a new meaning. The Resurrection Faith, as preached by the early evangelists, took on a definite form in no way related to the teachings of Jesus. The Resurrection Faith as taught by the Apostle Paul, holds that Jesus died taking away the sins of the world and giving us the promise of Eternal Life. We have but to be baptized in his name and follow in his footsteps. Because we are human, we will fail. But he died for us while we were yet sinners and we are saved by grace. We, too, will rise after death to join him in Heaven. So our life on earth is just a preparation for Heaven, a veil through which we pass quickly in order to get to a better land up yonder.

This is not the religion of Jesus. This is not the religion of Israel. In it, the concept of the Nation is destroyed. This is a corruption of the religion of Jesus by the Apostle Paul for the white Gentiles. Even though we have been confused by this corruption, when we go to the Bible, we must search for the religion of Jesus, the Black Messiah. We must separate it from these Pauline interpretations which tend to make us think that Jesus was something which he was not, and that he taught something that he did not teach.

Jesus undertook the Resurrection of the Nation. This is why the Disciples were not greatly concerned when the women went to the tomb and found that Jesus was not there. They were not primarily concerned with the Resurrection of Jesus as an individual. Jesus had taught that a Black Nation was to come into being out of a people who had ceased to believe in the possibilities of a new Nation and his Disciples had begun to catch a glimpse of this kind of Resurrection.

The crucifixion convinced the Disciples that the Nation was doomed to extinction. When they stood in the distance and looked at Jesus upon the cross, they were convinced that they had lost the only leader who could bring individuals together and make a Nation that could stand independent and free. So the Disciples were demoralized. They watched the crucifixion, and said, the movement is dead. The Nation can no longer exist. The only individual who had the power of revolutionary leadership has been killed. And they fled.

Only gradually did it occur to them that perhaps they could carry on the work which Jesus had started. Then they came back together and tried to remember the things which he had taught about building the Nation. They remembered how he had called them to discipleship saying, "Come and follow me and I will make you fishers of men." And how each time he called an individual, he made a test. How he told the rich young ruler, "Give your riches to the poor and come and follow me." But the rich young ruler was too rich. He refused to make the sacrifice. There was the young man who wanted to be a disciple but had to go back first and bury his father. Jesus said, "Let the dead bury their dead. If you want to follow me, come." The young man pleaded, "Give me a few days." Jesus said, "Forget it."

In each instance, the individual had to make a decision. Was he going to be a part of the Nation or was he going to stay outside the Nation? All of the teachings of Jesus were asking this one question. Every time he preached, every time he taught, he was asking men to make one simple decision. Are you going to be in the Nation or are you going to be outside the Nation? Jesus knew that the Nation could not include all black people because most of the children of Israel were corrupt. Just like most of us are corrupt today in our world. You can't say all black men are brothers today because some black men will sell you out in a minute. You know it, and Jesus knew it. He said, from those who have conviction, from those who are willing to put the Nation first, I will make me a Nation. I will make a Nation out of those who believe.

This was the meaning of the sacrament of baptism: to be baptized out of the corruption of individualism into the Nation. To go down symbolically into the water and say, I die to the old life and I rise in the newness of a new life. If you were baptized without a sense of dying to the old and being born anew into the Black Nation, then your baptism was useless and you'd better come back and be baptized into the Nation, a baptism which says openly and publicly, "I no longer believe that my individual life is important. I believe that the life of the Black Nation of which I am a part is the most important thing in the world. I'm willing to sacrifice for it, to work for it, to give of myself that this Black Nation may come into power."

It's never too late to be baptized into the Nation. I don't care how long you have been "Tomming." But you have to make a decision. You have to say, "I'm not going to live that way any more."

This is when the symbolic gesture of baptism is important: when you come before the Nation and say, "I've changed. I've 'Tommed' all my life. I've done everything the man wanted me to do. There have been hundreds of times when I've betrayed my brothers, when I could have spoken a word and I didn't speak it; times on the job when I tricked my brother to hold my job even if he lost his." Admit it, but say, "That's not the way it's going to be any more because now I'm going to be baptized into the Nation."

But you have to find a Black Nation to be baptized into. You cannot be baptized into the white man's nation, because you know what that means. You've had that for four hundred years. You cannot be baptized into the white man's nation because you know that we are enemies. You can say that that doesn't sound like Christian love. That's what confuses a whole lot of us. We can get to the point where we see that we ought to be part of the Black Nation, that we ought to be willing to sacrifice. We know that during the worst days of slavery, we could have done something. We know that all during the Reconstruction era when the Klan was riding, we could have stopped them with ten shotguns. In a sense, we have always known the importance of unity. I can remember when I used to go to meetings with my father, they all ended up on the same theme, "Negroes must unite." Every little tin horn politician would tell us how we had to get together behind him. Every little organization would tell us how we had to get together under their banner. But nobody believed in a Nation which included all black people. They didn't believe in sacrifice or giving up anything. But today, we are coming together as a Nation with a different kind of dedication.

But we're still hung up on this love business. Love your neighbor. Love everybody. We are all confused. If anybody ever tried love, we did. You remember those hordes of black men, women and children marching in Martin Luther King's Southern demonstrations, facing police dogs, cattle prods, fire hoses and every kind of indignity because they believed that they could redeem the white man through love. Many of you sitting right here are saying to yourself, "That's the one thing I can't work out. I just can't turn my back on love." Well, love for everybody hasn't gotten you very much during the last four hundred years. In spite of all the loving you've been doing, you're still second-class citizens. Your children are still getting a second-class education. They're killing all your young men in Vietnam. Within five years there won't be a black man working in this country unless basic changes are made. Automation and cybernation make it possible to run every factory in America with a small handful of men. They don't need us anymore. Those of us who figure that we're professional people and that makes a difference, will be the second to go, that's all. They fire the factory workers on Monday and by Friday, every professional man in Detroit will be in the breadline. We are in a situation where we must have a Black Nation. We must realize that talking about love does not change our problems. You can sing "We shall overcome," and you can talk about redemptive suffering, but neither of these will change your earthly condition.

I'm not concerned about what happens in Heaven. If there is a Heaven and I get there, I'll sing "Glory hallelujah," but in the meantime, I'm concerned about what's going on down here. I tell you, you cannot love everybody. You have been trying and you feel guilty because you have failed. Forget the guilt feeling. Nobody can love everybody. The white man does not love you. Don't feel guilty when you don't love him. You have less reason to love him than he has to love you. You've worked for him. You've ministered to his every need. You've provided a huge labor pool, ready for him to use you whenever he wants to and throw you out whenever he doesn't need you any longer. He has used your women, and still does. You've given him everything you have and he still despises you. So why are we sitting around talking about how we have to love everybody?

You can't love everybody. You have a hard time loving everybody even in your own home. A lot of times you think, "Maybe I made a mistake right here in my own house." You're not going to love the whole Nation even after you're baptized into it. I know a lot of you are going to be awfully hard to love, and if you haven't already guessed, I'm not too easy. We come together because we must. We're coming together in a Black Nation for survival, because if we don't, we are lost. We must build a Nation. We have no choice. You come in or die. That's the only choice you have. You must come into a Nation of black men who are dedicated to survival, who are dedicated to building dignity for themselves and their children, and this is that Nation.

You can't love your enemy. That is ridiculous. When I was a child I used to read the "Negro press." I still remember a picture in the *Crisis* that showed a black man being lynched, his body was charred, and a bunch of white clowns were standing around grinning and looking like idiots. I knew then that I couldn't love the enemy. We have to concern ourselves with justice, not love. We can't go to the white man and ask him to love us. We've done it too long. It's futile. We want justice, and we are going to fight for justice. We believe in justice. We don't even think about love. Love is only something for inside the Nation. We'll try to love each other as much as we can, as hard as it is, inside the Black Nation. Outside the Nation we are not thinking about love. We are thinking about justice.

We realize that we are engaged in a conflict that is going on forever. Your children and your children's children will still be fighting. It will never end. Don't think that you are going to do something mysterious that is going to change conditions overnight. You have been fighting, your children are going to fight, and your grandchildren are going to fight. We're going to fight until we win or we die. We have no other choice. Justice, that is all we are asking for. Don't ask for anything else, because if you do, we will be tricked. We want the Constitution enforced. We want the laws enforced. We want to be treated with justice by city, state and national public officials. We don't want inequality and injustice in the draft. We don't want all black young men killed in Vietnam because white men are on the draft boards deciding who is to die.

Jesus didn't spend all of his time walking around talking about love. He was trying to bring the Nation together. When he said, "Go the second mile, turn the other cheek," he meant inside the Black Nation. When he said, "Don't come to the altar and try to pray unless you've made peace with your brother," he was talking about inside the Nation. When a Gentile woman came to Jesus and said, "My little girl is on the verge of death. Do something for her," he said, "I don't know you. You're not in the Nation. I came to Israel." She fell on her knees and said, "At least give me the crumbs from the table." And he looked at her and said, "You have a lot of faith," and he healed the little girl. But he didn't come to the Gentiles.

Don't get confused about Jesus. When you read the Scriptures, try to pick out the things that really are Jesus. The things that Jesus taught. Separate his religion from the corruptions of the Apostle Paul and later writers who were trying to get along with the Gentiles, the white people.

So, as we unveil our Black Madonna, it symbolizes for us an important accomplishment. We now understand that Christianity is our religion, that Israel was a Black Nation. Go back and read your own history in Dubois' book, *The World and Africa*. All of the people in that part of the world were black. There wasn't any way in the world Israel of Biblical times could have been a white nation. We have made our discovery and we symbolize our new faith with the Black Madonna.

We issue a call to all black Churches. Put down this white Jesus who has been tearing you to pieces. Forget your white God. Remember that we are worshipping a Black Jesus who was a Black Messiah. Certainly God must be black if he created us in his own image.

You can't build dignity in black people if they go down on their knees everyday, worshipping a white Jesus and a white God. We are going to communicate with black Churches. We are going to talk to them, reason with them, shame them if nothing else works, saying, "Accept the historic fact. Christianity is our religion. The black Church is the beginning of our Black Nation. Baptize into the Nation. Make it clear when people come into the Church that they are coming into a Black Nation. Make it clear that the sacrament of communion is the sacrament whereby we symbolize the simple fact that for the Nation we must be willing to sacrifice even ourselves, even to have our bodies broken and our blood shed. The sacrament of communion is not some little empty thing whereby individuals are guaranteed a place in Heaven. It is the symbol that unites us in the Black Nation."

So the Resurrection that we celebrate is not the Resurrection of the physical body of Jesus, but the Resurrection of the Black Nation which he started, the Resurrection of his ideas and his teachings. The immortality which Jesus has lies in the fact that two thousand years later we remember, and two thousand years later we are trying to do the same thing he tried to do with the Black Nation in Palestine. Today, in the midst of corruption, we are drawing people one by one, two by two, into the Black Nation. This task and the faith that it can be done, this is the Resurrection.

8/New-Time Religion

"Give your eyes no sleep and your eyelids
no slumber; save yourself like a gazelle from
the hunter. . . .

"A little sleep, a little slumber, a little folding of the hands to rest, and poverty will
come upon you like a vagabond, and want
like an armed man" (*Proverbs* 6:4-5,10-11).

I want to talk about the Church and what it means to be black in a
white man's world. Our scripture reading is a very simple one. It
says, if you have come into your neighbor's power, you have to do
something to get out of it. You have to stay awake. "Give your
eyes no sleep, and your eyelids no slumber. Save yourself like a
gazelle from the hunter." Then, down a little farther, in the tenth
verse, "A little sleep, a little slumber, a little folding of the hands
to rest, and poverty will come upon you like a vagabond and want
like an armed man." I just want you to think about those words as
we consider the Church and its relevance to black people in today's world.

I was in a barbershop recently and everyone was arguing about
religion. The interesting thing to me was that each one was arguing
against some religion he had heard preached down home someplace. The one arguing the loudest came from West Virginia, and
he must have had a real wind-burner in his church when he was a
boy. The dangers of hell fire had scared him half to death every
Sunday morning, and he still hasn't recovered. As soon as anyone
admitted that he was a Christian, he would start arguing with things

that preacher back in West Virginia said thirty years ago. He didn't have any idea that Christianity could be anything other than the gospel preached in his little home town church.

The Church has come a long way in thirty years. I don't mean the whole Church. I know a lot of preachers who are preaching just like they were thirty years ago in some little country church in West Virginia. But we have come a long way in what we expect of a Church because we have come a long way in the kind of problems we face and the kind of questions we are trying to grapple with. "What does it mean to be black in a white man's world?" is a new problem for us. Just a little while ago we refused to recognize this. We wouldn't admit that it was a white man's world, because as far as we were concerned we were all white together. Some of us were just a little "dark white." So today, when we talk about the problem of being black in a white man's world, we have changed our whole position. We no longer identify with the white man and think of ourselves as being a part of his world. Now we know that we are a separate black people. We have a separate culture and a separate history. We realize this today and we are not ashamed of it. We have come a long way, and these changes which are taking place in our thinking impose strange new demands upon the Black Church.

What does it mean to be black in a white man's world? Obviously it means that we have difficulties everywhere we turn, because black people are powerless and white people are powerful, and are ruthless in the use of their power to maintain white supremacy in a white racist world. It means that in every area of life we are disadvantaged, and must be able to survive and move ahead against overwhelming obstacles. The Black Church must understand our dilemma, and must offer leadership in complex areas totally unknown to the down-home fire-and-brimstone preacher.

The Black Church must offer leadership in areas in which most of us are confused, if it is to survive. Few of us really understand what it means to be black in a white man's world. Many of us are just getting over the illusion that we are a part of the white man's world. Because we don't realize our powerlessness, we are confused. A black person will talk logically for five minutes and then he will say the most absurd things because he refuses to accept the obvious implications of things he knows to be true.

The most ignorant people I have talked to since the Detroit Rebellion have been black professional people. They could have been living thirty years ago. Many of them haven't changed one iota in their thinking. They can sit there in their silk suits and be just as out of touch with reality as a small town black preacher. Obviously we cannot expect them to play any part in the struggle to make the Black Church relevant.

One group kept arguing all night that I was unfair to them because I tell people that the black middle class is not doing its part. I said, "That's right, you're not doing your part." They contended that just living and maintaining their position was a real contribution. They hadn't even begun to face the implication of being black in a white man's world. They were black on the outside, but just as white as they could be on the inside. Oh, they knew in a vague kind of way that they were black. They knew there were whole areas of life which were closed to them. But they hadn't faced its implications.

The Black Church faces this kind of confusion in the black community as it seeks to face the problem of being black. These people will tear up a Church or leave it if the preacher talks too much about racial problems or the struggle to get Black Power. They will admit that they don't believe in anything all black.

What does it mean to be black, in a white man's world? A black mother called me last week. Her boy had gone to school dressed in an African Dashiki and the principal had called him in and told him that he couldn't wear it because it was disrupting the school. The boy said, "This is the dress of my people, I have a right to wear it if I want to." He tried to tell the principal about the black man's heritage, and suggested that if the Irish can wear green ties on St. Patrick's Day, he could wear an African Dashiki. The principal expelled him. So the mother put on her African outfit and went to talk to the principal. She told him more about the history and culture of Africa than he cared to know, until the principal finally said, "Let's forget the whole thing. He can wear anything he wants to wear." But the mother said, "I'm not about to forget it, now that you brought it up." And she talked to him all afternoon.

This is another response to being black in a white man's world. This boy was black. His African Dashiki and his African heritage meant something to him, and the white man is not used to any black person having something of his own that means anything to him. Now the boy is back in school, and a whole lot of other black boys and girls are wearing Dashikis because they know the man doesn't like them. The Black Church, too, must speak to the needs of black people who are proud of their African heritage.

But we are confused on so many things. The Black Teacher's Workshop, a very advanced group of black teachers, invited some black young people to present their ideas. Some of the young people thought that getting skills, learning something, was important, but some of the college age "black nationalists" thought that all you had to do was to "come out of your black thing." One of the kids suggested, "I still think it would be better if we 'came out of our black thing' knowing something." The younger kids were right in wanting the schools to teach them skills. They wanted Afro-American history and Swahili, but in addition, they wanted to be learning skills to equip them to fit into the 20th Century.

It is not enough to just learn how black you are. That's the problem of being black in a white man's world. You have to stop and figure out what's important at every step of the way. Both the young folks were sincere and the older folks were sincere. The problem wasn't that they were not sincere. It's difficult to be black in a white man's world and know what to do all the time. You have to figure it out, you have to think, to plan, to plot. Being black in a white man's world is not easy and the Black Church cannot survive if it tries to ignore the problem and pretend that it does not exist.

Our young people went down to the anti-war demonstration in

Washington. My daughter went. She said that there was a beautiful black contingent. They insisted on going in their own buses and when they got there they had a separate place to meet, a black caucus. There were hundreds of black young people from all over the country, from as far away as Los Angeles and San Francisco. And there they faced it again, how can you be black in a white man's world? Should they march on the Pentagon with the white kids and get whipped up in an integrated protest? And they had to sit down and argue it out right there before they could do a thing. They had gone to Washington, but they were not sure exactly what they wanted to do. Finally, they decided, "This is the white man's thing. Let them go get whipped up about their thing at the Pentagon, and we'll get whipped up about our thing somewhere else."

So they paraded and had their own separate black anti-war demonstration. They tied up traffic all over Washington. They marched to Howard University and held a rally there. Black young people had their own caucus and made their own decisions. Every time I see black folks getting together, trying to figure something out, I know it's a problem. And it's not going to be something that is all cut and dried. We have to think every minute, and we have to figure every minute. And we are going to have differences, but as long as we are trying to decide it in terms of what is best for us, it's going to come out all right. The Black Church must become a part of this important decision-making that black people are doing everywhere and in every area of life.

What is the role of the Black Church in all that is happening, where nothing is just accepted at face value? Can the Black Church adjust and survive, or must it be destroyed and rebuilt from the ashes? As black people begin to re-evaluate, they more and more tend to kick out religion and the Church. They say this is a white man's thing. He has used it to keep us in subjection all these years. We'll just put it aside and forget it. That is just one of the many problems we must figure out if we are to survive as black men in this white man's world.

I would like to suggest that we approach the problem of the Black Church in a much too unsophisticated way. The role of the Church and religion is always adjusted to meet the needs of a people. Religion is not just something that goes on the same way from the beginning of time right on down. Religion and the Church constantly shift to meet the needs of a people. Religion isn't the same today as it was thirty years ago, a hundred years or two hundred years ago. It is shifting and changing all the time. One of the things that confuses us when we talk about religion is that we tend to think of it as something fixed, final and settled. The man in the barbershop was arguing about a religion that he heard preached thirty years ago, but he thinks it's the same today.

Once there was a unified Christian Church which dominated the western world. The Church told kings what they could do, and if a king got out of line, the Pope made him crawl for miles to beg forgiveness. The Church was really running things then. That was the old Roman Catholic Church which existed before the Protestant Reformation. The Protestants broke away from the Catholic Church, and today, Protestants give a lot of reasons to explain why they broke away. The Catholics were corrupt and immoral and a whole lot of bad things were going on. But that wasn't enough to make folks break away. You know yourself that a whole lot can go on in a Church and everybody will just look the other way. There had to be a logical reason why so many people found so many reasons to get out of the Catholic Church at this particular time.

I am suggesting that this split had to do with the simple fact that the Church must adjust to meet the needs of the people. The Protestants, with their Reformation, placed a new emphasis upon the rights of the individual. In the old Catholic Church, the individual didn't have much in the way of rights. The Church, the institution, the group, had the power. The individual was forced to conform. People in general were getting tired of conformity and restrictions. The Protestant Reformation merely gave expression to the growing desire of people to free themselves from this monolithic Church which controlled everything. The Protestant Reformation declared the freedom of the individual.

Freedom is a funny thing. Protestants declared the individual's right to worship according to the dictates of his conscience. But freedom, once announced, could not be restricted. So the Reformation declared the freedom of the individual in many other areas: his freedom to get rich, his freedom to exploit, and his freedom to take whatever he wanted. The other side of Protestantism was capitalism, with each individual having the right to do almost anything necessary to make a profit. And in the artistic and intellectual areas, also, books, paintings, poems and music began to reflect the chaos of individual revolt. Obviously people wanted something new. They wanted a change. They wanted individual freedom from the restraints of an institutionalized omnipresent God.

The Church can always justify the changes it is forced to make. When the people wanted freedom from the control of a powerful Church, they went back to the Apostle Paul, the evangelist of individualism. Every time Martin Luther, the leader of the Protestant Reformation, sat down to search out an escape from Church power and domination, he would always go back to the Apostle Paul. Finally he found the phrase he needed, "We are saved by faith," and he said, "That's it! The Church can't save you. Each individual is saved by himself. We are saved by faith." He took this little concept of individual salvation and made a revolution out of it. Do you know why people paused to listen to this almost meaningless half truth? Because they wanted freedom from the control of the Church and here was a man who said: "You aren't saved by the Church, you are saved by your own faith." And they said, "Lord, that is what I have been waiting to hear somebody say." And so the whole Protestant thing came into being. "We are saved by faith." Each individual decides everything for himself. The Bible is a sufficient rule of faith and conduct, as interpreted by the individual. The Church doesn't decide. You read the Bible and the Holy Spirit tells you what's right and what's wrong.

This pure individualism was so extreme that Protestant Churches never really accepted it in practice, after the organization of Protestant Churches. In today's world, society borders on chaos as a result of this Protestant individualism. Individualism merely means that each individual feels that he is the most important thing in the world. Your whole life is built on getting what you can for yourself as an individual and getting ahead as an individual. Your concern for your little family is merely an extension of your self-centered individualism. Today the whole fabric of society is falling apart because there are so many individuals who have no sense of unity. There is no cement to hold society together. The Hippies reject a decadent society. Many motion pictures portray the step by step disillusionment of society, and contribute to it. In this kind of world, the Church seeks to hold back the tide by trying to come back together. The Church Universal broke up because people wanted to be free, wanted to be individuals. Today, people are sick of being free, sick of being individuals, and so the Church is trying to find its way back together. This is the ecumenical movement. Denominations merging and making little flirting gestures towards Rome, suggesting that maybe we can all come back together and have one big Church that can dominate the world again. Today, people are looking for the kind of security which a unified Church might offer. The very simple fact is that people make the Church serve their needs.

In the United States the Church was developed to meet the white man's needs. He decided what it should be. He decided the form, the structure, the theology, everything. The black man's Church has tried to work within the framework of the white man's decisions because we were so hell-bent on being integrated that anything he said had to be right. Only recently have we begun to understand that the whole development of the Christian Church has been something the white man was building for himself. We have been going along with the program and making only minor modifications to suit our own needs. Everywhere the Black Church tries to be like the white man's Church. They go through the motions and the more education black worshippers have, the harder they try. They even try to copy the dead emptiness of the white folks service, the little rhythmless songs with nothing to pat your foot to all through the service.

Have you ever heard a black preacher trying to sound white? He gets up and tries to whisper at you and tell you how nice everything is. That's only in churches for well-to-do black folks who don't go to Church often, anyway. This is the most ridiculous Black Church there ever was because it doesn't have any relationship to the needs of black people at all. We don't like the music. We don't like the preaching. We don't like anything about it and the only black people who attend are black people who have a need to pretend that they really like to do things the same way white folks do them. A black Church which is a copy of the white Church cannot meet any of our needs. Some black folks take pride in sitting through a service and saying to themselves as they suffer, "If white folks came in here they wouldn't know that this was not a white Church." They think that that's the highest compliment they can give themselves. Sometimes they even put a white preacher on the staff to make the illusion complete. It is as completely ridiculous as it is pathetic.

Now, the old down home Churches, Baptist, Methodist or what have you, were in a sense a replica of white folks religion. But there we took white folks Christianity, twisted it around and made it fit at least a few of our needs. When you worship in a down home Black Church, at least you feel good. The music is good, you can jump up and down, you can shout and feel free—free like you are home. To help you feel good and release tension is meeting at least some need. You caught hell all week. The white man was driving you, and all week you have wanted to tell him off but you couldn't because you didn't want to lose your job. You took insults because you didn't want to get whipped up and go to jail, and on Sunday you just let yourself go.

So the uneducated black preacher who can "shout" a congregation on Sunday morning is more meaningful than the most sophisticated middle-class black pastor who whispers a sermon that's unrelated to anything in the black man's experience because he is trying to sound like a white minister. If it doesn't meet the needs of a people, religion is nothing, and if it's geared to meet the needs of some other people, that doesn't help you any. There was a whole lot in the old time Black Church that was good. It was built wrong because we didn't know any better then. But it tried to satisfy the needs of black people. All the shouting and emotionalism that people laugh about offered an escape from oppression and we had to have some kind of escape. From somewhere we had to have some kind of escape. From somewhere we had to find the strength to get through another week.

We had sex and alcohol on Saturday night and Church on Sunday morning. All week we would be waiting for Saturday night and Sunday morning. We don't have to be ashamed of that because it is the truth. If we hadn't had Saturday night and Sunday morning, we never would have made it this far. We took the white man's individualism, turned it around and made it an escape from oppression. On Sunday morning we would feel good together. We didn't have to talk about the problems of the world. In fact, we didn't want to talk about them. We just talked about up yonder and Jesus taking care of us. And we knew that one of these days God was going to shake the white man over hell-fire and take us up to heaven through the Pearly Gates. It was such a wonderful thought that God was just. We knew that if God was just, there was no place but heaven for us. We could look at the white man all week and we knew where he was going. He was headed straight for hell.

Besides, we never had money enough to get from payday to payday, and that's still true for most of us. The Black Church offered deliverance. You came to Church, you were broke, you were hungry, you had no job, you were sick or whatever it was and the Church offered you deliverance. God delivered a whole lot of us a lot of times. You can't explain it, but things would happen, and we would say, "God did it." That is why the Black Church was valid. It related to the needs of black people.

Why did this down home Black Church put so much emphasis on

sin, little petty sins like drinking, fornicating and adultery? Because the Church knew that there was not only Sunday morning but there was also Saturday night. And a people seeking escape from oppression might very easily make Saturday night extend over the entire week. Then the Church could not have saved and delivered them on Sunday morning. The Black Church was preaching to the real everyday needs of black people. The Church had to keep black people from going too far in finding escape through sins of the flesh.

So the down home Black Church was not irrelevant to the needs of black people, but it met those needs only partially and superficially, because essentially it was but a slight modification of the white Church; it taught black people that they had been saved by a white Jesus because of the love of a white God. It could not come to grips with the black man's powerlessness. The white man's Church and religion are designed to meet *his* needs, not ours. We cannot borrow a Church which meets our needs from the white man. The white man's Church is inescapably an instrument for the preservation of white power. The Black Church must be something different—separate and apart from the white Church—because black people and white people have different needs.

Let me say it this way. The oppressor, the white man, needs a religion that gives him an opportunity to find escape from the guilt of his oppression. He knows that his oppression is destroying black people all week. He knows that he is responsible for a system of oppression that keeps little black children in inferior schools. He knows that everything he does is designed to reduce black men to permanent powerlessness and inferiority. He needs a religion that can give him escape from these feelings of guilt. His religion has to give him an individual escape from guilt. The white Christian finds the basis for this religion in the New Testament, in the Epistles of the Apostle Paul. He must find escape from the guilt of white racism in a faith in universal brotherhood. This faith provides "escape techniques" for the white Christian, without in any way endangering white power and domination.

A white Christian can go out into the community and do little brotherhood acts. He can fight for "open occupancy." He can do little, almost meaningless acts of face-to-face kindness which in no way touch the problem of the black man's powerlessness. That's his religion.

But our religion is something different. The black man's religion is essentially based on the Old Testament concepts of the Nation Israel, God's chosen people, and our knowledge that the problems of the black Israelites were the same as ours. When we read the Old Testament, we can identify with a black people who were guided and loved by God. Everything in the Old Testament speaks directly to our problem.

We know that Israel was a black nation and that descendents of the original black Jews are in Israel, Africa, and the Mediterranean area today. The Bible was written by black Jews. The Old Testament is the history of black Jews. The first three gospels, Matthew, Mark, and Luke, tell the story of Jesus, retaining some of the original material which establishes the simple fact that Jesus built upon the Old Testament. Jesus was a Black Messiah. He came to free a black people from the oppression of the white Gentiles. We know this now to be a fact. Our religion, our preaching, our teachings all come from the Old Testament, for we are God's chosen people. God is working with us every day, helping us find a way to freedom. Jesus tried to teach the Nation Israel how to come together as a black people, to be brothers one with another and to stand against their white oppressors.

There is no way in the world that a black man can teach the same thing in his Church that the white man teaches in his Church. The white man is not going to admit that Jesus was black. He is going to twist history to make it fit the pattern of white supremacy. He will continue to paint pictures of Jesus looking the way he wants him to look. He knows that all of those pictures painted during the Middle Ages are lies. He knows that the religious films which have come out of Hollywood are all white supremacy lies. Jesus was black, and he did *not* preach universal love. Remember the white Gentile woman who came to Jesus asking him to heal her daughter? "I don't have time to waste with Gentiles. I have come to the house of Israel," Jesus said.

Our whole religion, then, since we are black people, becomes different. There are many ways to say it. God is trying to help people stand up as men, and if anything in our religion makes us less than men, there is something wrong with our religion. God says that we are created in his image. That means that we have to have some kind of power. You can't stand up as a man if you are powerless. That means that the Black Church must dedicate itself to the task of building Black Power. Don't worry because white folks are afraid of the words "Black Power." Say "Black Christian Power," if you want, because that is what it amounts to. Black God-given Power. That is what we are talking about. God wants his chosen people to have power because if they don't have power, they are slaves. They are sick because there's no way to live without power and be well.

It is God's will, then. If God created us in his own image, he doesn't want us running around acting like lap dogs for white people. He wants us to stand up and be men, to fight for the things that belong to us, to build a heritage to hand on to our black children. This is what God wants. This is what we have to preach from the black pulpit. We can't really care what white people are preaching. They can be talking about brotherhood and love, day in and day out, but black people must learn to love one another. The white man stands separated from God by his oppression. God cannot look with favor upon the white man. If *we* can see that he acts like a beast, what must God think of him? When God looks down upon the white man, what can he say? He's oppressing everybody in sight, he's abusing people, he's robbing them of manhood. That is the white man's sin, so what can the white man do to rid himself of that sin? He must seek brotherhood and universal love. He must rid himself of this thing which he is doing. An oppressor is always in a peculiar relationship with God because he's filled with guilt.

Our relationship with God as black men also makes special demands upon us. God is disgusted with us because we have crawled too long. God did not intend for us to accept slavery and oppression for almost four hundred years. God has been ashamed of us for those four hundred years. God demands that we fight, that we throw off the shackles of bondage now; that we stand up as free men now; that we come together as black brothers now, in the cause of black freedom. We must fight, and die if need be, that black people may be free with the power to stay free. This is what God demands of black men.

So God is demanding different things of black men and white men. Don't let white people confuse you. Everytime I speak some place they say, "You're a preacher; you shouldn't be talking about power." I tell them, "You do what God wants you to do. You get down on your knees and ask forgiveness for all of the sins you have committed against black people, but don't ask me to get down there with you, because God is asking something different of me." That's why our Church here, The Shrine of the Black Madonna, is so important. We are pointing the Black Church in a new direction. We understand where we are going and why.

To the Black Revolution we bring the stabilizing influence of the religion of the Black Messiah, Jesus Christ. The Black Revolution is not going any farther than the Black Church enables it to go, by giving it a foundation, a philosophy, and a direction.

Angry frustrated black people running up and down the street are not going to make a Black Revolution. Our Black Revolution depends for success upon a people who are welded together into a Black Nation and who can fight together because they share a common faith. That's why this Church is so important. We are the wave of the future. The Black Church is in the process of being reborn, and we, here, are participants in that tremendous beginning. It is hard to be a black man in a white man's world. But if you don't have a black man's religion and if you can't be a part of a black man's Church, it's almost impossible.

Heavenly Father, we thank thee for this fellowship, for the opportunity of coming together in thy house as black brothers and sisters dedicated to the accomplishment of thy will, the freeing of thy people everywhere. Give us the courage, the wisdom, the unity, and the love for each other, necessary to accomplish this task. Bless this Church and bless this house, that we may be in fact thy chosen people. Help us that we may follow in the footsteps of the Black Messiah, thy Son, our Lord and Savior, Jesus Christ. Give each of us the courage to do the things which must be done. Give us the courage, if we are not yet a part of the Black Nation, to come forward, as we open the doors of the Church, and become followers of the Black Messiah. Give us the courage to wipe from our hearts and minds those little twinges of Uncle Tomism that still linger there. Help us to come forward and say: "I am not ashamed to worship a black Jesus." Help us, God, as we open the doors of the Church that people here and now may feel the persuasive touch of thy spirit. These things we ask in his name. Amen.

9/No Halfway Revolution

"And Samson said, 'Let me die with the Philistines.' Then he bowed with all his might; and the house fell upon the lords and upon all the people that were in it. So the dead whom he slew at his death were more than those whom he had slain during his life" (*Judges* 16:30).

Our Scripture lesson is taken from the Book of Judges. While the riots were going on down in Watts, I preached on the same text. Samson is a good Biblical figure and he fits into the framework of riots and rebellion.

The Book of Judges has to do with the early leaders of Israel who presided over the young Nation Israel and were called "judges." Samson was never a leader of Israel in the sense of having an official position. Yet his story is included in the Book of Judges because he was a leader in the fight against the Philistines.

The Philistines conquered Israel, it is said, because of the sins of Israel, and ruled over it for forty years. During this period when Israel was in bondage to the Philistines, Samson was the person people looked to. He was a kind of center, the outstanding personality. Yet he was different from all the other judges, essentially because the times were different. Israel needed somebody like Samson.

I remember when the riot in Watts was going on, the front page of *Life Magazine* pictured a young black militant with a do-rag around his head. He was a symbol of what was happening. He represented rebellion against oppression. So I have selected

115

the same Scripture lesson now because that which started in Watts two years ago and which is now sweeping the nation is the same kind of rebellion against oppression which Samson represented in Israel. The same kind of hoodlum character emerges as some kind of peculiar hero because he does the things which have to be done at a particular time in human history.

Samson wasn't any hero kind of person in normal circumstances. Normally people would have frowned on him. They would have called him a hoodlum. They wouldn't have listed him in their religious scriptures as a "judge" of Israel. But during this particular time, he had what everybody wanted. He wasn't afraid, he didn't mind dying, he was emotional, he struck out against oppression. So everybody called him a judge of Israel.

Samson married a Philistine woman and he spent a whole lot of his time chasing around after Philistine women. He was just an ordinary kind of person, except that he loved to fight, and when he got mad he would fight anybody, even a thousand people. Walking through the countryside, attacked by a lion, he would fight single-handedly. He was that kind of person, and so in a day when people were oppressed, they tended to look to this kind of person for leadership.

A riot becomes a rebellion when people tend to support the little group of people who begin some kind of violence. In America today, we have riots or rebellions taking place in almost every city across the country. They had a riot or rebellion in Kalamazoo. Now those of you who have visited Kalamazoo would agree that Kalamazoo is the last place from which to expect that kind of thing. But they were carrying on in Kalamazoo. They carried on in East Harlem also. That wasn't so hard to understand. In fact, we had been wondering why Harlem was so late. It started in East Harlem, but they expected it to sweep across all of Harlem. A policeman shot a little Puerto Rican boy.

This is the kind of times in which we live. We had our own riot here in the City of Detroit. Riot or rebellion, you pick your own word for it. I think what we had is a riot. I think it has been participated in by relatively few people—so far.

The radio stations called me and asked if I wanted to issue a statement asking people to cool it. I said I had been trying to get white people to do something that would make it possible to cool it for years, and nobody had paid any attention, so I didn't have any statements about cooling it now. I tried to explain that if everything is alright in Detroit, if nobody is alienated, if nobody feels oppressed, if all black people feel that there are other things they can do to change the situation, if they are confident that they have alternatives to violence, then it is just a little thing that broke out and it won't last for long. But if all black people in Detroit feel that they are helpless and hopeless, and that there is no chance of solving their problems peaceably, that they can't solve them by the ballot or by organizing or by economics, then you have a rebellion on your hands—because, in that case, more black people are going to join in, once it has started.

There is a difference then between a riot and a rebellion. A riot is a little group, perhaps more interested in looting than in freedom. But a rebellion is a community that has decided that it will no longer tolerate the kind of racial oppression that it has been forced to tolerate. So across the country we are getting a combination. In some communities there are riots. Little bands hear about what is happening somewhere else and think it might be good to have one here. And in other communities, it is not a riot at all; it is a rebellion. People look around and say, we are tired of these slums. We are tired of all the conditions that we have to put up with. We are tired of the whole situation and we are not going to tolerate it any longer. And then a whole community erupts, and other people say, we don't know why it happened. That is a rebellion. And more and more of these eruptions are rebellions, rather than riots.

Now in any period of rapid social change (that is what this really is; the conditions in America are changing more rapidly than ever before in American history) you are going to get all kinds of people participating, and everybody who participates is not going to be a great freedom fighter. If you start a fight on a corner because your freedom has been transgressed, there is going to be somebody who comes up just because there is a crowd of people and picks all the pockets he can. That doesn't mean that freedom wasn't involved in the first fight. That just means that somebody else who was broke or knows how to pick pockets utilized the situation. But when that happens, and we all stand back and say, "there was nothing going on but some people picking pockets," that isn't true. And usually that is not true in a community, no matter how much emphasis is placed upon the looting. Usually there are other things that are important to the people. There are people who loot, just as there are people who do every other kind of thing that they want to do for their own personal satisfaction.

Riots everywhere, rebellion everywhere. The *Detroit News* ran a very interesting editorial recently. They were talking about the civil rights rampages. "Wrongs spark riots," which is quite a great admission for the Detroit News. They say, "Why Newark, why Plainfield, why Buffalo? why not other cities?" And they say the answer lies in "a paradox: an upsurge in spirit and a lack of hope. The spirit reflects the change of the 60's in race relations." And then comes the most interesting sentence: "there were no such riots when Negroes everywhere knew their place." You know that's true. There *were* no such riots when Negroes everywhere knew their place. As long as we had a place and we knew where it was (the man had made it for us), and we were afraid to get out of it, there was no possibility of a riot or a rebellion or whatever you call it.

I point this out to show you that there is some good in what is going on. It must mean that a whole lot of black people no longer believe that they "have a place." And whether you like the expression that this new feeling takes or not, this change is a fact, and that is good. I prayed for, lo, these many years that there would come a day when we wouldn't know our place, and if that's what is indicated throughout the country, that increasingly black people no longer know their place, then I say that is good. If not knowing our place leaves us for the moment confused so that we do some things that are not constructive in the sense of planned campaigns for freedom, then that is a part of the struggle, an inevitable part of the struggle.

There was another little article in the paper on riots too. It was Roy Wilkins holding forth in his Saturday column. This is a very interesting column. He gives a very touching description of a scene: "Two little boys sat with their mother and father in the National Airport in Washington, D. C., after one of the nightmare nights of the Newark, N. J., rioting. Both handsome and under 12 years of age, one slept in a chair as he awaited the plane, but his brother greeted me with alert eyes, a ready smile, excellent use of language and the now old-fashioned courtesy towards older persons. Their suits were linen and their ties were tributes to their mother's taste. Their father was an officer in the Air Force and their mother a college graduate. The Major said quietly that he had done a stint in Vietnam and was now looking forward to Germany."

I presume he was talking about a black family. The father has been in Vietnam, killing Vietnamese. Now he is on his way to Germany, and he is sitting in the airport in Washington, D. C., with his two well-trained clean little boys. It is a beautiful little picture, the kind of family everybody thinks he wants.

"Sunday night, while in Plainfield, New Jersey, a white policeman was being brutally stomped and shot to death, (this is another Negro family now) a Negro father and his two sons were strolling on the observation deck at LaGuardia airport. The boys like all boys everywhere were zooming with each jet takeoff and they hovered with each helicopter which settled down as it made its way to the gate."

Wilkins has picked here two middle class bourgeois Negro families, put them both in airports because that is a sort of status thing right there, and he is very much concerned that all this riot and turmoil and fighting is going to hurt these nice little boys in Washington, D. C., and at LaGuardia airport. He is concerned that this stomping of a policeman in New Jersey is going to rob these little boys of their chance, their opportunity, their hope, their dignity, that all these hoodlums carrying on in Newark are really hurting these nice little colored boys. He is apparently primarily concerned about these little bourgeois, middle class boys. He doesn't say one word about the fact that a little black boy was killed by the policeman in Jersey—*he* didn't have on a linen suit and his clothing was no tribute to his mother's good taste! He was just a little black boy who lived in a slum. A riot was going on and he was running around trying to see what was happening and a policeman in his fear shot and killed him, so crowds of black people stomped the policeman to death.

But Roy Wilkins isn't concerned about *that*. He is just concerned about these nice little boys with the father who has been dropping bombs in Vietnam. He doesn't like violence, but he doesn't see anything wrong with this middle-class Negro who is an Air Force officer and who can participate in complete wholesale violence in Vietnam. He doesn't see anything wrong with that. All he sees is these nice little boys who are polite, well-mannered, well-trained, and well-dressed. He is going to evaluate the total struggle from coast to coast in terms of what it is going to do to these little well-dressed, well-mannered little boys.

You know, these two little boys are not the sum total of what we are fighting for. We are fighting for little boys who don't dress nicely, who don't know how to talk, who don't know what manners are, who don't come up with what he calls this old-time courtesy to elderly people. Little boys who are nasty, who steal, who are darting around in the slums, learning the hard way, who don't have any opportunity. That is what the struggle is for. These two little boys in the airport have every advantage that a black person can have—which isn't too much. But they have a little money, a little position. We want dignity for those other little boys in Newark, New Jersey, in Harlem, in Bedford-Stuyvesant, in Birmingham, in Detroit. We want dignity for all of these boys. That is what is involved in the total struggle—not dignity just for a middle-class black society.

Roy Wilkins has picked his role. He is going to be the spokes-man for bourgeois black society and anything that hurts *that* is going to be bad. Some of you think that isn't too bad because you figure you kind of identify with that, too. You are identifying yourself with what is about gone. A middle-class black society can-not maintain itself, and it cannot free black people. It is impossible —essentially, because the middle-class is selfish. Each is concerned about his own family, and his own little children, his own job, his own advancement, his own self.

In a rebellion or riot, a lot of people are concerned about things other than self. I am not talking about the looters now—those who are trying to steal what they can and get it home for them-selves. They are just like the middle-class. I am talking about those who are outraged, whether it is a sensible outrage or an irrational outrage, outraged at the indignities that black people have to live with. Those people strike out not selfishly but because they identify with a group. They identify with black people, and a policeman doesn't have to shoot them before they are outraged at police brutality. A policeman doesn't have to beat them over the head personally before they become involved in a reaction against po-lice brutality. In Plainfield they stomped a policeman to death be-cause he shot a little boy. That little boy didn't belong to all of them in a family sense, but in the sense of a Nation, a people, they were involved, they reacted, they responded, they were indignant.

It is a complex thing, this struggle for freedom. It is so easy after we become involved in a struggle to say, "Well, we have gone far enough now, let's cool it. I got some of the things I wanted. I got my job, I have been promoted, I got a poverty program job now. Let's call it all off now." But essentially what we were trying to get from the very beginning wasn't something for you. It was equality for all of us. And when we once started it about 13 years ago, there wasn't any calling it off. Now you have been talking all this time about "I want freedom, I would give anything for freedom, I am tired of whitey, I am tired of him being on my back, I want to run my own community." You have been saying it, but it is harder to say it now because they have fought on 12th Street and it may be on your street soon. It is not over by any means. And it is harder to say today, "I am for freedom and I think black people ought to strike back; I think they ought to fight for freedom," than it was when they were fighting in Newark.

We were all for the people in Newark because we said they were striking a blow for freedom. We said, "Isn't it wonderful, what they are doing?" And this Sunday some of you say, "Are those Niggers crazy? There they go, just acting a fool, up and down 12th Street, robbing and stealing." That's right. Plenty of them are acting a fool up and down 12th Street. And soon they are going to be acting a fool up and down Linwood Street. They are going to be acting a fool all across town, up and down Dexter, up and down Joy Road. But that is a part of what you started. You didn't think you were going to have a rebellion, a freedom struggle, and nobody was going to get hurt, did you? Did you think it was going to go on everywhere else, and they were coming to Detroit in the end and say, "You all are black, too. We are going to give you the things that these other people were fighting and dying for. We are going to give it to you because you all were so good." It doesn't happen like that. When it started, it started for everybody.

Some of the people who holler so much about violence had a part in starting it. Roy Wilkins doesn't want to be reminded of it now, but when they started taking these cases to the Supreme Court, when the NAACP won the case to outlaw segregation in schools throughout the South, that was one of the first gunshots of the rebellion. And Wilkins can say now that he doesn't like what is happening, but he had a big part in starting it because at that time we didn't know what we were. We didn't know what the possibilities were in human life. We didn't know what we could do. When the Supreme Court said you have to give equal education, we said if we have to have equal education, there are a whole lot of other things we have to have too.

Martin Luther King said he didn't believe in a whole lot of things which are now going on. But when he had the bus boycott in

Montgomery, that was the second shot. When black people started marching in Montgomery and white folks couldn't stop them, black people all over the country said, "Look here, the man hasn't got as much strength as we thought he had." That was the beginning of our changed conception of ourselves, and a changed evaluation of the white man.

Then some people said, "We are not going to ride in the back of the bus anymore." So we had the Freedom Riders. The whites burned up busses, they turned them over, they whipped black men and women over the head, but the Freedom Riders didn't stop. Another shot. The rebellion is going on, people's ideas are changing. And when your ideas are changing, the way you act changes, too. Montgomery bus boycott, Freedom Riders, you saw the pictures. College kids, high school kids just sitting at the lunch counters and white folks doing everything to them. But they refused to leave. They were demanding equality, demanding that black people be treated like anybody else in this country.

These things went on and we cheered all the time. Greenwood, Mississippi, mass demonstrations, Birmingham, the dogs, the cattle prods, the firehoses, we cheered them on. But you know those people had to have gone through a big change or they couldn't have done that. A few years ago a black man stepped off the sidewalk in one of those Southern towns if a white man looked like that was what he wanted him to do. When you come from the stage where you step off the sidewalk to the point where you are ready to let police dogs and everybody else try to stop you but you keep on, you have come a long way in your mind. Your emancipation is in progress. When people begin to think of themselves in a different way, they begin to act in a different way. Black people have started thinking differently. All along it has been happening.

Even in Detroit, provincial and backward as we are, we have been thinking differently the last few years. You can see it with every issue that has come up; black people have reacted differently in Detroit, not the same way they would have acted five years ago, ten years ago. So we have been caught up in change. You remember the Freedom March in Detroit when more than 300,000 black people marched down Woodward Avenue? What happened at Cobo Hall when we got there is something else. But we marched in protest, 300,000 of us. Even then, we were in the process of changing. Our thinking was changing. When you start this process, when you start black people deciding that they are going to be equal; that they are going to change conditions; that the white man is not going to keep them in bondage and slavery and oppression; that if he does, he is going to have to do it with force and naked power, then a whole new world is being born. That is what we are in the midst of now.

When Stokely Carmichael screams "Black Power," he is only putting into a phrase the change which has been going on for almost fifteen years. Things had reached the point where the change could be put into a phrase. And so Stokely said "Black Power," and everybody screamed "Black Power," and the white man said —"uh-uh." Then the white man began to ask, "What is Black Power, what do you mean? What is the philosophy of Black Power?" But the white man knew that some big and basic change had already taken place, or Stokely Carmichael could not have cried "Black Power" and gotten a Black Power response.

This is the kind of thing that we are in the midst of everywhere in these United States. You look at the paper now and you wonder at the places that rebellions or riots are breaking out. Little communities that don't have enough black people for you to feel comfortable in are fighting—3,000 in a community of 80,000, and they are tearing up the town. But those 3,000 have been systematically mistreated and oppressed, and when they get ready to strike back, they don't always care whether they win or whether they lose. This we have got to understand. Most of you are rational. You are for freedom, for justice, for equality. You make rational decisions, you are going to fight in a rational kind of way, you realize that there are certain things you can do. But you know this freedom thing is exploding in people's heads. And everybody is not going to be rational about it. When someone decides, "They have been mistreating my momma and my grandmomma, they have been mistreating all of us, and I don't like it," they are not all going to be rational about it.

Some of you saw the TV report from the Black Power Conference in Newark. You saw about twenty-five of them walk up the street and break into the place where the press conference was taking place. They were delegates but they had had a little caucus and they had decided what they were going to do. These delegates broke in there and tore up everything, kicked over the TV cameras, ran everybody out of the place and threw the furniture out after them—just had a ball. They were expressing their indignation.

You know, when you say over a period of time, "Oppression comes from the white man. We want to get the white man off our back. We want to have communities in which we have control." When you say that over and over again, some people will say, "I don't want to have anything to do with white people at all." That is what those people walking up and busting up that press conference were saying. They didn't even want them in a separate room in the building where the conference was taking place. That wasn't rational. You can say they were crazy if you want to. But that is a part of the thing in which we are engaged. They needed publicity in the sense that that they needed to get out to black people everywhere the message about what they were doing. We all know that the press, the TV and radio won't take it out exactly as it is. They are going to slant it. But that is about the only way we all are going to know about what they do in Newark. They could have set up and used press conferences. They could have gotten a lot of information to us through the mass media. But this little group of young black militants just said "whitey has go go" and threw everybody out. That wasn't sensible but it is one of the things that you can expect in this kind of a rebellion.

Everything that happens in a rebellion is not sensible. You don't have to participate in all parts of it. You try to develop all of the sensible aspects of rebellion that you can. You try to give at every step a sensible alternative to violence, as we do here at the

Shrine of the Black Madonna. We believe in political action. Now a lot of black people say, "I don't care about political action, that is just the white man's bag." Well, that is what they think. We have got to try political action because that is an alternative to violence. We have got to use picket lines, boycotts, all the things that offer the possibility of power without the necessity of violence. We try to do those things. That doesn't mean that at the same time we look with disdain on these other people who are fighting in this country for the same cause that we are fighting for.

We have got to understand that it takes all kinds of people to fight a rebellion, and a lot of them are not going to be doing it the way you are doing it at any single moment. And a whole lot of people are not going to agree with the way you are doing it, either. It won't be too long before they will be calling you "Uncle Tom," because unless you throw a brick you are an Uncle Tom. That would be a logical development, wouldn't it? But you understand why people do what they do. Because essentially we are trying to get free and we want justice and we are no longer talking about love and all those other things that cluttered up people's minds for so long. We want justice and we are going to fight for it. But there are a lot of ways to fight. Because we fight one way, let's not join in some universal denunciation of people fighting in some other kind of way.

The rebellion goes on. There is no halfway revolution. When it starts, it is going to go to its logical conclusion. Either we get free or we end up in concentration camps. You can understand that. There is no turning back, no stopping. You may wish you hadn't started, but you did. It is going on and there is no way you can stop it. You can try to utilize reason, you can channel power, but you can't stop it. Either we get free or we end up in concentration camps. We are increasingly useless to the white man. Economically he doesn't need us, politically he wishes we would drop dead. It is not going to stop. So we have got to do everything possible to get free because this is what we started and this is the process in which we are engaged. And you don't stop a process. It goes on.

For years now we have been engaged in a process of trying to break the black man's identification with the white man, so that a black man says, "I'm a black man and I am not ashamed of it. I am a black man and I don't feel I have to go along with anything the white man says." That has been the process of years, breaking our identification. More and more it is being broken. Fewer and fewer black people feel that they are a part of the white man's world. Alienation, the understanding of oppression, the realization that the white man is an enemy against whom we have to do some kind of battle if we are going to exist, to survive—all of these are realities we have to face. There is no halfway revolution.

I hope most of you saw on TV the young man from Newark who tried to explain what he thought they were fighting for. He was wonderful. He wasn't a leader, just an ordinary person they picked up, but he knew what he was fighting for. Maybe he did some looting. I don't know. You couldn't tell. But he also knew what the freedom struggle was all about. He didn't give one wrong answer, and that is more than you can say for most black leaders on TV who are always trying not to say too much, not make somebody mad. He didn't say one wrong thing. Asked what he was trying to do, he said he was just trying to run all the white people out of the district. There was no equivocation about it. He didn't say, "Run the bad ones out, leave the good ones in." He was just going to tear up everything until he got them all out—a simple clear-cut statement.

All over the country we have young men now who are aware of the problems, who are participating in a rebellion, who understand what the nature of the rebellion is. They fight one way here and another way some place else. But the rebellion goes on, and whether you want to be in it or not, you are part of it.

The times determine our heroes. Recall, again, in the Book of Judges, how Samson was considered one of the judges of Israel because he lived at a time when they needed that kind of person, fearless, strong, with a deep hatred for the enemy. And how Samson fought. And remember the end of the Scripture lesson this morning. Sometimes you wonder, "What are they trying to do, what do they hope to accomplish?" Remember when Samson was in the Temple and the Philistines were all around, making fun of him, robbing him of his dignity. They brought him out because he symbolized the enemy whom they had fought against, the enemy who had humiliated them so many times. They were going to humiliate Samson. They were going to make sport of him. And a little boy brought Samson out and put him in between these two big pillars that held up the Temple. His hair had begun to grow back because he had been down in the dungeon so long, and with it his strength returned. He asked the little boy to put his hands on the two pillars because he couldn't even see. They had blinded him. And the little boy put his hands on the pillars so Samson could support himself. And when Samson got his hands on the pillars, he knew what he was going to do. You may not like it, you may not agree with it, but Samson spoke right out to God about it. "Let me die with the Philistines. Oh God, that I may be avenged upon the Philistines for one of my eyes."

You have to understand that indignation, anger, hatred, all of them stemming from systematic oppression, can develop to the point where an individual says, "I am willing to die if I can take a whole bunch of them with me." That is what Samson said. I am not quoting from anybody in Detroit or Newark. That is the Bible. " 'Let me die with the Philistines.' Then he bowed with all his might and the house fell upon the Temple and upon all the people who were in it. So the dead he slew at his death were more than those he had slain during his life."

This you are going to have to understand because this is a part of the rebellion. There are people like this in Detroit, Newark, Birmingham, California, New York, Chicago who are willing to destroy even themselves if they can express antagonism, if they can strike out against oppression. So to the Hebrew people, the Jews, Samson is a great hero. Who knows but that a hundred years from today we may remember as heroes some of these very individuals we call hoodlums today, who are striking out for freedom? We don't know. But they fight for freedom in their way and we in ours, confident that God will see that freedom comes.

Heavenly Father, we seek thy blessing upon black men, women and children in their struggle for freedom everywhere. Not only in our own community, but in Harlem, in Newark, in Birmingham, in Chicago, everywhere throughout this nation, we pray that thy spirit, thy strength, thy wisdom be with thy people as they struggle for freedom; that they have a sense of the tremendous magnitude of that for which they struggle, that they seek to build on earth thy kingdom, that they seek thy guidance. Be with them everywhere to sustain them and to lead them. This we ask and we pray that we may be identified with them fully, that we may be a part of the struggle for freedom, whatever form it takes and wherever it may appear, because we are one people, one Nation and we struggle for freedom for black people everywhere. This we ask in his name. Amen.

10/Grapes of Wrath

"Then I will make this house like Shiloh, and I will make this city a curse for all the nations of the earth" (*Jeremiah* 26:6).

A march which began almost fifteen years ago in Montgomery, Alabama, has now reached Newark, New Jersey, Detroit, Michigan, and almost a hundred other cities from coast to coast. This is the same black revolution that started when Rosa Parks refused to move in Montgomery, Alabama. The same one. The same black revolution that drew black college students to the South for freedom rides and demonstrations. The same black revolution. The same movement, the same freedom struggle. It is the same thing going on now, today, in New Jersey and Detroit and a hundred other cities. The same thing. But people are reacting differently because a movement grows up. A movement comes of age, a movement one day begins to come to grips with reality.

The President of the United States has asked us to join with Christian Churches everywhere in America in a big prayer for racial peace. By racial peace I know he means the end of racial violence. And I know that in many black churches all over the U.S. there will be pious exhortations to black congregations. Black preachers will read from the Bible and misinterpret what Jesus said and misinterpret the message of the Old Testament. And they will caution people that "this thing has gone too far." It hasn't gone too far, it hasn't gone far enough yet. Because we are still in chains. It hasn't gone far enough, and black preachers in black churches who try to make it seem that the message of Jesus Christ is a message of reconciliation with injustice, misunderstand the Old Testament and the message of a Black Messiah.

We cannot pray for racial peace yet. Not in this church, because we know whom we serve. We are followers of a Black Messiah who two thousand years ago tried to bring black men together so that they might fight for their freedom. So we do not join in prayer for racial peace. We pray that struggle and conflict may go on until black men and women are free. We do not judge the struggle in terms of its costs but in terms of the value of that for which we struggle and die. And there is no price too high to pay for justice and freedom.

We do not pray for racial peace. We pray for our brothers and sisters who were killed during the rebellion in Newark and Detroit and other cities. We pray for those who are still herded into filthy cowpens like cattle today because they are black. We pray for their spirit. We pray for our own spirit that we may not grow weak, that we may not, in the face of difficulties, turn back, that we may not become frightened, that conflict may not make of us Uncle Toms. We pray for that, and we pray that black churches from coast to coast will some day, and not too far in the future, become like we are, churches dedicated to the freedom of black people, centers of black culture. We do not pray for racial peace because justice has not yet come.

In all that is happening we can see the hand of God, the kind of God we worship. You remember the Battle Hymn of the Republic. White folks used to sing it. I don't know if they will sing it anymore. You remember the words: "Mine eyes have seen the glory of the coming of the Lord./He is trampling out the vintage where the grapes of wrath are stored./He has loosed the fateful lightning of his terrible swift sword./His truth is marching on." We can sing that kind of song. We don't have to be ashamed of it. We don't have to keep the doors closed tight lest the brothers think we are that kind of Toms. We can sing that kind of song because that is the kind of God we worship.

I have seen him in the watchfires of a hundred circling camps. I have seen him in a hundred watchfires of a different kind. *"They have builded him an altar in the evening dews and damps./I can read his righteous sentence by the dim and flaring lamps./His day is marching on.* His day is on the way because we are participating in bringing it closer every minute and every day. *He has sounded forth the trumpet that shall never call retreat.* I don't think they are going to sing it anymore. *He is sifting out the hearts of men before his judgment seat.*

He is sifting us. When you get home and look out and say, "I wish those hoodlums would stop," when you get on your little street and say, "I am afraid those folks will come over here and get us," it is because you are scared, because you've got guilt feelings. That is just your identification with the man, coming to the surface. You know that living on your street, you ought to have done more than you have been doing, and you feel like, "If I was out there rampaging I would come over here and get me." That is what you are feeling. He is sifting out the hearts of men, all of us.

You were sifted during the riots. You had to make some kind of decision. When you crept back to work, and the man asked you what you thought and he said, "It sure is terrible," you could say, "Yes, it sure is terrible." You know you had to make a decision and some of you made one decision and some of you made another. But he is sifting our hearts in this sort of thing. I am talking about my kind of God. He wants to know where you stand when things are happening. On what side?

Some of you are too old to participate in this way. You would just be in the way. But you don't have to talk like an Uncle Tom because your feet are slow. *Oh, be swift, my soul, to answer Him! Be jubilant, my feet!* You know what he is talking about. *Our God is marching on.* And then it ends up, *Glory, glory, Hallelujah!* Sometimes you look back at the spirituals. In "Nobody Knows the Trouble I've Seen"—you know what trouble they were having—they could still sing *Glory, glory, Hallelujah!* We can say the same thing today—"Nobody knows the trouble I've seen. We are going to keep on fighting. Glory, glory, Hallelujah!" It is a state of mind. It is an attitude.

Our Scripture lesson is taken from Jeremiah. Jeremiah is telling them, "The way you folks have been acting (he is talking to the Black Nation Israel), I have to tell you what God said. He is going to tear up the temple and the city because both of them are wrong. 'I will make this house like Shiloh.' " That is the temple in the north that they desecrated and destroyed so that everybody would have to come to the temple in Jerusalem. He is telling them it doesn't matter how big the church is, how much money you have, how many people you've got shouting "Amen." God will destroy the temple as well as the city. "I will make this house like Shiloh and make this city a curse for all the nations of the earth." When you understand the things that God was trying to tell us through Jesus Christ, then you understand that all men in the sight of God have a right to dignity, and when somebody decides that he is going to build a civilization, a world, and deny black men the right to dignity, then God is going to act to destroy that very civilization and that very nation.

"I will make this city a curse to all the nations of the earth." That was true then. Jeremiah said, "Babylon is going to come in here and destroy this temple, make desolate this temple and this city and take you all into captivity." That is what Jeremiah told them. They didn't believe him. They met, they talked around, held meetings and said that couldn't be. But it happened. Anytime a people try to destroy God's chosen people, they are bound to find that desolation is their reward.

We are God's chosen people, God is with us in our struggle. Our freedom struggle, our movement, our Black Revolution is in the hands of God. And the things we do, we do with the guidance, the strength, the support of God—we have to understand this, because there is so much nonsense and foolishness now being spoken and written in the newspapers that we are getting confused.

I have talked to so many confused people. I know a Tom when

I see one, but this is just outright confusion. This lady called me up and talked for a solid forty minutes.

She said, "There is nothing racial about this disturbance. White folks did it."

I asked her to explain it to me.

"Well, the John Birch Society went into our neighborhoods and got our boys all excited. They did it."

I said, "What are you trying to do, explain away the revolution?"

She was trying to explain away what the white folks were saying. The white folks are saying this was a criminal action and she wanted to disassociate herself from this so-called criminal activity. So all she could do was say, "We didn't have anything to do with it all. It was the white man did it." That is the old kind of slavery talk, isn't it? We haven't even got sense enough to revolt by ourselves. Somebody else must come in and tell us what to do. She didn't understand what she was saying. I would rather be a criminal than be somebody who didn't even have sense enough to revolt by himself.

I want to say one thing about this criminal thing because that is what they are going to be talking about from now on. White folks have got to establish in our mind that those who participated in the freedom struggle are criminals and, therefore, we have got to separate ourselves from them in order to be nice, decent Christian people. They have got to make a division down the middle of the black community. They have got to separate one group of black people from the other. They have got to make *you* believe that those people over there are criminals. And you don't want anything to do with them, do you?

That is the purpose of the President's Committee. That committee is supposed to run all over the country and come back with all kinds of homemade evidence that there is some kind of conspiracy, and that criminal elements are running this thing all over the country. Not that they believe it, and no one will believe this report anymore than they believe the Warren Report on the assassination of President Kennedy. But we will be the ones to believe it because we are the target. We will be trying to decide who is a criminal and who is not. It will all be done for our benefit. It is really amazing the number of black people who have been calling up their friends, the police, during the riots telling on their black brothers and sisters, trying to get straight with the man, trying to let him see that he is a good one. As though the man is going to write down, "This was a good one. He reported something over there. I went over there. There wasn't anything going on but I knocked hell out of everybody anyway. So he was a good one, he was trying."

That is what they want us to do. Let us understand. We are trying on the other hand to build a Nation that takes in all black people, where we are fighting for the freedom of all black people and where we understand that there are a lot of different ways of fighting and where we try to include everybody in what we are trying to do. But the white man doesn't like that. That is what scares him. We begin to talk about black consciousness and they get scared. Then people begin to believe it enough to fight for it. Then they really get scared and they say we have got to separate them, divide them, we have got to make them like they used to be on the plantation. We have to make us some more house niggers, and that is what they are going to try to do.

So when you read, when you listen to radio, when you look at television, understand what the man is trying to do to your mind. He is working on you to confuse you. Because there was strength and power demonstrated in these disturbances from coast to coast, which shake at the very foundation of this country. That is why they are all saying, "We are going to rebuild America and make it like it was."

Let me tell you, they are not going to rebuild it like it was. We didn't like it the way it was, and they are not going to rebuild it like it was. They are going to rebuild it like we want it. We are going to keep on participating until they rebuild it like we want it. Now understand, we are talking about rebuilding our own community, controlling it, rebuilding it the way we want it. All of us. Don't try to separate yourself, because we will come get you!

Let's go into this criminal business that they are trying to make so much out of. Any effort on the part of the powerless to take power is criminal. Isn't that right? If you don't have any power and you try to take power, anything you do is criminal—understand that when you read all this stuff, when you listen to all these learned professors making statements, or watch all those press conferences. Any effort by the powerful to hold the powerless in bondage and oppression is the preservation of law and order. Do you understand me? This is their interpretation. *They* decide what is law and order, and *they* decide what is a crime. We don't have any power. So whatever we do that disturbs their power, that is criminal. Whatever they do that keeps us like we are, hopeless, helpless, oppressed and exploited, that is law and order.

We have seen many illustrations of their law and order during the recent revolt. The Inner-City Organizing Committee sent a telegram on the first day to the Justice Department, the Attorney General, the Bar Association, demanding an investigation of the way prisoners were being treated. Most of you probably understood what was happening, but most of the people up and down the street took it like they got it. Those arrested were criminals. They were supposed to be treated like dogs; the very judges who are going to try them were issuing statements about what a mob and a pack of swine they were. The judges declared them guilty and they hadn't even been examined. One judge issued his statement, a denunciation of prisoners before they had even been examined, saying, "*We* (the judge talking now) will prove them guilty." As a judge, he is only supposed to decide a case on the basis of evidence presented. Yet the court is already prejudging black people who have been picked up by a cracker police department that has discriminated against black people down through the ages.

It wasn't only the words and acts of the judges. It was the very procedure by which arrests were made. Grab anybody in any kind of a situation. He is automatically guilty. If he doesn't act like he is guilty, kill him in the street. Take him down, give him none of his constitutional rights, don't let him communicate with anybody or make a telephone call, don't let him have a lawyer. All of these things were done by the power structure. All of these things are criminal. At the very time that they are denouncing black people for criminal acts, they are downtown in the halls of justice, in the City-County Building, in the State Capitol in Lansing, carrying on criminality much worse than anything any black man has ever been charged with. A prisoner's right to a lawyer is a time-honored constitutional right, and yet it has been and is still being refused.

Excessive bail is another thing. They put bail of $10,000 on little children who picked up things in the street. If he is down there, it is $10,000; I don't care how old he is. If he is an adult, it is $15,000 or $20,000. If they thought he was anywhere near a gun, it was $100,000 or $200,000. This is not bail. This is the court using its power to oppress, to participate in oppression and to keep black people off the streets. Criminality! Who is the criminal?

Now we go back and look at America and America's whole fabric and ask who is the criminal? Who is the criminal in Vietnam? The United States. "Our" government, this United States, is the criminal in Vietnam. They have invaded a nation, they are killing people daily. America is the criminal in Vietnam. And yet they talk of criminal acts in Newark and Detroit.

Who is the criminal? America was a criminal nation from the very beginning. The dungeons and prisons of Europe were emptied of criminals in the first place to make this nation. They stole the land from the Indians, which was a criminal act. Everything that America has, was stolen from somebody. America was built on criminal activity. You don't understand that? Everything in the world is built on criminal activity.

The French Revolution was criminal. A group of people who had nothing, fighting against the government for power. It was criminal until they won. Do you understand? When you win, then the thing you did is not criminal anymore. America was engaged in criminal activity taking the land away from the Indians until they got the Indians all crowded into concentration camps (reservations). Then it ceased to be criminal.

The Russian Revolution was a criminal act, the effort of people who were oppressed to throw off the shackles of bondage. It was criminal until they won. Now the dignitaries of Russia sit in the highest councils of the world because they won.

The difference between a criminal act and an acceptable act lies only in whether you lose or win. During this whole period of our struggle we have got to bear this in mind. If we lose, we are criminals. While we are fighting and until we win, every act that we do is going to be defined as a criminal act. This is a part of the system that the man controls. While he is in power he decides what is crime and what is not crime.

It was true in the Old Testament. When Israel was struggling to enter the Promised Land (God gave Israel the Promised Land, you remember), they fought their way out of Egypt, stealing everything they could before they left, killing the first-born of the Egyptians. When they got to the Promised Land, they had to fight their way in. God said, "I give you the Promised Land." But he didn't just open the gate and let the people in. He said, "If you want it, go get it." Their activities were criminal until they took it, until they won. The difference between a criminal act and an acceptable act has to do only with whether or not you win. Understand that and you won't get so excited by "the man" talking about how many of our people are criminal.

Black people are engaged in a freedom struggle and a lot of the things they are going to have to do are going to be defined by the man as criminal. If you don't understand that and you are going to run every time he starts calling someone a criminal, you better start running right now, and it will be a long time before you find a place to stop. The sit-in demonstrations in the South were criminal acts. Now we accept them. They were against the unjust laws of a particular community. Every step of the freedom struggle has been filled with criminal acts because the very power structure that controls everything decides what is criminal and what is not criminal. They write the laws and they define what is and what is not criminal.

Walter Reuther was down in the City-County Building at this great meeting to which twenty black people were invited. I called down and asked would there be any great objection if I came down. Would I have to fight my way in and incite a riot to get into the meeting? They said they would rather I didn't come, but if I promised not to say anything . . . I said, "Just forget it. I am coming anyway."

But when I got there it wasn't worth saying anything. It was complete nonsense from start to finish. Walter Reuther stood up —you know he is our great black leader—to explain the whole thing and said he was going to come in and rebuild everything. The first ten minutes of his talk were about how opposed he was to any criminal activity, how criminals must be punished and how he can't stand anything criminal. I thought back to when the CIO was being organized. He is respectable now, all of his officials are respectable now. They live in nice houses, they go to dinners at the White House. Everything they did to build the CIO was criminal in the days when they were struggling. They fought, they looted, they burned, they killed, they did everything they could do. You remember the first sit-in demonstration. It was the UAW. That was against the law, that was criminal activity. Now Reuther stands up, all honest and sincere, he wrinkles his brow, he is so sincere, and says he can't stand criminal activity. Nobody can stand it after they win. And let me tell you when we win, we are not going to stand it, either.

We ought to understand what happened in this whole thing. Don't get all mixed up in the "events." Understand this was a struggle. Black people are fighting against oppression. The white man has put the oppression on us. He can send all the canned food he wants into the ghetto now. That doesn't remove the oppression which he put on us and which he still controls. We are fighting against oppression, against white men controlling our communities, controlling our schools, controlling all of our public services, controlling the businesses we have to patronize. That is a struggle against oppression. That is rebellion.

I don't care how many white people participated for kicks or how many white criminals went out under cover of the confusion to steal all they could. We know white folks can steal. We didn't need a disturbance to prove it to us. But at the foundation of the whole thing is the simple fact that black people are fighting against white oppression. And don't let anybody tell you it was something else. You look up and see these houses that were burned and black people lived in them. Paramore's house was burned down; he is a member of this church. I am sure he's got sense enough to know that black people didn't burn his house down on purpose. It just was unfortunate because he lived up the street from this exploitative white business and they were going to get rid of that business and the wind blew the sparks down his street. No use his getting mad and saying, "Negroes got no right out there burning down their own houses." They were not burning down their own houses. The wind sometimes is uncontrollable.

Every business that was burned down can be explained. You go and look at the places and think back, what kind of store was that? That was one of the stores that was cheating everybody who came in the front door. You know, charging ten, fifteen, twenty cents higher on every item, bringing in meat after the other store couldn't use it anymore, old vegetables, and still not hiring black people except to clean up the place. That was the kind of store that was burned. And it didn't take a national conspiracy or Stokely Carmichael beating drums off some place to tell black people that somehow those stores had to be gotten out of our community.

In every community that has been the pattern. Black people, as they come of age, as they become sophisticated, understand that these businesses have got to be removed. We have tried to talk to them. You know I am peaceful. We picket Sears, we try to talk to them. We try to tell black people, "Don't buy at these stores until they hire black workers in proportion to black customers." We will be back, we will be picketing Sears and other stores with unfair employment policies. White folks won't listen to a non-violent approach to the problem. I know because I have been using it. They don't listen to me.

I tell them down at the school board that they are turning out black kids who can't do anything because they are not equipped. They are not educating our children. They argue with me: "We can't do anything because they come from nothing—they are culturally deprived." So they can't go to college and they can't get a job. Now I tell you, the kids that were fleetest of foot and knew what they were doing out there during the rebellion, were sixteen to twenty-six years old. Those were the ones they refused to educate. Those kids had no choice but to fight for freedom here or in Vietnam. Now if the Board of Education can see that they have failed, that this whole thing need not have happened if they had been willing to listen to black people when we told them what had to be done, then something might still be done in Detroit.

But let me tell you, brothers and sisters, they still have not gotten the message. They think they can talk us to death. They haven't gotten the message that they have got to give over the control of the black ghetto to black people. This has to happen in Newark, in Detroit, everywhere. If there are enough people to have a black ghetto, they want to control it. Now we are not going to control only the black ghetto. You will be surprised, since this thing has happened, at the exodus of white people from the city and houses that are up for sale or are in the hands of real estate brokers. We are going to control this city faster now than we would have before, if we have sense enough to use our political power and not be confused and go to the polls and vote for these so-called "liberal" white friends, who come out every election and talk about "what I have done for you people."

We must have a black man in the mayor's seat in the City of Detroit. I know how it is going to be—and this discourages me—not the struggle, but I just know when the election comes, black people will be out working and voting for a white liberal just because they don't know any better. Crockett was one of the best judges down there. They fought him every way they could, and I thank God they did because he learned a lot from white folks fighting and trying to stomp him. He learned a lot because no matter what hysteria was going on he was down there in his court practicing law. He was being a judge, one of the few on the bench. We must remember that.

I want to remember another man—Poindexter. In spite of white folks who put him in office, he was down there in his court turning black folks loose with all the white folks saying he was crazy. Everybody down there was acting a fool and he was saying, "It isn't legal. We got nothing on him, turn him loose." He certainly didn't have anything to gain because we didn't give him two votes. This whole thing means that the white folks downtown must realize that the whole movement has changed, that we are going to be free, and that they must do certain things. If they realize this, it is going to save a whole lot of trouble. If they don't realize it, there is going to be a whole lot more trouble.

Heavenly Father, we thank thee for the opportunity to come into this thy house. We thank thee for protecting it during the week from the defenders of the law. We thank thee for the fact that this building is still situated here. We thank thee for thy guidance, thy counsel, and thy strength, for all that thou hast helped us to do during the past days. We thank thee that thou hast protected us, that we can gather together again and rededicate ourselves to the struggle for freedom. Heavenly Father, be with us to build and strengthen this Church, that it may be a beacon, a light upon the hill, that we may call black people from coast to coast to the sure and certain knowledge that thou art our God, that thy Son Jesus Christ was a Black Messiah, that we are dedicated to following him, that this is his house, that we are his disciples. Be with us that this Church may become increasingly meaningful in the freedom struggle, and let us remember that it is not a house made with hands but a people dedicated to thy will, and even if we must meet on the corner or in a barn, we will do thy will and struggle that our people may be free. Amen.

11/But God Hardened Pharaoh's Heart

"But the Lord hardened Pharaoh's heart, and he did not let the children of Israel go" (*Exodus* 10:20).

After another week, with four or five meetings and interviews a day, I am convinced that the white Establishment has decided that the rebellion or riot or revolution, or whatever it was, really was not terribly significant, and that they will return the city to conditions as usual. This is my opinion after talking to any number of people who are in a position to decide whether or not there are to be changes made in the city of Detroit. I do not feel that any significant changes will be made, and I think this is most unfortunate.

Recently, I talked with a member of the New Detroit Committee. A couple of attorneys were there. We tried to outline a number of basic things that should be done if the committee he heads is to be meaningful. We tried to point out that it had to be the kind of committee on which black people had some equality of representation so that it could speak on the committee and the committee could then use its power to do the things which the black community demanded. He was very pleasant, very nice, very friendly, but he didn't do any of the things which we suggested, and this is very typical of the white Establishment. They talk to you, act friendly, suggest all kinds of concessions which are about to be made, and then go right along doing everything just like they always have.

I talked with a lot of other people in key positions. The Justice

Department people took copious notes, just as they did all over the South while black people were being whipped to death. The next day they came back and brought Cyrus Vance with them. Vance took up another afternoon, and he, too, took copious notes. Everybody wanted to know, "What should we do?" and then they nodded and wrote it all down. But nobody has indicated any intention of actually doing what the black community wants done.

Mr. Doar, of the Justice Department, came and said that he had gathered from my published report on the Detroit schools (which had somehow gotten to him) that perhaps the Justice Department could be helpful to us. He wanted me to take him around to the schools and show him what ought to be done. But then he had to leave for Mississippi before we could even begin the grand tour.

It is a very peculiar kind of thing that white people carry on in their dealings with black people. We went down and talked to Neighborhood Legal Services to find out what was being done with prisoners. It is terrible. A white minister told me that he went to a precinct police station when they were bringing prisoners in. The ones who hadn't been bayoneted in the streets were bayoneted off the back of the truck at the station house. This was just a part of the procedure. A pregnant black woman was trying to climb down off of a truck and they told her to jump. She said, "I'm pregnant." They said, "Jump." She jumped and had a miscarriage in the street. They dragged her into the police station and threw her into a cell with all the other black prisoners. She screamed and yelled and cried, and they just didn't hear her. The white minister said he went out into the street and threw up. It was more than an individual who has been playing at civilization for a number of years could stand.

This is just one incident. The treatment of black prisoners was inhuman everywhere. Some were lucky. But on the whole, it indicated that the white Establishment or white power structure has decided that no basic changes are to be made yet. It is a peculiar thing. I met with the Interfaith Emergency Council which includes clergymen from all parts of the religious community. They were the only group of the many groups I talked to which had any sense of the urgency or the magnitude of the crisis confronting the city of Detroit. Everyone else had already decided that it was time to put the city back like it was. Just pick up the pieces, clean up the streets, wash away the glass and bricks and act like it didn't happen. Let's tear down old pieces of buildings so that there will be nothing to remind us.

The merchant on 12th Street with his sign painted across the plywood covering his broken windows, "WE HAVE COME BACK," symbolizes the attitude of the white community. Standing in front of his looted store, he said, "This is a good place to do business." Sure, it is a wonderful place to do business. A little hole in the wall makes $20,000 a year for the man who has nerve enough to stand there and say, "We have come back. They are nice, friendly, colored people and I have known them for years." White people are peculiar.

I see that the *Detroit News* has started a series of articles by Louis Lomax. I haven't had time to read them carefully, but I glanced at the first article to see what commercial approach Lomax has taken to exploit our crisis. "Seeds of Riots Planted Here by Salesmen" is his headline for the most utterly fantastic story you can imagine. It seems that black people came here from some place (you know, wherever it is that we have our national riot headquarters) offering subscriptions to black magazines, and then leading the discussion gradually around to Black Power. After offering subscriptions to *Ebony, Jet,* and *Negro Digest,* they would ask such questions as "Why do you let Whitey run that business up at the corner?" In this peculiar way they planted the seeds of rebellion in a few weeks.

I want to talk to those salesmen and learn that technique. How do you do that to black people? I have been talking for fifteen years and *I* couldn't get them to go down to the corner to run Whitey out of our community. How can some kid come in, talk to them in the parlor of their homes, and suddenly plant in them this intense desire to throw off the shackles of bondage?

How can Lomax write it down and expect the white man to take it seriously? Yet they did. He wrote it down, they printed it and you will hear folks quoting it for weeks. "Yeah, one came to my house." Of course, magazine salesmen came to their house. They have been coming every summer for the last twenty years. Some white racket, that's all it is. Some poor black boy or girl says, "I am working my way through college and I *want* you to subscribe," and you subscribe because you are trying to help somebody. Now they are trying to make that the basic method for planting the seeds of riot. There is something weird about the white man's thinking. Our rebellion had to be some kind of foreign plot or conspiracy, someone looking like Rap Brown had to come in from somewhere to tell us that we were not satisfied.

This really means that white people still feel that "us good Niggers" in Detroit don't have any resentment. They tell us we are happy, and don't mind paying more for everything we buy. We don't mind the things that are being done to us, the police brutality, the total fabric of oppression. That is what the white man is trying to say, and he is saying it through his boy, Louis Lomax. We find it hard to understand that the man could believe it, that he could look at us day after day, know the conditions, see brutality everywhere, and yet believe that because we lived here in Detroit, we were such "good Niggers" that we couldn't be upset, and that there wasn't anything that could make us fight. That is what he believes and that is why he thinks that this city can go back to normal, back like it was on the 22nd of July, 1967.

You have got to put together little things to see what the white man really thinks, because he rarely says out loud what he thinks. But you can tell by the way he treats you in little situations. For example, the big memorial service at Friendship Baptist Church. The Governor and the Mayor are sponsoring it. All the big white folks are going to be there, memorializing "our dead." The Mayor and the Governor thought it would be good to heal the wounds and help us get back to normal.

Yesterday someone from the Council of Churches called me and said, "We would like to have you participate in the service." All the announcements have gone out and then they called me. "What would you like me to do?" I asked.

"We would like you to say some kind of prayer."

"Who is speaking for black people?" I asked.

"Rev. James Chambers of the Negro Interdenominational Ministerial Alliance."

"Anybody else black on the program?"

"Well, we have one doing a benediction, or invocation or something."

I said, "I am sorry, I can't participate. I am not going to sit on the platform and act like I support this kind of thing. If Jim Chambers is speaking for the black community, I don't want to be anywhere near the building where the whole thing is going on. Of course, I could come and say, 'Let us pray,' and then get up and really tell God all about it. But I am not going to use the subterfuge of talking to God about something that white folks did. God didn't do it."

So the man from the Council of Churches said, "We will call Mrs. George Romney, who is getting the service together, and let her make the decision."

A few minutes later somebody from the Governor's office called and asked whether or not I would talk to Mrs. Romney. I said that I would talk to anybody. After a little while Mrs. Romney called and asked, "What is this about the Memorial Service?"

I said, "The service as it is now is a farce. It is way over there in the Urban Renewal area where we can't even find it. It ought to be over here where the action was. Rev. C. L. Franklin's Church, New Bethel Baptist, is right here and just as big or bigger than Friendship Baptist. I know you don't want it at my Church, but you could have had it right up the street."

"Well," she said, "we left it to the Council of Churches and they wanted a Church that had a big parking lot."

I said, "New Bethel is full to the ceiling every Sunday, and they park some place, and when white folks are coming over to memorialize our dead, they can park just like we do."

She said, "We can't change that. What else can we do?"

I said, "If you can't figure that out, I have nothing more to say."

She said, "Would you participate if we let you speak?"

I asked, "No strings attached? Say anything I want to say?"

She said, "Not too long. You can say a whole lot in five or six minutes."

I said, "Is everybody going to speak five or six minutes?"

She said, "Yes."

I said, "I will be there because from what I hear about this service, somebody ought to be there saying what black people want said."

So I will be there, but the whole thing indicates that they still don't understand. They still want to have a little service off some place and keep it isolated from the black people who are concerned about the problems and about the crisis. I'm still not sure that when I get there they will let me speak.

I asked Mrs. Romney, "Are you sure the other people on the platform will participate if I speak?"

She said, "I am sure they will be happy to."

But she hadn't checked, and when I get there I don't know whether they will let me speak or not.

It is not a personal thing that I am talking about. I told her, "There are a whole lot of black people in this town who can speak and articulate what black people want said and that is all I want." We don't want a leader telling us what to do and where to go, or acting as a sounding board for white people. We want leaders who are in essence speaking for us, and if they are not speaking for us, they are not our spokesmen. White people do not yet understand. Nowhere in the city do you get a sense that they understand. All week I could hear the words of our Scripture lesson in my mind. "And the Lord hardened Pharaoh's heart and he did not let the children of Israel go."

It is an old story. You have heard it whipped up so many times and in so many different ways it has become almost meaningless. "Niggers" catch hell and black preachers preach about the children of Israel and the Red Sea. Well, I am telling you it is the same situation. That's why we talk about it. Egypt had suffered every evil there was. The locust finally came and ate up everything. Every time there was a plague Pharaoh would say, "I am going to let these people go. I can't stand this much longer. I can't stand all the suffering and misery that is coming to us because of these Israelites." And the Egyptian people would come to Pharaoh and say, "Why don't you let these people go? We can't go on year after year like this. They are destroying us."

They were not talking about letting the children of Israel go because they loved them. They said, "We can't stand it much longer. We can't stand these plagues that are coming year after year after year." And each time, right in the middle of the thing, when Pharaoh could look around at the damage and talk to his treasurer and learn how much it had cost, he would say, "I am going to turn them loose because it costs too much to keep them in bondage. It is too expensive for me." Then, after a few days, he would sit around and say, "You know, I believe we can take care of those Israelites. We will just be harder on them. Take away the straw. Make them make bricks without straw. That will teach them." And the Bible says, "God hardened Pharaoh's heart."

Let me tell you, anybody who has power and is faced with the necessity of giving up any part of that power has his heart hardened time after time after time. God doesn't have to do it. This was a black Jewish historian writing and he wanted it to sound a certain way. He said, "God hardened his heart." God was going to use Pharaoh to show the world that you can't hold his chosen black people in bondage. Maybe that's true. Maybe God is going to use these white folks to show that you can't keep black people in bondage even in this 20th Century.

Year after year after year these white folks harden their hearts. In Watts they looked around and said, "We can't let this happen again. This is terrible. Black people are looking different and talking different. We got to do something. These black people are dangerous." That is what they said in Watts. And they trickled in a little poverty money and took a few little black organizations and gave them a pittance, and said, "Now, I guess we have taken care of that."

Then more cities exploded here and there and everywhere, and they said again, "This is terrible. Chicago, New York, this is terrible. We have got to do something. We have got to make some new plan."

Then when fall came and it cooled off, they said, "I don't think we have to do too much. A little anti-poverty money, a few little concessions. Let's find out who the leaders are and give them a job." Then, during the summer, here it came again. Everywhere. A hundred cities broke out almost simultaneously. They could hardly keep up with one. Do you know that if we had done it all on one day there wouldn't have been enough troops, federal or state, to take care of it? That is a worrisome thing that stays on the white man's mind. When it comes down to force, how much force does the man have? He has atom bombs, but it is hard to use them in this kind of situation. He has napalm, and oh, how he would like to use it. But how much does he have that he can use without exposing himself for the beast that he is to the whole world?

So he says, "Suppose there is a Riot Center. Suppose Niggers are organized. Suppose they do know what they are doing. Suppose next summer they pull it all at one time. Then what are we going to do?" You know this is a horrible thing, this hardening of the man's heart. He thinks about it, he worries about it. Then he says, "No, it can't be." He puts it in the paper about the big conspiracy. Then he goes back and thinks, "No, it can't be conspiracy. I have known Niggers all my life. They never organized nothing." That is what he says. "Just a few hotheads and criminals got mad and wanted to steal something, that's all it was. I am not going to let that kind of thing drive me out of my mind. I'll just get a bigger police force with bigger guns, that's all."

But he is not sure. The Justice Department didn't spend all week sitting around here talking to me because they were sure there was nothing to it. They were trying to find out whether or not I was Riot Central. And I told them straight out, "I am not Riot Central. You have got to look elsewhere." But they keep coming back, talking and taking notes. They are doing that all over the country because they can't face the simple fact that all of us black people are tired of the way white folks have been treating us. That's all there is to it. We are tired of it everywhere and we are not going to stand it any longer.

They can harden their hearts again just like Pharaoh. You know what happened after the locust. Next time they killed all the first-born, and Pharaoh and his army got killed. They can harden their hearts if they want to, and they can put signs all up and down 12th Street, saying, WE HAVE COME BACK. "You are all good friendly colored people." And it will all be burned down again.

I know that the Justice Department has agents here this morning. Understand me now. I am not telling you all to burn it down again. Understand that. And you little children who go home and tell your mammas, "I get scared sometimes when Rev. Cleage talks," understand me, little children. I am not telling you to go out and burn down anything. I am only saying that unless changes are made, there are people who will burn it down again. I am just saying that the conditions are such that if they don't do something soon and do it big, it is going to be burned down again and the next time more of it is going down. That is what I am saying. That is the truth. It could be before it gets cold this summer because this thing isn't over at all. It could be next summer or it could be three years away. But each time they put it back like it was, it is going down again.

Do you notice how black people, even without real organization, are learning? Every year it is more thoughtful. Every year people are learning. And we are not going to stand for the things that are going on. There are some very easy things that could be done. They seem so obvious that you wonder why the white man doesn't say, "I am going to do these things that ought to be done." You wonder why he goes on pretending that he doesn't understand anything that we are talking about.

The whole rebellion is so simple. Black people want to control black communities. Anybody can understand that. You can look at the buildings that were burned and know that black people were trying to get rid of somebody. Black people want to control black communities. That ought not be hard for white people to understand. They control their white communities. Nobody thinks it weird that the city of Dearborn wants to "Keep Dearborn Clean," that is, keep us out. No one is much disturbed by the city of Grosse Pointe's "point system," to keep us out. Why is it so strange, then, when we say that we want to control our communities?

We are going to organize our consumer power. Some of the big stores and producers we may not get to right away, but they are either going to put all black people in those stores or they have got to go. We have the power. And "downtown" is now a part of the black ghetto. They, too, have got to hire black managers, personnel managers, everything from top to bottom. For them to be sitting there and saying, "You don't have anybody ready," is a whole lot of foolishness. We have people who are as ready as they are. We are going to control the economics of our community.

We are also going to take political power. This city cannot continue to exist with a Mayor downtown who thinks that he doesn't have to talk to us. Not once during this whole situation has the Mayor contacted anybody who is really representative of the black people in this community. He is still talking to the same old functionary Uncle Toms. So we have got to change the whole political structure. We have got to have a ward system where we can elect a council that is responsive to us. And that council can control the budget, which means it can control the police department, which means it can control everything in the city.

You say we might not have a majority on it. I don't care. The white man will make a deal anytime and anyplace. His whole life is dealing and trading. If we have seven men on the council and they have eight, they will still have to deal. If we get some sensible black people on there who will deal for us, we can get what we want. And we don't care what white folks get out there in their community, just so long as they don't get more out there than we get in here.

Our school system must come under community control. We have to have district election of the School Board. We have to have men and women on it who represent us and who do not represent the newspapers, the TV stations, City Hall and the UAW Solidarity House. We want black teachers, black principals, and black administrators throughout inner city schools because we have got to set up a different kind of educational system. We have got to set up an educational system which is teaching our black children black history and black culture and which gives them a sense of pride in being black.

We can no longer leave our black children in the hands of a white enemy to educate. I don't care how nice he talks, how nice he sounds. He is not educating black people. You don't have to take my word for it. Just check the city-wide achievement tests. Your children, I don't care where they go to school, are two, three or four grades below white children in the same grade. If your child brings home an "A" in the 8th grade, he probably is doing 4th grade work. We can't stand for that. We have got to take over control of the educational system in our community. Those are things we must do. And we must do them right away. That is the meaning of the revolt. That is why people were willing to die. I am not saying there were not some people out there trying to get a TV. I know that. And some of them who wanted a TV also wanted freedom, also believe in freedom, also want to control the black community. But the man won't listen, won't talk about it, won't accept it.

I talked to a reporter from New York last week. Like most white writers who interview you, he had his own theory all worked out. They just want you to say "That's right." So he was telling me his theory. He talked for two hours and he hadn't heard anything of my theory yet. He was in New York when the whole thing broke out. He said, "Black people revolted (I had conditioned him to say black people by the end of the interview) because there is a golden door through which you can pass and escape from being a Negro—I mean black person. And the thing that made black people revolt was the fact that some were getting through the golden door before others. So the rest got irritated and frustrated."

I said, "You must be some kind of fool. What kind of golden door are you talking about and who are these black people who have gotten through the door?"

He said, "Jones. You know, Jones—special advisor for the police department."

I said, "Jones? He's through the golden door?"

"Yes," he said, "He has a nice home, a nice car, he doesn't have to fight for freedom."

I said, "His very job is a flunkey job. He has neither dignity nor power. It doesn't matter which side of that mythical door you are on. In this country you are a Nigger wherever you are. There is no door that stops you from being a Nigger in the eyes of the white man, and anybody who thinks that there is some door through which he can escape will find that he is only going from where he is into Uncle Tom Land. That is the only door there is. He can stop identifying with black people and he can go through some door to where the white man is going to accept him as a good old Uncle Tom. There is no other door. There is no other escape."

White people try to pretend that there is some golden door someplace and that all black people have to do is act right and then they will make the door a little bigger so that more of us can get through. We don't even want that golden door because it is destroying us. We are a Nation. We want to build a unity of all black people so that we work together as a unit, so that we stand together, fight together, and die together if need be. That is what we want. There is no golden door that an individual can slip through into the white world, but if there were any such door and we could find it, we would tear it down.

Heavenly Father, we pray, understanding thy power, under-standing the message which has come to us through thy Son, the Black Messiah, Jesus Christ. We understand the task that is ours. We must learn how to stand up and be men. We must learn how to be a Nation and work together. We understand that this, thy Church, is dedicated to this accomplishment and this task. And so we have come together to worship and to go forth from this place, rededicated to the many unfinished tasks that lie ahead. Be with us, God, to strengthen us and support us in all that we undertake to do. Help us to do all those things that are necessary that we may be free. This we ask in his name. Amen.

12/"An Enemy Hath Done This"

"Another parable put he forth unto them, saying, The kingdom of heaven is likened unto a man which sowed good seed in his field;

"But while men slept, his enemy came and sowed tares among the wheat, and went his way.

"But when the blade was sprung up, and brought forth fruit, then appeared the tares also.

"So the servants of the householder came and said unto him, Sir, didst not thou sow good seed in thy field? From whence hath it tares?

"He said unto them, An enemy hath done this. . . ." (*Matthew* 13:24-28).*

All of the parables of Jesus are really parables of the Nation, although they have been consistently misinterpreted and misunderstood because it is impossible for white people to understand them. Jesus was black and he was speaking to a Black Nation. He was always telling black people how to fight white people. So there wasn't any way in the world that a white man could read Jesus and know what he was talking about. If he did, he would know what we are talking about today, and he finds it just as hard to understand one as he does the other.

* King James Version

The parables of Jesus are very interesting, particularly if you remember how you heard and understood them before. The parable of the tares had to do with a farmer planting his crop. Jesus was a Black Messiah trying to bring together a black people. He had all kinds of problems, the same kind of problems we have today. He was trying to get people to understand what is involved when you are trying to build a Nation, when you are trying to bring together a group of people who are oppressed, who have all kinds of ways to try to get along with the man. When you try to deal with them and bring them together and unite them, it is a problem.

So Jesus tried to explain it all kinds of ways. He was primarily dealing with life here on earth. If he talked about a kingdom of heaven, he was talking about a kingdom here on earth that is compatible with what God wants this earth to be. We get all tied up with the kingdom of heaven, like we are going to fly off some place. But Jesus was dealing with the problems of building a Nation here on earth. He was concerned with the problems of a black people who were oppressed by a white people.

This is the parable of the tares: "Another parable put he forth unto them, saying, 'The kingdom of heaven is likened unto a man which sowed good seed in his field.' " That is true of any farmer. He sows the best seed he has in his field.

"But while men slept, his enemy came, and sowed tares among the wheat and went his way." Tares are a certain kind of weed that looks like wheat. You can't tell it from wheat except that it is poison. It will kill you. So an enemy came and sowed tares among the wheat.

"But when the plant was sprung up and brought forth fruit, then appeared the tares also. So the servants of the householder came and said unto him, 'Sir, didst not thou sow good seed in thy field? From whence then hath it tares?' "

"He said unto them, 'An enemy hath done this.' "

"The servants said unto him, 'Wilt thou then that we go and gather them up?' "

"But he said, 'Nay; lest while ye gather up the tares, ye root up also the wheat with them. Let both grow together until the harvest; and in the time of harvest I will say to the reapers, "Gather ye together first the tares, and bind them in bundles to burn them [maybe this is where "burn, baby, burn" started] but gather the wheat into my barn." ' "

It is a very interesting parable if we understand it correctly.

"An enemy hath done this." That is Matthew 13:28. The householder has planted good seed in his field, and an enemy came in the night and planted the tares. And when the servants see the tares, they come to him and the first thing they ask is, "Didn't you plant good seed in your field?"

This approach is very interesting. What they are saying is, "You must have done something wrong. You must in some way be responsible for this field."

In other words, explain this mess that is out in the field. That field is just a mess. Didn't you plant good seed? You must have done something wrong. This is a natural human feeling. When something goes wrong, your first inclination is to say, "I must have done something wrong." If things mess up in your house, you think either you or your wife did it. That is natural. I don't care how carefully you have planned. The moment things go wrong, you begin to wonder, "What did I do wrong? Where did I make my mistake? How did this mess come into being?" This is so typical. How did you plant good seed and get this kind of crop? And the answer of the householder is equally simple.

"He said unto them, 'An enemy hath done this.' "

Most people don't have any conception of an enemy. You hear old wives' tales about witches and things like that with which people try to explain things. But this is a simple statement that it was an enemy who came in here and did this. An enemy is responsible for this. I am not responsible and you are not responsible. The householder's explanation of what happened was a realistic one. We live in a world where we have enemies. Enemies can do things that disrupt our plans, that tear up the things we are trying to do, that destroy the Nation.

This was a necessary message for the Nation of Israel. Jesus wasn't just telling parables because he didn't have anything to do that afternoon. He was talking to a people about the problem of their own thinking. As he looked around at the Nation Israel, he saw a mess. Someone had done something to the Nation Israel, because it wasn't a nation any longer. People were fighting each other; they were against each other; they mistrusted one another. Some were using others. They were exploiting each other. All of them were caught up in this vast web of oppression and in the midst of oppression each individual tries to look out for himself. In looking out for himself, he walks on anybody he can. He will lie about his neighbor, about his brother, he will cheat his brother, he will do anything in order to win a place for himself, in order to have the enemy recognize him and accept him.

This was true in Israel. This was the problem that Jesus was speaking to when people came around him. He was trying to get them to look at this thing that was happening to them. Why do you think you are in this kind of condition? Why do you think you are betraying each other every day? Why do you slip off to the Romans and try to take advantage of the fact of our slavery here? And he used the very simple little explanation of a farmer who planted good seed and then when he looked around, found his field filled with tares. And he said, "Don't blame yourself for this. An enemy hath done this to us."

This was necessary for Israel to understand. It is necessary for any people who are oppressed to understand that they do have an enemy. It is very easy for a child who grows up in bondage to feel that there is some logical reason for his condition and to feel that the logical reason is his own innate inferiority. Your children feel this unless you do something consciously to make them understand that an enemy hath done this thing. They see your condition and how you are treated. You say, "I am doing pretty good." Maybe you are doing pretty good according to your standards, but there are so many people doing better and I don't care how well you are doing, your children have a wider horizon. If you are doing pretty good, they wonder why you are not doing better. How does it happen that Henry Ford is doing so much better? How does it happen that white people live out in those suburban homes that are so much newer and fancier than our homes here? Your children tend to think there must be a reason for this. They look at you. You are their reason. Somehow you didn't have it. Then they feel they must not have it. They look up and down the street, at their friends, at their relatives, and feel there must be something wrong with all of us. We just don't have anything. People couldn't treat us like this if we were equal.

I can remember a few years ago when black folks were forced to ride in Jim Crow cars, I went down South. It was a horrible thing to sit in a Jim Crow car and wonder why all of us should be jammed into this little car just because we were black. It was the first time I had been down South and I was very ignorant. I couldn't even find the car to begin with. When you climbed into that car you had to have some kind of sinking feeling that there must be something wrong with you. You knew the man was right because it was his thing. It was his station. He was letting you ride. He had to be right. So you couldn't help thinking that the man wouldn't be putting me way back in his old beat-up piece of car unless there was something wrong with me.

Even then, on a Jim Crow car, there was a better feeling than in the plush cars in which the white folks rode. Sometimes we overlook those little things, but honestly, the first time I rode on a Jim Crow car I said, "This is the nicest train I have ever been on." I was going down to Fisk, my first year in college. It was the nicest car I had ever been on because the people had something together. We ought to have been tearing up the train because we had no business back there. But instead, we were laughing and talking and sharing our lunch, you know, the shoe box with fried chicken and soul food. You know how white folks act on a train, everybody taking care of his own business and looking all evil at everybody else. Well, these folks were saying, "Won't you have some?" and walking up and down the aisle making sure that everybody did have some. With no white folks around, everyone was relaxed and friendly. I thought to myself, this is another kind of train. It is a Jim Crow thing the white man has put us in but even here we have something that he doesn't know anything about.

That didn't justify it because we had no business in there, sweet as it was. There was something wrong with it, and deep down inside all of us we knew it. One of the things that made us friendly was the fact that we were sharing the same kind of oppression. We all hated the same man. I know you would like me to say it another way, like we were unfriendly to the same man, or something. But we were together because the man had forced us together, and this little Jim Crow car symbolized it. When we got off the car, it didn't matter where the station was, we all headed for wherever it was that black folks lived. The car was just a symbol of the life that we lived. I had never been on a Jim Crow car but I had lived in a Jim Crow community all of my life.

When we look around us and see the way we have been forced to live, we feel something, and if we don't understand what Jesus was trying to tell Israel, that an enemy hath done this, we are in bad shape. And as much as you hate to admit it, I know a lot of you still have that old feeling that the way we are mistreated proves that something is wrong with us. So you don't talk much about race in front of your children. You don't want them to know about their inferiority. You had better start talking about it in front of your children, because if you think that because you don't talk about conditions, they don't know about them, then you are crazy. They know what is happening. They see how you are treated. They know how they are treated. You have got to explain it to them so that they can understand: "An enemy hath done this."

You say, "I don't want to raise my child so that he will know that he is living in a country where so many people are his enemy. I would rather my child just grew up like a normal child." That is what we all wish. But we cannot escape from reality. Our condition doesn't look quite as bad here in Detroit as it does in Harlem. Somehow Harlem seems to symbolize the white man's oppression of black people. We are segregated in Detroit. We have bad conditions and rats too. But when you give a rat plenty of room to run in, he doesn't look quite so bad as when you pen him up. Walking around Harlem at night, I feel just like I did in that Jim Crow car. I wonder why we let the man do this to us. I know that he is charging all kinds of rent for these old beat-up buildings.

Go into one, and it's like going into Fort Knox, just getting into the front door. A black man took me to dinner at his home in Harlem. He started turning things, and bolts started turning on the inside.

I asked, "What you got all that for?"

He said, "We got to do it. Everything's got to be bolted."

Then you begin to think we sure must be a thieving people. A man can't even leave his house. But we've got to remember, "An enemy hath done this." You go out in New York and try to get a decent job and you understand why you've got to bolt everything if you are black. You walk around for three weeks looking for a job and spending carfare to get there and you finally say I ain't going to live like this. You start kicking down people's front doors. You've got to remember, "An enemy hath done this."

The thing that always bothers us is the sinking feeling that maybe this means that there is something wrong with us. You fight that in yourself most of the time. You fight it when your child goes out to get a job, after the white folks have educated him. When he comes home without the job, you think that rascal hasn't been studying. You blame him. You say, "I knew you weren't doing your work all the time. Now you done flunked that little test." Don't fuss at him, the enemy hath done this. But you've been going along day after day, year after year, thinking that you didn't have any enemy. But the enemy was there all the time destroying your child. So when your child comes home ignorant and can't pass a simple little test, don't blame him. "An enemy hath done this."

You worked with the enemy because you didn't help very much. You didn't explain to your child that an enemy hath done this. The white man has created every black man's problem. Why do you think we live all jammed up in Harlem and other black ghettos across America? Because we have no other place to live. An enemy hath done this, a system. You don't have to walk around and wonder about it. Like the servants asked the farmer, "Didn't you plant good seed?" Yes, we planted good seed, but an enemy hath done this. When we talk about building a Nation, we are trying to build a unity that will enable us to change this situation. An enemy hath done this. Everything was wrong in Israel and Jesus knew it. That is why he was trying to get the people to understand that they had an enemy, and that they had to do something about it. And the same is true of everything that is wrong with us today in America.

So the parables of Jesus apply just as if Jesus were standing right here talking to us. Two thousand years haven't made a bit of difference in oppression. We are oppressed exactly the same way today, and the enemy hath done this. We must understand that and do something about it. We have got to understand how to fight the enemy, but you can't fight him unless you know he is there. That is the first step, just being willing to say in your own heart, I've got an enemy. Get up in the morning and say, "I've got an enemy." Keep reminding yourself because you will forget it, and the man who helps you forget it is your worst enemy. That is the white man who pretends to be your friend.

He is your worst enemy because he confuses you. He will come up and discuss the problem with you. You know, at work he will come up and say, "What do you think of all this? You know I am on your side, really." He isn't on your side. There is no way in the world he can be on your side. But you go home and you say, "That is a good white man. What he said made a lot of sense. If we would all just straighten up and make our own people act right, things would work out." He was lying and you know he was lying, but you go home all confused. An enemy hath done this, and you have got to remember that all day long.

When the man comes up and talks all his sweet talk (they have been doing a lot of sweet talking since the rebellion), just tell him

like it is. "We are tired of it. We are not going to have it any more."
He will step back then. He doesn't know how to talk then. And before you take it back, add to it. You have got to do it because he is
your enemy and you want him to understand that you understand
it. We have a lot of enemies who don't understand it themselves.

There was a poll taken which showed that 65% of the white
people consciously think black people are treated just like white
people in the United States. It is a lie because they know they themselves don't treat black people just like they treat white people.
They themselves don't, but the mind is a weird thing. Just like
we've got a whole lot of mixed-up ideas in our minds, a whole lot of
white people have that same kind of mixed-up thing in their minds.
They will get a questionnaire and mark it YES, everybody in the
United States is treated the same, and they think they mean it.
But you try to live next door to them, you let your son go to call on
their daughter, or you let your little child, I don't care how little he
is, go to their school, and you will see whether or not black people
are treated just like white people.

They are confused and we help confuse them because we seem to
go along with the whole thing. When the man starts giving you that
soft-soap at work, you have to tell him how it is. It is good for you
because it helps protect your own mind. You must keep consciously before you the simple fact that you have an enemy. You
can't let him soft-soap you into thinking that you don't have one.
An enemy hath done this.

All these things about black people that we are ashamed of, all
these deplorable conditions that they write about in their Moynihan
and other reports, an enemy hath done this. And you have to remember it. Of course, we are ignorant, we are uncouth—an enemy
hath done this. It is almost impossible for a black person to get a
decent education in these United States. If he gets one, he is going
to get the man's kind of education. First they are going to try to
weed you out altogether by not giving you anything in school.
From the first to the twelfth grade, no black child is going to get an

education unless his parents educate him. After the twelfth grade they say, "He made it this far, so he must have a whole lot of stamina."

Then they try to brainwash him. From the twelfth grade through graduate school, I don't care how far you go, you are in the process of being brainwashed. When you step out with a doctor's degree, they have guaranteed that there is nothing real left in you. This is the process and it works. We don't have to go out and apologize for being ignorant because in our ignorance we will figure out something to help ourselves. But it is better for us to be ignorant figuring it out than to be going to him asking him what should we do. If we remember that an enemy hath done this, then we realize that in dealing with the enemy we can't ask him for advice and counsel.

I am not saying don't use him if you can. But when you use him, be careful, because he is a pastmaster at using you. He has been using us longer than we have even dared think that it was possible to start using him. An enemy hath done this. We are poor, we are unskilled, we don't have any training. We can use that as an excuse to hate ourselves, or we can remember that the enemy hath done this. He owns everything, the factories, the banks, the stores, but that is no sign of virtue or brains. We are poor because we came over here disadvantaged. He brought us over on slave ships. He held us in bondage. He released us only to do the hard work. He refused to educate us. He built a system of oppression to keep us outside of everything that was going on. Yes, we are poor, but the enemy hath done this.

As long as the enemy can masquerade as a friend, he is going to keep on doing it. The only way we can stop him from doing it is to know he is the enemy and start doing things for ourselves. So don't be upset because we are poor. There is a certain value in being poor because you have so little to lose. As we go along I think we are going to discard a lot more of this foolishness that ties us down. If we don't own too much, we are free to move anywhere and to do the things that have to be done. There is a certain strength in our poverty. He kept us poor, he kept us down, he kept us outside, and now the very thing that he has done to us is our strength, and we will use it to take power.

It is easy to understand the white man's confusion, but his confusion doesn't really concern me. In fact I would just as soon he stayed confused for a long time. He doesn't understand what is going on. But our confusion is something else. We have got to straighten out our own minds and our own thinking. We are trying to build for ourselves and our children a decent place to live here on this earth. We are trying to build a Nation. We recognize the fact that we are together, that we must be united. We recognize the fact that our problems are one. We recognize the fact that no individual black man can solve his problem by himself. We have got to solve our problems together, for all of us.

It is our confusion that we must take care of. The man is almost helpless in dealing with us now. He can't do much more to keep us enslaved. We are beyond the place where he can say, "You all do this," and we do it. That is not the problem. The problem is to figure out together what it is that we ought to be doing. It was safe and comfortable as long as the man told us what to do and we did it. He headed our organizations, he sent workers into our communities. He had it all worked out so that he could tell us exactly what we were supposed to do. As long as we thought he was our friend and we just did what he said, we got along pretty well. If we got out of line, he punished us. If a black politician in Detroit got out of line, the man saw to it that he got stomped. The man thought of everything.

But now we have decided that he isn't going to tell us what to do. This is a whole new thing. We are going to do it our own way, ignorant, poor, stupid as we may be. But now we face a new problem. We sit down and look at each other. I look over at you and I say, "I can't trust that fellow. I don't know if he is really with us." Then I look over there and say, "I don't know about him, either." Then you both look at me and you say, "I don't know about him, either." So there we are. When we decide that the man is not going to tell us what to do, then we have to come together and this is a bigger job than just deciding that we have an enemy.

We went through certain stages getting here. It didn't just happen overnight. Everybody tries to act like this was an instant rebellion. It wasn't. It took time. A whole lot of people worked for years on this. It is a long way from Dr. King in Montgomery to Twelfth Street. We all traveled that road together and a lot of things happened along the way. We suffered with black people we had never seen before except on TV. We saw the police dogs, the cattle prods, the fire hoses and we came to understand that we do have an enemy. We stopped thinking that something was wrong with us, and that the white man was good, honest, and kind, and that if we ever started doing right, he would reach out and accept us. We got over that because we saw him on TV here, there and everywhere, and everywhere we saw him he was acting like a beast. Don't be afraid to say it. You know it. You saw him all over the South.

Then we said, "There are two kinds of white men. There is the bad southern white man and there is the good northern white man." And black people had to march into Cicero before we could say, "There isn't but one kind of white man, just one kind." From Montgomery to Twelfth Street was a long journey and we made it together. Some traveled it at one pace and some at another, but we all traveled that road, and on Twelfth Street all black people came together. The white man can talk whatever he wants to talk about the black middle-class not being a part of the rebellion. But there wasn't a middle-class black man who wasn't proud and happy when all those white people he had been crawling for and knuckling down to all these years were getting it at last.

Don't think that you have to go into some barbershop on Twelfth Street to find the hatred that we have, as black people, for the white man. The greatest hatred for the white man can be found among bourgeois Negroes when they get off by themselves, when they shut the door and get a cocktail in their hands. White folks would be amazed. I don't care who you are; if you are black, you know everyday that the man hates you and that he is discrim-

inating against you. You hate the fact that you have to crawl on
your belly to get the little bit that you are getting. You hate the
man who makes you crawl, and you would cut his throat in a
minute. White folks who keep watching *me* had better start watching some of those "good Negroes" they think are their friends!

An enemy hath done this. We are trying to get together now.
That will be the basic emphasis for the whole next period. We are
going to make all kinds of mistakes. We didn't understand the
whole thing in Montgomery. We didn't understand too much in
Birmingham. But there was a whole lot of courage. You remember
Dr. King standing up and saying, "If blood must flow, let it be our
blood." We don't fully understand about getting together now, but
this is the next step, and we have got to understand it first here, in
this place, because we are the Black Nation that is coming into
being. We must lead the way in this movement towards black
unity.

Organization is a part of it but it is more than formal organization. It is the ability to sit down and work with other black people
and trust them, trust them as long as they can be trusted and when
they mess up . . . ("Mess *them* up!"—from the audience). I
want to state, for the F.B.I. tape, that that was not *my* voice. But
we have to try to work together. We have to try to understand. We
have to build on these basic principles. We have an enemy. We have
to help our children rise above feelings of inferiority. We have to
find the avenues by which we can work together.

We must develop a discipline and a unity that the white man
can't break. This will be much different from just getting up and
making speeches about unity. It must mean that when you do
something, I am with you. When you do something, we are all with
you. When I do something, you are with me. We must be working
together so that the man cannot come between us. That is a wholly
new approach, a wholly new philosophy, a wholly new UJAMMA.
We have to be together.

It is not easy. We have reached a place now where some of us think that the job is all done. "We have power and the man has to back up." The man isn't backing up any place. Any place we go from here we must go ourselves because we are together, speaking with a united voice and moving with a united program. This is the hardest thing yet. We have come now to the difficult part of the struggle. We have now come to the point where we must each somehow give up a little bit and not try to be a prima donna or a star. We must come together and work together because we are trying to build a Black Nation.

We are trying to build it here at the Shrine of the Black Madonna and we hope that eventually black people will be building it everywhere. The kind of feeling that we have here as we work together, sacrifice together, share together, has to be a new mood for black people. The white man is now building up the idea that there are two Detroits, the east side of Detroit and the west side of Detroit. He wants us to believe it. It is a lie. There is just one group of black people in this town. I don't care where they live. We must be together. He will send a man out to southwest Detroit and he will say, "You all are separate. They don't pay any attention to you out here. You have to build your own little leaders out here and not pay any attention to them." We have to understand this kind of thing and fight against it.

There is no other message for us today but this trial and error, working together. And don't try to hang a man the first time he makes a mistake, so long as he is working for the Black Nation. I would rather have a black man make forty mistakes in the next year if he was doing it out of love and unity, and the fact that he is black, than have a white man doing everything right for me. Let's remember as we go into this new phase of our struggle that even our disunity and our inability to trust each other and work together is the work of an enemy. We are going to overcome it the hard way, each individual trying to get together, trying to remember that every black person is his brother, trying to make that a reality in the everyday things that he does and says. Let the other black man know that you trust him and see if he will trust you. This we have to do. This is all from the Bible. In his parable of the tares Jesus said, "An enemy hath done this."

Heavenly Father, we thank thee for the opportunity of coming into thy house. We thank thee for our new understanding of the teachings of thy Son, Jesus Christ. We thank thee for the knowledge that we are sustained and supported by thy strength and thy power. Be with us in everything we do in our efforts to unite and come together, in our efforts to fight against the enemy who would destroy us. Be with us in the difficult task of uniting and building a black brotherhood which has meaning in terms of today's world. We pray to thee with a sense of confidence in the future. The things which must be done, we will do. Sustain and support us as we go about our task. Amen.

13/Great Gettin' Up Morning

"And when you hear of wars and rumors of wars, do not be alarmed; this must take place, but the end is not yet. For nation will rise against nation, and kingdom against kingdom; there will be earthquakes in various places, there will be famines; this is but the beginning of the sufferings" (*Mark* 13:7-8).

I ask you to look at all of our black leaders who have suffered and died and remember one simple fact. It is hard to lead a people who are waiting for God to intervene and do everything for them. It is hard to lead a people whose basic orientation to struggle is not in terms of what they can do or must do but rather in terms of God's intervention to do for them that which must be done. When we think of "a city called Heaven," do we think of a place which we must fight to possess, to hold, and to build, or do we think of something which God is to usher in for us? If most of us think of the solution to our problems in terms of something God is going to do for us, then what can a leader do? Normally, leadership has to do with providing a sense of direction and with manipulating power. But what leadership can a black leader offer black people if they are oriented in terms of God ushering in a new world?

It is hard to lead a people who are waiting for an apocalypse. That's just a word that they use in the Bible to refer to the end, the latter days when God will break into human history. Do you remember the scene in the Book of Daniel, in the Old Testament, where the king and his corrupt court are enjoying a big banquet and suddenly there is a flash of light, and a hand points and writes on the wall: "MENE, MENE, TEKEL, and PARSIN . . . You have been weighed in the balances and found wanting . . . your kingdom is divided and given to the Medes and Persians" (Dan. 5:25,27,28).

This sense that ultimately God will break in and put things right is one strand of religious faith. In both the Old Testament and the New there are those people who are constantly waiting for those great moments when they feel that God will break into history, when God's handwriting will appear on the wall, separating the just from the unjust, the sheep from the goats. This is the apocalyptic approach. It is the approach of the Book of Revelations, which no one really understands, but which essentially says that there will be a time when God will break into history and the beast will be destroyed. It is the kind of thing which the Honorable Elijah Muhammed describes so vividly. God has set the world up in a certain way. For six thousand years the white man is the beast who will hold sway and have power. Then at the end of six thousand years God will reach down into history again, stir things up and place the black man on top. This approach has a natural attraction for many people. If we just keep the faith, things are going to work themselves out, because God is going to do it for us.

People who are constantly waiting for divine intervention find it very difficult to develop and keep leadership because leadership depends upon people who are expecting to do something for themselves. Leadership is created by people who are demanding and ready to struggle for certain things. But what role is there for leadership when a people are waiting for God to break into history? Leadership is reduced to mystical incantations, magic dances, and other rituals designed to induce God to do more quickly that which he has already decided to do.

I call your attention to the 13th Chapter of the Gospel of Mark, where the kind of conditions that exist in the world today are described. "And when you hear of wars and rumors of wars, be not troubled. This must take place. But the end is not yet, for nation will rise against nation and kingdom against kingdom. There will be earthquakes in various places. There will be famine, but this is just the beginning of the sufferings." This is a biblical description of the kind of world in which people live. All Jesus is saying is that you live in a world in which there is hell everywhere, and don't think, just because things are bad, that the end is near. This could just be the beginning. Don't think that just because you're in such bad shape, that this means that God is going to come quickly. Don't think that he knows just how much you can bear and that he wouldn't let you get so close to the end of your rope if he wasn't ready to step in and act. Jesus said this could be just the beginning. That's the Bible, the 13th Chapter of Mark. Then he says, "But in those days after the tribulations, the sun will be darkened and the moon will not give its light and the stars will be falling from heaven and the powers in the heavens will be shaken. And then they will see the Son of man coming in clouds with great power and glory."

Now you may not know it, but that is what you have been waiting for. When white folks treat you like a dog, when they discriminate against you, when they persecute you in every way and treat your children as though they were mentally retarded, that is in the back of your head. Not "what can I do," not "what must I do," but "one of these days I'll see 'the Son of man coming in clouds with great power and glory.' " You may not realize it, but that's what you think all the time. You don't feel that you have to take any kind of meaningful action because there's going to come a day when God in his infinite wisdom will rain down hellfire on our enemies and pick us up and put us on high.

Do you know where we got that idea? Way back in slavery days, Old Master gave it to our grandmothers and grandfathers on the plantation. And they handed it down just like you're handing it down today to your children. What kind of leadership can be given to that kind of people? You can't lead a people who are sitting around waiting for Jesus to come back on clouds of glory. All you can do is prepare a landing field for him.

So, generation after generation, we have waited for God to

come back on clouds of glory, on that great gettin' up morning when he'll send out his angels to gather his elect from the four ends of the earth. We know we're going to be among the forty and four thousand elect. He's going to round us up and we can endure anything until that day because when that day comes we're going to have our reward. You are just waiting to be rounded up, aren't you? You won't even have to come out; he'll go in and get you.

But there is a little mistake here, a few verses later. Some of you don't like to admit that there could be a mistake in the Bible. But it says, "Truly I say to you" (this is reportedly Jesus speaking), "that this generation will not pass away before all these things take place." Now we'll have to admit that was a mistake, wasn't it? Because that generation certainly did pass away before these things came to pass.

Then comes another little statement that goes just beyond that. "But of that day or that hour (you know that great gettin' up morning when Jesus comes back) no one knows, not even the angels in heaven, nor the Son, (that's Jesus) but only the Father." So we've been sitting here waiting for almost four hundred years for that great gettin' up morning, even though Jesus told us way back there, that even he didn't know when it was coming. You may think that this isn't true, that we haven't been waiting for it. You think that we've been doing a whole lot of things. But let me tell you, almost everything we have done has essentially been in terms of waiting for God to take care of everything for us. Instead of working and struggling to build a Black Nation here on earth, we have been waiting for God to usher in his kingdom.

Now the Bible, the New Testament and the Old, says that individuals who have been touched by the spirit of God are going to change the world, that we have a job to do. But we don't pay much attention to that part because that means that we have certain responsibilities. It's so much easier just to wait for the Son of man to come back in clouds of glory. But that's not the Bible. You take the Bible and read it. Even the Apostle Paul doesn't tell you to just sit there and wait for something to take place. The Bible just doesn't say that if you sit long enough, God is going to solve all your problems for you. But that's what we've been doing.

It's not just the Christians and the people who come to church that have this attitude. I'm constantly amused at the number of people who think they're emancipated from Christianity, who wouldn't be caught dead in church but who still have this same basic idea in the back of their heads. They have stopped going to church, but they can't get it out of their heads. They are still waiting for the intervention of God even though they think they're radicals. They talk about revolution but they don't mean a revolution where they're going to do anything. You listen to most black radicals talking and you try to deduce just what it is that they're going to do. You won't be able to pinpoint a thing that they're really going to do because they don't have a program of action or struggle in their own minds. They're talking about what *ought* to be. This precisely is the same as waiting for God to usher in what ought to be.

We had a meeting trying to figure out what black people in Detroit could do to protest the racist treatment Congress was giving Adam Clayton Powell. It was a good meeting. All the black militant radical leadership came together and their whole approach was "Those white folks shouldn't have done this. It's bad and therefore if we issue a call, if we just make a gesture, everybody's going to rise up because God will see to it that this condition is rectified." They didn't actually say that God would see to it, but that's all they could have meant because they didn't have any other plan for doing anything about it.

One of the serious proposals was to ask all black people not to go to work for thirty days. This will show them. It sure would, but it was the same as waiting for Jesus to come on clouds of glory! Can you see black people staying home from work for thirty days for Powell or for anything else? We couldn't afford it in the first place. The second week, we'd all be starving because we hardly have enough to last from pay day to pay day. The argument was, "There is no sacrifice too great to hit back at this thing." No sacrifice too great for whom? We're living in a dream world in which we think that anything that is right is bound to triumph and anything that is wrong is bound to fail.

You know you believe that. "Give the world the best that you have and the best will come back to you." "Sin, and God will certainly pay you back." But we don't live in that kind of world. Right may prevail and evil may be punished on the other side, but right now, we're living on this side. And when we run around in circles on this side with our minds on that side, nothing results but utter chaos and confusion. It is very difficult for black militants to see that they're still going through the same old religious thing.

We can see it when we listen to the radio on Sunday night and hear the deliverance preachers. "Come in on Monday at eight o'clock and bring your 'trinity offering.' I've just been down to Mississippi and I brought something special back. I want you to have it. So be here on Monday morning." They have dates all through the week when you're supposed to be there for your deliverance. Obviously people who support these deliverance preachers, those people are not trying to do anything to solve their problems. If you spend your life jumping from one of these deliverance preachers to another, you're not going to solve anything. Your whole life is geared to waiting for God to do it for you.

If you're broke, you just run around hoping that you'll luck up on some deliverance preacher who'll give you the right number. If you're sick, you go to the deliverance preacher or you sit at home and listen to him say, "Put a glass of water on your radio and when I get through praying, drink that water and put your hands on your misery and it will go away." You know, there are black people doing that all over this country from coast to coast. Every Saturday and Sunday night half of us are sitting around with glasses of water on the radio and our hands on our misery, waiting for God to take it away. You can laugh, but that's the way we are. We're waiting for God to do it.

Now do you think we're going to sit there on Saturday and Sunday night with our hands on our misery and a glass of water on our radio and the rest of the week, Monday, Tuesday, Wednesday, Thursday and Friday have sense enough to try to do something about our other problems? If we're foolish on Saturday and Sunday, we're going to be foolish the rest of the week as well. It's one life. If you go to church on Sunday morning and all you want to hear is how wonderful it's going to be up in heaven, you're not going to do anything to build a Black Nation on earth during the rest of the week.

Some of you complain that when you come to this church, I don't give you any sense of peace and comfort. I'm not trying to. I'm trying to involve you in a daily struggle to change the world because you follow Jesus, the Black Messiah. You've had too much peace. Oh, it's easy to see it in other people. You see them with their glass of water and their hands on their misery and you laugh. But you go to a meeting where black radicals are saying we've got to do this or we've got to do that and you know that it doesn't make any kind of sense but you go along with the program. Why? Because it sounds good, that's all. Sounds like it might be, maybe God will do it.

It's not just us though. It's a basic weakness in religion. In the surburban churches where the white folks with their ranch-style houses and everything go, they have the same idea. They don't have a glass of water on the radio, but they go through the same kind of ritual, thanking God for white supremacy. That's why they build those big churches and pay fabulous salaries to ministers to keep them convinced. They raise hell all week, keeping things the way they are, and then they go to church on Sunday morning to be reassured that it's God's will that white supremacy endure. This is the same kind of foolishness, except they just want to know that God is with them in what they're doing here on earth; they don't have to worry about the hereafter. What do you think those Bible Belt preachers are thinking about when they pray for the Klansmen at Klan meetings? They are asking God to do for them what they haven't been able to do for themselves, "to keep Niggers in their place."

But as black people, we have to figure out how we are going about building this City called Heaven. What are the methods to be used? Are we just going to talk about it? Are we going to put glasses of water on radios? Do we just go through incantations and mystical dances, or do we have a method? Is there something we're going to do? You know, there's a whole lot of foolishness hooked up with everything we do. We're constantly trying to find a new messiah, and we discard them if they don't produce. All of our leaders have to be little messiahs. If they don't arrive on at least a little cloud of glory, we don't have any time for them. All we want is a Black Messiah and we go through one generation after another trying to find him.

You go back as far as Booker T. Washington. He wasn't just a leader in the sense that he was leading a people. He was going to do something for us. He was the symbol of God acting for us. Then came DuBois and Marcus Garvey and we were in a dilemma because we had two Black Messiahs who were fighting each other. More black people followed Marcus Garvey than DuBois because Garvey himself believed that he was a Messiah. It's a big help if you can believe in yourself. Millions of black people believed that somehow he was going to pick them up from here and put them down in a great kingdom of Africa. He was a great leader, but essentially he was a Messiah. And then Dr. King and his promise that "we shall overcome." What was he saying? God is going to break in. We shall overcome because God is on our side.

Powell, too, at one time, was the Messiah. You know when Powell was really a leader? It was when he was organizing and leading picket lines for jobs in Harlem when nobody else was doing anything. But he had such a flair. What do the white folks say? He was so flamboyant. That just means he had a style about him. He wasn't like an old ordinary white man going to Congress. He knew how to dress, he knew how to act, he knew how to walk, he knew how to talk. He was a wonderful character. So we made a hero out of him. The whole significance of Powell is not Powell. It is *us*.

We can see most clearly in Powell our shortcomings because we made Powell act the way he acted. We wanted a flamboyant representative. We wanted somebody who could act just like the white folks. We didn't want him to do anything sensible. We wanted him to play around the world, to dress nice, wear good clothes, spend his money, have beautiful women. We wanted him to do that because we identified with him and when he did it, it was almost like we were doing it. Not quite, but almost. And we were so proud. Oh, he showed them white folks! We didn't mean he showed them with legislation or anything. He just showed them by being Adam Clayton Powell and we were with him. If he had beautiful women all over the world, we had them.

It's not Powell. It's us. A people create the kind of leadership they deserve. You can look at the leadership of any people and tell what's wrong with them. When we look at Powell, we can tell what's wrong with us. That's what we wanted, that's what we produced.

That is why it's so difficult to work with an oppressed people. Masses of people who are oppressed want a hero-leader who represents for them a symbolic escape from their oppression until God can make the changes which are required. Basically, oppressed masses are sick. The theoretical adulation of the masses began with the Communist fantasy, that everything that is wrong in the world could be straightened out very easily if we were just willing to take our lead from the masses. It was a lie the first time they said it and it continues to be a lie when black militants drop out of college to find the "truth" in ghetto streets. Masses of people who have been oppressed, discriminated against, who have lacked opportunity, who have in every way been shut out of the mainstream of life are sick because of their oppression.

This gives us an entirely different approach to life. If we approach the masses of people not as heroic individuals being held down by the strong hand of violence and oppression, but as sick people who have inside themselves the disease of powerlessness and around their minds the chains and the shackles of slavery, then we will not let our actions on a leadership level be determined by the thinking of masses of people who have been destroyed by the white man's vicious system. We must engage in a course of action designed to change conditions, to change the masses, and to change the system.

Here at the Shrine of the Black Madonna we are engaged in group leadership for black people and our program of action does not depend for its validity or its success upon what the masses of black people are ready for at any particular moment. I am not speaking disparagingly of the masses of people, but there is a sickness which comes from oppression. Over a long period of time, you are driven down, you are beaten, your humanity is taken from you, you are given no sense of dignity, no opportunity, no hope for the future, and so you live then in terms of dreams and fantasies, doing what the white master wants you to do, thinking what the white master wants you to think.

It takes a long, long journey for people to find escape from this kind of basic elemental sickness. We find this sickness in the Northern ghetto slums and we find it in the rural ghetto slums of the South. Black masses who have suffered systematic discrimination and oppression, whether their discrimination has been at the hands of a rednecked Southern sheriff or at the hands of a sophisticated Walter Reuther and the white establishment in Detroit, end up sick. It is a long journey from this kind of sickness to a realistic struggle for freedom and equality. Do not expect that the masses of people, sick as they are, are going to move quickly and easily to participation in any realistic struggle for freedom and equality. They will wait upon the Lord, and lean upon an earthly hero-leader-messiah if one is at hand.

Sometimes we wonder why many of those who do struggle for freedom and are part of the organizations that are engaged in the struggle for freedom evidence the same obvious signs of sickness. There is no speedy cure for the effects of oppression and powerlessness. Those of you who participated in the Michigan Freedom Now Party in 1964 will remember how out of a city of seven hundred thousand black people, a handful came together to organize a Black Political Party, and yet in that little vanguard group from this great mass of people, there were still all kinds of sickness which hampered our efforts to achieve meaningful independent black political action. You may think that we just happened to run into this kind of internal conflict because there is something peculiar about Detroit. That is not true. You go to any black meeting, East or West, where little groups have come together dedicated to freedom for black people. Listen to them talk and you will find in the first half-hour that 90% of those present are using the freedom struggle as a therapy by which they hope to cure the inner sickness with which white oppression has infected them.

That is why, when you get right down to it, there is no real black leadership in this country, no individual, no black man in this country who has any power. Powell came out and stood on the steps of the Congressional Building, looked out at the thousands of black people who had come to Washington to support him. That wasn't power, that was love. We all said, "they put him off the committee, they put him out of Congress because he had too much power." Powell didn't have power except an individual kind of power to mess around in Congress. He was chairman of a committee. He could hold up legislation. He could mess around with things. But he couldn't do anything, he couldn't pass a bill, he didn't have any influence on other congressmen. Harrassment power was all he had. But we didn't care. We didn't insist that he have power because the only power that he could have had would have been us.

Powell never organized Harlem. That would have been power. Black people would go out and vote for him because he was a Black Messiah. Black people never controlled elections in New York City or New York State. He never organized them. He never made a serious effort to organize the Negroes all over America. Black people are no closer to power today than they were when Powell first came on the stage 23 years ago. We are still sitting around with a glass of water on the radio.

The significance of Powell ought to be the very simple lesson that individual hero-leaders cannot emancipate us, and God is taking an awful long time, so perhaps we ought to do it ourselves. We must organize and struggle to take power. Only through struggle can we escape from the disease of powerlessness. Powell was never responsible to us except in the image sense. We liked the way he looked, the way he walked, the way he dressed, but he was never responsible to us. He was the Messiah. Let the people of Harlem fall down and worship. Let the black people of America say, "Amen."

But now we've come to another stage. Powell is the last of an era. A. Philip Randolph said he's calling a summit conference of civil rights leaders to do something about Powell. What can they do? They don't have any more power than he had. They can meet, they can issue a statement. They can beg. They can go ask Walter Reuther to do it for them. Congress says that they didn't get any communication from civil rights leaders before Powell was removed. Why not? Because civil rights leaders are just like the rest of us. They have a glass of water sitting on the radio, waiting for God to deliver us. They had sold themselves on the myth of Adam Clayton Powell's power. They said those white folks won't dare touch him—"Powell is one of the most powerful men in America." But do you know, you never see the names of the most powerful men in America in the newspapers. They buy political parties; they buy candidates and control presidents. They make Congress jump through hoops. They have power and nobody dares touch them.

But they can touch any of us. Anybody. No black man is safe in this country as long as we are powerless. That includes Powell, Roy Wilkins, Whitney Young, A. Philip Randolph, and all the rest of them. Because they are the leadership which we have created in our powerlessness. We do not have a leader with power. We can cry over Powell. People in Harlem are saying, "It's like somebody in my family died." O.K. then. Let's have a funeral. That's what it amounts to. It is in no way involved with our destiny in terms of power.

If all over America black people suddenly decided to retaliate because white folks have used Powell to strike at all black people, that would be something else. It could be anything realistic and possible, and it would indicate that at long last we were on the way to recovery, because we had decided to do something ourselves. It couldn't be a thirty day strike or anything that drastic. We must use the experience of Powell to understand how powerless we are and to begin to build power. The day of the national black leaders is over. King, as long as he lived, maintained a certain position, but he was not a national black leader because he had no way of giving a program on a national scale to black people. We will find more and more that black people must organize from community to community. We'll have to be content with struggle and conflict in which we are all engaged rather than hero-leaders. This involvement and participation is the medicine for our sickness. Whenever you get tired of trying to build co-ops for economic strength, whenever you grow weary of daily struggle and conflict against white oppression, just remember Powell. Let him be from this day on a symbol of what happens to black people when they are powerless. Anytime the white man gets ready, a powerless black man can be destroyed.

Then let us be about the struggle. Let's take the glass of water off the radio and come to the conclusion God doesn't deliver that way and he never did. We must be about the task of building the Black Nation here on earth. The Black Church must offer leadership in the Black Revolution. Instead of selling "deliverance," the Black Church must become a center for education, organization, and the involvement of black people in meaningful struggle and conflict. The Black Church must become more than a place where black people perform magic dances in an attempt to induce God to perform miracles. That's why the Shrine of the Black Madonna is setting a trend which other churches must follow. It's not a question of choice. They either follow us or they die.

Powell can stand there on the steps of Congress and say that somewhere in the Old Testament it says, "if you strike a man down, he will rise again." Baloney. You strike a man down who doesn't have any power and he's not going to rise again. If he does, you just strike him down again. That whole concept has got to be wiped out of our minds. We must realize that we build from day to day, each one of us, day by day. We don't wait for Jesus to do it for us. We don't wait for God to do it for us. We don't wait for Dr. King to do it for us. We try to do it for ourselves.

We can pray for Powell. I know that it must be a horrible feeling that he has, because he too had come to feel that he was, in a sense, a Messiah and that he had power. They said there were tears in his eyes when he looked at his colleagues, because he couldn't believe that they could do this to him.

Do you remember the old movie, "Little Caesar"? Remember the end, when Edward G. Robinson was behind the signboard and they shot through it and he fell to the ground. He'd been a big time gangster, but he just lay there, looking bewildered and asked, "Mother Mary, is this the end of Little Caesar?" There's much of that feeling in Powell now, I think, as he wonders, "Is this the end of Adam Clayton Powell?"

It's not the end of Adam Clayton Powell, because he is making in this moment his greatest contribution. We see now that he was powerless. And through him we can begin to see that we too are powerless. We must help black people throughout the country to see it because this is the moment to start building Black Power for tomorrow, so that our children will not come to this same moment when they wonder, "Is this the end of me?" This is our task. No little messiah, no glass of water on the radio. Just hard work and the Church at the center of the Black Revolution and all of us building a Black Nation together.

Heavenly Father, we thank thee for the vision which is ours and we ask for dedication and renewed strength that we may continue to do those things which must be done. Help us to avoid the pitfalls of building false messiahs. Help us to realize that each individual is important as he contributes to the welfare of the group, as he becomes a part of the Black Nation, as he is willing to sacrifice to build Black Power. Help us to see clearly as we have never seen before the pitfalls and the dangers of powerlessness. Be with us here and now. Give us a sense of thy presence. Help us to have the strength to do for ourselves the things which must be done. All this we ask in the name of thy Son, the Black Messiah. Amen.

14/Brother Malcolm

"Thou art my beloved Son, in whom I am
well pleased" (*Mark:* 1:11).*

Each year we pay tribute to Brother Malcolm, Malcolm X. It is
wonderful to have this opportunity each year to look objectively at
the struggle in which we are all engaged, and to try to see where we
have been and where we are going, in the light of Brother Malcolm
and what his life means for us. It is strange how the life of a man
takes on new meaning in terms of the changing conceptions of a
people. His life means more and more as the years go by. We can
say, in a sense, that the shooting down of his physical body a few
short years ago brought to pass a kind of miracle. Brother Malcolm, his message, his personality, the things for which he lived and
died have not changed, but we have changed.

I cannot resist the temptation to compare Brother Malcolm to
Jesus, the Jesus whom we worship, the Black Messiah. The conditions which both faced in many ways were so similar. The conditions faced by Jesus in trying to bring into being a Black Nation two
thousand years ago were in many ways similar to those faced by
Brother Malcolm just a few years ago. Both tried to bring black
people toegeher, tried to give them a sense of purpose, and to build
a Black Nation.

Yet in many ways their situations were very different. At the
time Jesus was born, men were expecting a savior. The Nation
Israel realized that it was fragmented, that its people were despised, that they looked down on each other and upon themselves.

* King James Version

186

They realized their oppression, and even though they betrayed each other to the oppressor, even though they did what the white man wanted them to, they knew that they needed someone to save them from this kind of degeneration and make them a Nation.

So they longed for a savior. Every prophet talked of the coming of a savior. The people organized and waited for the coming of a savior. The most depraved individual in Israel still hoped and longed that a savior would come who could bring him back into a Nation of which he could be proud. This was the kind of a world into which Jesus came, a world anticipating the coming of a savior.

Remember how, at the time of his baptism, it was recorded that a dove lighted upon his shoulder, and a voice spoke from heaven saying: "This is my beloved son in whom I am well pleased." This was the reaction of men who were thinking, "Perhaps this is the savior we have been waiting for, the Black Messiah who can make us a Nation again." As he came forward to be baptized, John the Baptist is reported to have hesitated saying, "I don't think I should baptize you," because he, too, had a sense that this might be the Messiah Israel was waiting for. The sense of expectation was everywhere. The disciples had to tell the children to stay away and let the master alone. They were taking up too much of his time. Even the little children were waiting for a Messiah.

Remember the shepherds on the night that Jesus was born? According to the Christmas story, they heard the angelic choir, and said, "The Messiah has come, this must be the night of his birth." Wise men came from the East, seeking the Messiah who was to be born in Israel, the Black Messiah who was to bring back into a Nation the black people of Israel. The people were waiting when Jesus came. They did not receive him only because they wanted a different kind of Messiah.

How different it was for Brother Malcolm! The same fragmentation of black people, divided, exploited, oppressed; the same white Gentiles with their system of oppression; the same degeneration of a people who had lost pride in themselves—who fought against each other, who had no sense of dignity or of their future as a people. The Nation Israel waited for a Messiah that they might again become a Nation. But Brother Malcolm came to a people who waited that they might disappear as a people, a people who prayed every night that God would make them cease to be a people. You know what I am talking about. You didn't want to be a black people. Every night you said your prayers and hoped to God that you would wake up in the morning white. Everything you believed in was white. Everything you tried to imitate was white. Everything you had been taught was white.

No, Brother Malcolm didn't come to a people who were waiting for a Messiah. He came to a people who were tired of being a separate people. Fragmented as they were, disorganized as they were, each man looked upon his brother as his enemy. He hated him because he was black. It reminded him that he, too, was black. He hated his own children because they were born black and wished that there had been some kind of miracle that could have permitted at least his children to be born white.

This is the kind of people that Brother Malcolm came to, a people lost beyond any comprehension that Jesus might have had of how lost a people can be. The people that Jesus preached to wanted to hear the message of the Nation. But the last thing in the world the people Brother Malcolm came to wanted to hear was any word about a Black Nation. They wanted to forget everything black they could forget, as fast as they could. Each individual had a dream of escaping from his blackness. Get enough money, get an education, dress nice enough, talk nice enough, get a white man to like you and you can stop being black. That is what everybody was looking for, "integration." Get out of that old black ghetto and get over there where the white man is, where things are good.

Don't look surprised! Admit you felt like that yourself! When you hoped that your child wouldn't have it as hard as you did, you meant that you hoped he could get over there with the white people. You worked and scraped to send him to college so he wouldn't have to be a Nigger, he could be just like white folks.

That's what you were working for, that's what Brother Malcolm had to deal with!

We can look back now and say, "Oh, it's wonderful to be black! Black is beautiful!" but that is not what Brother Malcolm faced. When Brother Malcolm went anywhere to speak, most black people were ashamed even to go in and listen to him. Some would slip in and try to hide in a corner some place, saying "That's right! That's right!" but not saying it too loud. We were a black people who had been debased as far as a people can be debased, because when you stop loving yourself and your brothers and sisters, you have hit bottom. That's where we were. We hated ourselves, we hated each other, and we were looking for some way to escape from ourselves, some way to get out of this thing we were in and to pretend that we weren't black. All the wigs, and processes, and bleaching creams were to help us fool each other.

I remember Brother Malcolm would be talking and the women would reach up and pat their wigs every once in a while because as he talked, they began to know something was wrong. And the Brother in there with the beautiful processed curls hanging would kind of reach up and touch them. He knew something was wrong because of what Brother Malcolm was saying. Malcolm didn't have to say, "Take off your wig." He didn't have to say, "There is something wrong with your process." He just began to give people a sense of pride in being black, and this was hard to do.

Jesus had it hard; the Uncle Tom preachers were all against him. They betrayed him; they went out and organized the people against him. They were afraid because the exploitation they were carrying on was getting more and more difficult, as Jesus began to awaken people. Brother Malcolm faced all that, too. Remember, we had to go to court in Detroit to permit him to speak at King Solomon Baptist Church. After the contract was signed, they tried to call the whole thing off when they found out Malcolm X was to speak. All over the country, black preachers were warning black people, "Don't follow that man who is so filled with hate and who is preaching separation." Everywhere you went black people were saying, "He's preaching hate. He's talking about separation." For black people to say that a black man was preaching hate because he wanted separation from white people who had done everything possible to destroy black people, was weird.

They said, "He's preaching hate against the white man; he's telling us to hate the white man." They thought there was something wrong with that. It just shows you how far down we were. We were even ashamed to hate a people who had hated, oppressed, and exploited us for almost four hundred years, who had brought us to America in slave ships, sold us on slave blocks, raped our women and lynched our men! Not to hate people like that was a sign of mental illness. But you couldn't say that to black people. "He's preaching hate," black people would say, Brother Malcolm did not preach hate, but when he got through telling it like it was, you did your own hating. He didn't have to do anything but preach the truth.

"He's preaching separation," the white folks said, and black folks started echoing, "Oh, he's preaching separation." And they had been separated all their lives by the white man. You were born separate, you will live separate, you will die separate, and you'll be buried separate. Malcolm didn't have to preach separation. All he had to do was say, "Look around you, fool. You run around talking about integration. Everything you've got is separate." And that's what we did—we began to look around.

Remember, that was just a few years ago. We have come a long way in a few years because all those wrong ideas I'm talking about are not just things that other people used to believe, but things that most of you believed. Some of you still have a lot of it in the back of your head right now, today. You know how the thing goes, "We settle the whole thing by integrating, one by one. You get your family straight; I'll get my family straight, and we will all be taken care of one of these days." We were hemmed in by a separate existence which the white man had given us, which we thought was temporary but which he knew was permanent.

Inside this all-black thing which the white man had given us, we kept talking, each one saying, "I don't believe in anything all-black." We were in a black ghetto together, hating ourselves and hating each other, and looking enviously out at him on the outside, because wherever he was, that was the place we wanted to be. We wanted to look like him, and we wanted to live over there with him. We wanted to get away from these people who looked just like us. We were separate, but we were ashamed of our separateness. We were ashamed of everything that made us what we are, we wanted to be like the enemy who was oppressing us.

As long as we felt like that, we were helpless, we couldn't do a thing. That's the way we were in every community. Everything we had was just a temporary, stop-gap operation. We didn't really want it, we wanted to get out of it. Even if we were running a business, we didn't have any idea of making it a first-class business. We operated it from the very beginning on the premise that "I'm just operating a nigger business here, you can't expect too much from me." We didn't wash the windows. We just sat there trying to get by because we didn't want that kind of business anyway, we wanted to be in some kind of integrated business. We knew that a black business, even if it was ours, had to be no good because it was black and black is automatically no good. Our houses, our streets, our neighborhoods were all temporary—we were just staying there with these inferior people until we could get out, so we didn't work too hard at fixing things up. Our whole community life was geared to this feeling that we were living a kind of temporarily separate life.

We thought that it was temporary because we believed in the American dream. The white man told us that America is a huge melting pot. Everybody comes in and wherever they come out, they are American. We just couldn't seem to find the spot where you come out. But we had faith that there must be some way to escape from this blackness. If we had a child who showed any promise at all, what did we dream about, day and night? We were going to get him out of these black schools, we were going to move to some neighborhood where he could go to school with white children and really learn. That was a dream. Parents would sit down and talk about how they were saving, how they were trying to get out—for their children. We were not concerned with improving the schools in our black ghettos, with improving the situation for all black children. Each one of us by his own little lonely self was going to find a crack in the ghetto wall and get out some way. That was the dream.

That was the kind of thinking, or useless dreaming, that Malcolm had to deal with. That is why it's so important to remember him and the things he said.

Jesus was distorted by the institution that was set up in his name. Jesus didn't organize anything except a few people who believed in him, some revolutionaries who followed him in a nationalistic movement. Jesus didn't organize any kind of Church. He brought together people who believed in doing what was necessary to create change. That's what Jesus did. But after Jesus was killed, they organized a Church in his name. The Apostle Paul, who was really a great organizer, set up Churches everywhere and said, "This is Christianity. All of you who follow after Jesus, come right on in here." And then he changed the whole thing around. No longer was it building a Nation, it was tearing down a Nation. It was leading people right back to the same old individualistic kind of thing which Jesus had fought against all of his life. In the name of Jesus they created a new kind of individualism. "Come into the Church, be washed in the blood of the lamb and you will become white as snow."

We did all that. We came in and were washed in the blood of the lamb. But we stayed black, and the white man kept us in black Churches. That old individual thing had us. You said to yourself, "Well, I'm white on the inside, even if I am black on the outside." And no kind of washing seemed to make any real difference. That is what they did to Jesus and to his teachings about the Black Nation. The teachings of Jesus were destroyed. The Church which carried his name went back to individualism, telling people, "You can find escape from your problems in heaven, after death."

That is why the text which opens the fourth chapter of Ecclesiastes is so important. It says, "Again I saw all of your oppressions that are practiced under the sun. And behold the tears of the oppressed, and they had no one to comfort them. On the side of their oppressors there was power, and there was no one to comfort them." This was true during the lifetime of Jesus; it was also true during the lifetime of Brother Malcolm. Two saviors came to a black people. The people were different in each instance, but both saw the oppression that black people suffered and each saw the power of their oppressors—and they saw that there was no one to comfort those who were oppressed. So today as we remember Malcolm, and as we remember our weaknesses and how far we have come, let us remember the basic things that Brother Malcolm taught that are so important for us. Because we too can forget, we too can distort Malcolm's teachings as the Apostle Paul distorted the teachings of Jesus. We can make something else out of them to suit our purposes if we forget what Brother Malcolm actually taught.

Brother Malcolm taught us that the white man is the black man's enemy. He didn't beat around the bush and try to say it in some acceptable way. He just looked at black people and told them simply that the white man is an enemy. This was basic because you can't engage in a battle until you know that you have an enemy and you know who he is. Brother Malcolm explained the whole thing. It is not accidental that black people everywhere are poor, that black people everywhere are uneducated, that black people everywhere live in slums, that black people everywhere are exploited. It didn't just happen, it's a system. It's set up that way. The white man doesn't leave anything to chance, he organizes your oppression. You are systematically oppressed. You are supposed to be oppressed. You think that it just happened because you are unlucky or that there is something wrong with you or you made a wrong turn some place. You tell yourself, "I should have gone on to school, then I would have had it made." I tell you, if you had gone to school for a thousand years, you would still be oppressed in this white man's country. Don't drop out of school, but don't think that school is going to solve anything. We are oppressed by a total system of oppression which includes all of us.

You can't escape from it until we can all escape from it together. When you are overcharged three or four thousand dollars for a house, that means that the banks, the insurance companies, the mortgage lending agencies, the Real Estate boards, all of them together have arranged for your exploitation. They confine us to an area, open up a new area when they want to, and let us in at the price they want us to pay. It's a system. You go into a ghetto store and you pay ten to twenty-five percent more for everything you buy. You drive five miles out to the white suburbs and you pay less. That's not accidental either. You send your children to school and their achievement is two to four grades below grade level. That's not an accident. In most of Detroit schools there is a teacher shortage, so they are transferring the good teachers out of inner city schools, and putting in unqualified emergency substitutes. Do you think that just happens? Do you think they don't know that they are dealing with a black school when they take the good teachers out and put in inexperienced and untrained teachers? Do you think that when they transfer a principal who has been kicked out of five schools to your black child's school, they do it by accident? They know what they are doing. They are doing it on purpose. You ask, "Why would they want to do that?" Because without a good education your child is economically and socially disadvantaged in the 20th Century. Your child is less of a competitive threat to white children with a better education.

They want your child ignorant because it's easier to oppress an ignorant people. They want to break his spirit so that he'll accept oppression, so they treat him like a dog in school day after day, ridicule him, rob him of his dignity, don't let him see a black person in a position of authority or power, make him feel inferior. It's not by accident. When your child comes home and everything he says is ridiculous, that didn't just happen. They are programming him for inferiority.

The white man is an enemy. I know that you wish we could

say the same thing some other way. But there is no other honest way of saying it! That's why Malcolm said, "The white man is your enemy." That's why Brother Malcolm frightened white people so much. That was the last thing they want the black man to know. As long as you think that he is not your enemy, that he is just as concerned about you as he is about himself, and that he is trying to do right by you, but that you are just a little slow-witted, you cannot possibly change conditions, because you are blaming yourself for a situation over which you have no control. You can hate yourself, but you cannot change a thing. Self-improvement will not change the way a black man is treated by white people. As long as you go along that path, he doesn't have to worry about you. But when you stop and recognize the simple fact that the white man is your enemy, then he faces an entirely new situation.

Now you are saying, "I have got to draw some lines; there are some good white people." Then you can start naming them: this one that died down there, and that one who was run over by a tractor lying down on some construction site in Cleveland, those were good white people. Go on, you can name them all on two hands and have some fingers left over. The "good white people" in this world are so insignificant that we don't even have to worry about them. They're not going to solve our problems. They are individuals without either power or a power base. Where do they operate, these good white people? In our neighborhoods, at our meetings, in our organizations. What can they do out in Bloomfield Hills or Grosse Pointe or Dearborn? What can they do against organized white racists? Nothing. But they mess us up because they make us think that there are a lot of different kinds of white people. For all practical purposes, there is just one kind, and that kind is out to destroy you and your children, and your children's children.

That's why it was a turning point when Malcolm would stand up and say, "You've got an enemy, the white man is your enemy." And you would sit there and squirm and twist, but you would know that it was true if you sat there long enough. And some people couldn't stand it. They would squirm and twist and then they would get up and go out. Sometimes they would get a drink of water and smoke a cigarette and tiptoe back in. It was hard because they had never faced it before. I have heard people who come here to visit say, "I couldn't go to work the next day. Those white people I work with—I didn't know how to face them, I didn't know how to look at them."

Well, just look at them as they are, as you would look at any enemy. Perhaps two people who can face each other honestly as enemies will someday face each other honestly as equals. So Brother Malcolm taught us. He said it out loud, he went everywhere and said it, "The white man is our enemy." It was important. It was so important, that as far as I can gather from all the evidence, white people had to have him killed. I am not worried about the charges we heard against the Honorable Elijah Muhammed. Malcolm wasn't hurting Mr. Muhammed. He wasn't that important to Mr. Muhammed. But he was that important to the enemy.

Malcolm was willing to accept the implications of his statement. You might say that the white man is your enemy, so be careful. But that's not enough: he is our enemy; therefore, we must confront him, we must fight against his oppression. We must protect ourselves against genocide. When you recognize an enemy and you know that he is trying to destroy you, you must do whatever is necessary to guarantee your own survival. That's why Malcolm said that we must forget all this non-violent foolishness in a violent world. The white man has had one basic attribute ever since he climbed down out of the trees, and that is a love of violence, a genius for violence, a commitment to violence, and a willingness to use violence to take anything he wants.

And so, you have an enemy and your enemy believes in violence. Those two things have to be considered together. If you had an enemy who was off praying against you somewhere, you wouldn't have to worry about him. But this enemy believes in violence. You can see what he is doing in Vietnam. He is treating the Vietnamese people just like he has treated us for four hundred years. White people have a peculiar sex thing with their violence. I'm sure Freud could have explained it. In Vietnam the torture method used by American soldiers is a sexual thing. They attach batteries and generators to the genitals of Vietnamese prisoners to torture them. The same sexual torture was used against us during slavery and reconstruction. Don't look so horrified. It was your own people they did it to. They would cut off a man's genitals and make him eat them while he was still alive. "Good white people" may be good for white people, but they cannot be good people for us. They are an enemy, and they believe in violence.

Then Malcolm said that our struggle against these people who are an enemy, who have a system built up to oppress us, and who believe in violence, must be a power struggle. That's why we ourselves were so afraid of him at first, and why white people were so afraid of him. He was developing a concept of struggle. Our struggle is a power struggle. We didn't have to wait for Stokely to scream "Black Power" down on some country road. Malcolm had defined "Black Power" when he said that our whole struggle against the white man as an enemy, is a power struggle. We are not going to solve it if we are powerless. We must get power if we are to participate in a power struggle. You can't get down on your knees and beg the man, "Please give me equality. Please give me freedom." You will never get it. Our basic struggle, then, is to get some kind of power. We must not be ashamed of power. We must mobilize the entire black community to secure political and economic power. Without power we are helpless and psychologically sick.

So Brother Malcolm had a message that hung together. You could listen to him and you wouldn't find a hole in it. You might not like his words, and you might wish that he had said it more gently, but you had to say, "That's right." Gradually people began to understand that not only was it true, but Brother Malcolm's message offered the only basis for salvation for black people. To identify an enemy, to understand him, to realize that he is violent and to recognize the fact that we are engaged in a power struggle —this was Brother Malcolm's message. You can picket and march and scream and sing. If those things lead to power, then they are good. If they do not lead to power, then they are a waste of time. So he gave us a yardstick by which we can judge our organizations, our Churches, and our institutions. Do they lead to power for black people?

That's why this Church, The Shrine of the Black Madonna, is building a Nation, because we believe in Black Power. We are trying to organize for power. In every area, we are trying to secure power for black people, so that we can deal with white people on a basis of equality. We believe in it, and we believe that this was the message of Jesus as well as Brother Malcolm. That's why there is no inner conflict when we have a memorial for Brother Malcolm in a Christian Church which is dedicated to rebuilding the Nation of the Black Messiah.

We believe that the things which Brother Malcolm taught, Jesus taught two thousand years ago. Our struggle is a struggle for survival. Malcolm knew that. You can think of many little things he said that were terribly important. He talked about the "house nigger" and the "field nigger," to illustrate the problem of identification with the enemy. That has always been one of our basic problems. The more you get, the higher you climb above your black brothers and sisters, the more your identification with the enemy becomes a problem for you. That's why the people who serve the Black Nation best are usually those who don't have anything. You wonder why some brothers don't have any qualms about fighting the enemy any time and any place. Usually it's because they can see the problem clearly because they don't have too much to lose. But give them a job (that's the reason for the poverty program) and let them buy a house, or a car, and their whole attitude changes. So we have to be careful, all of us. We have to be wary of any position where a few little possessions tend to separate us from the struggles of black people. A power struggle demands the total involvement of all black people, identification with black people, accountability to black people, and the severing of any identification with white people.

In his last days Brother Malcolm was trying to do the most diffi-cult of all the tasks which he undertook. He was eloquent, he had a philosophy, he could make people understand it. The basic task that he was not spared to do was that of organization. He didn't leave any organization. He left a revolutionary spirit. There are certain benefits to that. If he had left an organization, probably the organization would have distorted his message because they would have tried to use it. He didn't leave anything but a spirit and a memory, and a love in the hearts and minds of people. But this revolutionary spirit must be channelled into a knowledge of organ-ization. How do we organize to struggle for survival in this second Civil War which has already begun? If the white man is getting ready for genocide, it's not enough for us to just walk around saying "Brother." We have got to organize. That is the point to which Brother Malcolm brought us. If we can't move beyond where he left us, into the kind of organization which is essential for struggle, then we still will not survive. We must organize to secure power, and we must organize to use power.

Organization is one thing that we don't know too much about. We have never done it. Our organizations are all loose, helter-skelter, and harum-scarum, and we tend to tear up any organiza-tion on a personality basis. We can get a thousand people together, and two people will tear it all up, for no better reason than the simple fact that they don't like each other. In almost every north-ern urban center, you will find black people fragmented a thou-sand different ways. We're closer together right here in Detroit, in the Nation, than black people are anywhere else in America. We are also learning the lessons of organization. We have our differ-ences, but we try to avoid fighting each other up and down the street for the entertainment of the white man. When we move into real organization, we are moving a step beyond Malcolm. Mal-colm couldn't do it in New York and all across the country. We haven't been able to do it. This is the next step in the Black Revolution.

On this occasion, when we remember Malcolm, and review how

far we have come, let us keep clearly in focus the simple fact that unless we can learn to organize and submerge ourselves in a Black Nation without regard for individual self-interest, we will not be able to survive the critical decade ahead as black people. We can no longer afford the luxury of individualism. The question is now one of survival. Even if you don't like somebody, if he is black you must work with him because it's the only way you can survive. Our survival will depend upon our ability to work together, to organize and to trust each other.

So on this occasion, in memory of Brother Malcolm, we say that the Black Nation which we are building here, is carrying on his spirit and teachings which we believe to be compatible with the spirit and teachings of Jesus, the Black Messiah. Within the framework of this philosophy, we are trying to do the things which he would have done if the white man had let him live a little longer. Some of us are going to live long enough to finish the job.

Brother Malcolm was tremendously important to all of us because he articulated what we felt. He spelled out a philosophy and we are building on that philosophy.

Heavenly Father, be with us. Give us a sense of the importance of this moment in history and of our importance as a Nation. Help us to submerge ourselves in the cause of black people. Be with us to guide us and strengthen us in all that we do. Keep bright our remembrance of Brother Malcolm. These things we ask in the name of Jesus Christ, the Black Messiah. Amen.

15/Dr. King and Black Power

"And some of the Pharisees in the multitude said to him, 'Teacher, rebuke your disciples.' He answered, 'I tell you, if these were silent, the very stones would cry out'" (*Luke* 19:39-40).

We have come together to commemorate the triumphal entry of the Black Messiah into Jerusalem two thousand years ago, and to pay tribute to Dr. Martin Luther King, a black leader. It is a profound tribute to Dr. King that so many have come here this morning, since few of us really agreed with his position. We respected him for his sincerity, for the dedication which he brought to the task of leadership, and for the things which he accomplished. And so we have come together to pay him tribute. A mighty oak has been felled in the forest, and there is an empty space against the sky.

Early last Thursday evening, Dr. King was murdered by a white man in Memphis, Tennessee. I suspect that many of you have forgotten by this time that he was murdered by a white man. The simple fact has been obscured by the copious crocodile tears which are being shed everywhere. His murderer has not yet been apprehended, I think that's the way the police phrase it, but momentarily they expect an arrest. At the time he was killed there were hundreds of police officers present, and yet his murderer seemed somehow mysteriously to slip away unnoticed.

Since that time, we have been constantly reminded by radio, television and every branch of the mass communications media, that Dr. King believed in non-violence. You would think they were afraid we didn't know that. All right, Dr. King believed in non-violence. But then they add something to it, "Dr. King believed in non-violence, and any retaliation for his murder would desecrate his memory." They say Dr. King would not want us to be violent. How do we know this? Because white folks have been telling us every day, all day, ever since white folks murdered him. "Dr. King died to prove that non-violence can work." Now that's an absurd statement if I ever heard one. White folks killed Dr. King because he was black, and then they come right back at us, saying that Dr. King died to prove that non-violence can work.

There's no kind of logic in that statement, no kind of way. If Dr. King's death proved anything beyond the shadow of a doubt, it proved that non-violence will never work in a violent white racist society. I have a feeling they are very much afraid that we will see this is what has been proven conclusively by his brutal murder. They are afraid we will now see that this is the real meaning of his life. He tried in every way possible to be non-violent. He took no steps to protect his life. He believed in the power of non-violence. He hoped, and he prayed, that the black man's non-violence could somehow redeem white people. He believed it. And you know what white people did to him? They killed him!

They tell us that Dr. King believed in America. He believed in the goodness of white folks. They keep reminding us. And all we can say is we know he did, and we see what it did for him. He believed in America. He believed in the goodness of white folks. And there he lies, dead. Dead. No use making it fancy. He's just lying there dead, shot, killed, murdered.

I heard Roy Wilkins, Sammy Davis, Jr., and Reverend Wyatt T. Walker last night. White folks have a way of bringing their black leaders together in crisis situations of this kind to tell us what they want us to know. There they sat, looking pious and unctuous. Sammy looked so pious he could hardly talk, just carried away with grief. But he had a message, they all had a message, and they all had the same message. They were denouncing the sub-teens (whatever that means) who had betrayed Dr. King's memory by perpetrating violence. Now sub-teens, according to the dictionary, means those lower in age than the teens. So it must be the nine, ten, eleven, and twelve year-olds who have been carrying on all this violence across the country, the sub-teens. That's what Mr. Wilkins said. And then they proceeded together to read these violent sub-teens out of the race. They said, "We can't call them brothers if they are going to act like this and betray Dr. King's memory."

Now I'll tell you something. If all the action which has been going on in more than forty cities across America, if all the fires and everything else that has been reported, was done by black sub-teens, we have the most powerful nine, ten, eleven and twelve year-olds in the world!

More than forty cities have been torn by violence and are in flames, and the violence is not yet finished. Are we ashamed of the violence? Is it possible that black people in America could have let Dr. King's murder pass without some kind of retaliation? Even if you feel that they shouldn't have carried on like this, is it possible that black people in America could have let this dastardly deed pass without some retaliatory measures? Even as you sit in your home scared, aren't you glad that somebody did something about it?

And when you go back to work, when it's all over and you aren't scared any more, won't you look at white folks with some pride because somebody, somewhere, did something about it? I have heard so many of our leaders, dragged to the microphones and television cameras, talking about how much they loved Dr. King, and how ashamed they are of the destruction of property, and how a revolution does not consist in looting, that I must make one comment. We live in a materialistic society. You actually hit the white man hardest when you tear up his property. Perhaps those who loot and burn don't have any real revolutionary philosophy, but they do know one simple thing: tear up the white man's property, and you hurt him where it hurts the most.

We have all kinds of black people. Some go around talking

about non-violence, and some don't go around talking about anything; but when something happens, they do something. And there's no point in our so-called leaders' apologies for what's happening. Somebody had to do something, we had to retaliate in some way, America had to know that we did not like it. What we are saying to America quite simply is: "You can't go around murdering black folks that you don't like. You can't go around murdering black folks, period."

That's what we are saying. We can't be ashamed of that. We had to say it, somebody had to say it. So don't go around apologizing for those who are saying it and have said it. America is a different place now, because forty cities were in flames. They say, "We are going to make some big changes now." If they make any changes, it will be because now they see that black folks are human enough to feel anger.

This is a national thing. All over America at one time black people suddenly erupted. That is the last thing they wanted to happen. And now all kinds of plans are on the drawing board. The church denominations are saying, we are all going to come together because we can't fight this racism alone. They weren't saying that last week. Everybody's got a program now. Forty cities. Something had to be done. Can we say to Black America: be silent? Stifle your tears? Mourn quietly so that you don't disturb the white folks? Mourn quietly because white folks don't like unseemly noises from the black ghetto.

Our Scripture text this morning is taken from the Gospel of Luke, the 19th Chapter, the 39th and 40th verses. Jesus, the Black Messiah, was going into Jerusalem. He knew that he was going to be killed, that the Toms and the white folks, the Gentiles, were going to get together and kill him. He knew, and yet he had turned his face steadfastly towards Jerusalem. It was a beautiful passage that we read this morning, and it is somewhat strange that the scripture we read last Sunday was the same one that Dr. King used in his last speech. We talked about Moses going to the mountain top. He looked out and he saw the Promised Land. He could not enter it, but it was there for his children and his children's children.

We read that last Sunday. And we talked about the difficulties you face when you get all tied up thinking about entering the Promised Land, and forget all about the importance of what you are doing for your children and your children's children. The night before he was murdered, Dr. King said, "I've been to the mountain top and I have seen the promised land, I don't expect to enter in, but I know that my people will enter in.' 'You know, on that last night he sounded like he belonged to the Nation. "I believe that my people will enter in."

Today our Scripture has to do with the Black Messiah entering Jerusalem. A lot of his followers were there because it was a political thing, this entrance into Jerusalem. And they were screaming and yelling, "Blessed be the king who comes in the name of the Lord!" because they expected him to take power. They were with him, they were supporting him. A multitude of his followers had come together, and there was loud rejoicing.

Seeing this, the Pharisees, or the Toms, came over and whispered to Jesus, "Don't you think you ought to rebuke your disciples? The things they are saying are going to make the Gentiles mad." In other words, the white folks don't like a Black Messiah coming into Jerusalem with his disciples screaming about taking over. Jesus looked at these Uncle Toms, much as I believe Dr. King would look at these Uncle Toms who are around supposedly representing him now, and answered simply, "I tell you, if these were silent, the very stones would cry out."

Do you know what he was saying? There are some things that cannot be silenced. If these people shut up, the very stones would cry out. This thing is in the very heart and nature of the universe. It is the will of God that black people should be free. I'm going into Jerusalem, trying to free black people and black people are shouting that they believe that they are going to be free, and you tell me to hush them up. If they were silenced, the very stones, the mountains, the skies, the stars, would cry out.

That is true right here today. You know that if black people hadn't done something to retaliate for the murder of Dr. King, the very stones would have cried out, because some things strike at the very meaning of the universe. If black people are men, created in the image of God, then in a situation like this, they could not but strike back. That is what Jesus meant. If these were silenced, the very stones would cry out.

Jesus' entry into Jerusalem was a triumphant entry, triumphant only in the sense that Jesus was willing to go to the end with what he believed. Throughout Holy Week, from Palm Sunday through Good Friday, the Black Messiah went through a series of confrontations with the white Gentiles. He did those things which pointed out to black people the enmity and the distance between them and their oppressors. He did it day after day. So Holy Week is a series of confrontations that Jesus set up. He was making clear that some things just have to be done. They can't be avoided, no matter how afraid you are. Someone must do them because they must be done. And so Jesus refused to rebuke his disciples. If they were silenced, the very stones would cry out.

I was not a follower of Dr. Martin Luther King. I respected him, but very early in his ministry, I differed with him in his approach to the problems of black people. He was not my leader in that sense, and yet I respected him for his position. I remember that he came to Detroit when we were organizing the Freedom Now Party, he came to fight against it, to sabotage it. It is no disloyalty to recall what Dr. King did at that time because we all do things from time to time that are wrong. He came here at the behest of white people, along with Adam Clayton Powell, to destroy the Freedom Now Party, which black folks were trying to get together to elect black people to office. The white folks were very fearful, so they brought in heavier guns than they really needed. I remember that Dr. King issued a statement denying the endorsement, which he had made previously, of independent black political action. So I say, he wasn't my leader.

I had prepared to speak on Dr. King this morning even before he was murdered because he had an article in last week's *Look* magazine on "The Last Stand for Non-violence." He went into all kinds of detail about what he was getting ready to do in Memphis and with the Poor People's campaign in Washington. He was going to take three thousand poor people and camp on the mall there between the Lincoln and Washington monuments and stay there for three months if necessary, to focus attention on the problems poor people are facing in this country.

Somehow he thought he could do that non-violently. He was wrong. There was no way in the world he could have stayed there in Washington non-violently. We can all see it now. You saw it last night. Those folks wouldn't have stayed non-violent for three months, I don't care what Dr. King said or how eloquently he might have appealed. He could not have kept control of such a demonstration for three months. But he thought he could, and what he was trying to do was an honest and sincere thing.

Here is what would have happened. He would have set up a confrontation situation. All the world would have been looking at black people in Washington, D. C., and in the middle of it the white man would have acted a fool the way he always does. He would have started whipping heads one evening, or one morning, or one afternoon. He would have gotten tired of the whole thing, and he would have gone wading in just like Bull Connor, right there in Washington, in the shadow of the White House. And when he did, everything in America would have broken loose. It was a confrontation that Dr. King was setting up.

Now Dr. King believed that he was preparing for redemptive suffering. He thought, "We will go there, we will camp, and we will suffer, and white folks will be moved to do something by our suffering." That is what he had been thinking all the time, for the last thirteen years. But just go back and look at the history of the things he actually did. He has a tremendous history. I never agreed with most of the things he said, but I have loved everything he did because the things he did had no relationship to the things he said. What happened was never redemptive suffering; every time he set up a confrontation, black folks and white folks stood and looked each other in the face, eyeball to eyeball.

It started in Montgomery. Think back to Montgomery, thirteen years ago, how disunited we were, how fearful we were, how without courage we were—when that little bunch of black people in Montgomery came together and said, "We're not going to sit in the back of the bus anymore." Dr. King was willing to take leadership of that little movement that seemed to have no chance of success. He led it non-violently, but black folks stood face to face with white folks and said what they were going to do, and what they were not going to do. And they did what they said they were going to do, and did not do what they said they were not going to do. And black folks won, one of the few victories that black folks have had in recent history. Black people won in Montgomery. They beat the rich white folks. They won the bus boycott. They forced them to let black folks sit anywhere on a bus in Montgomery. That was success.

Now I suppose we can say that he was engaged in redemptive suffering. You're suffering when you walk all the way across Montgomery, after working all day. You're suffering, and your suffering redeems white folks. But it wasn't really redemptive suffering. It was black courage. Black folks were learning that they had power, and they were willing to do the things that were necessary to use it. And they won.

Then Dr. King set up mass demonstrations in Albany, Georgia, Greenwood, Mississippi, and Birmingham, Alabama. The mass demonstrations were very simple; he just asked all black people to come out, to march, and protest, until white folks did something. You know what white folks did? They beat them, they locked them up, they did every cruel, inhuman, bestial, barbaric thing that white folks can think of. They did it day after day, because day after day black folks would come out of their little hovels and shacks and march. They knew what it meant to march. They knew that it meant jail, they knew that it meant clubs, cattle-prods, fire hoses and police dogs. They knew what it meant but they still marched—black men, women, and little children marching and confronting white folks daily in a way that black folks had never confronted white folks in this country before.

Dr. King was still talking every night about redemptive suffering. He was still saying, "If blood must flow in the streets, let it be our blood and not the blood of our white brothers." But what he said had no relationship to what was happening in the hearts and minds and souls of black people. Black people marching every day felt more and more that they were a people. As they marched they felt "I'm not a part of these white people." Every day as they marched and sang "We shall overcome," they were saying deep down in their hearts, "I have got to separate myself from these people. I have got to recognize the realities of my existence."

Dr. King was saying one thing and they were learning another. He set up the situation, he set up the confrontation, and black folks, as they stood up against white people, saw that these people were not invincible. These were no super-beings. "Even if they beat me over the head, knock me down, stomp me, use cattle-prods on me, and lock me up, these people are not invincible. Even without striking back, I can beat them."

This was a movement inside black people. It had no relationship to what Dr. King was saying, either in his speeches or in his books. It was something that black people were learning. They were learning that they could stand up against the white man, that black people could come together as a group, that they could find unity in their struggle against oppression, and in their desire for justice. We were discovering something, and it had no relationship with what he was saying.

White folks remember what he said, his words. But we remember where we were thirteen years ago, and where we are today. Not that he did it by himself, but he created the confrontation situations in which we could learn, in which we could work, and which Brother Malcolm could interpret. Everything was working together. The white people couldn't see it because they thought that they had two antagonistic elements here, splitting the black community, Malcolm X on one side and Dr. King on the other. So they gave all their money to Dr. King to keep his voice speaking, but he was at the same time creating the very situations which Brother Malcolm could interpret. White folks didn't understand it, but looking back, we can understand it. We needed both of them. It wasn't enough to say, "We've got our enemy. We've got to fight." No one would have listened to Brother Malcolm until Dr. King had created the confrontation situations in which we began to learn, step by step, that black people can unite, black people can fight, black people can die for the things they believe in.

This is the kind of thing that Dr. King actually accomplished. I criticize the things he said, but I have only admiration for the things he did. We learned from the struggle and conflict which he made possible. In Albany, Georgia, they said Dr. King was through because he didn't win anything in Albany. They were looking for some kind of settlement, for some concrete solution, for the setting up of some kind of interracial committee. But the victory was not in what white people did; the victory was in how we were changing and in what was happening in our minds. This was Dr. King's victory all through this crucial period in the Black Revolution. He didn't win anything in Greenwood, Mississippi. People were beaten and lots of people were jailed. He didn't win anything, but we were all changed. Birmingham was no victory, either, in a sense that can be measured, but certainly we were changed. With Birmingham, black people all over America began to feel a part of what was happening. Not that any real solution was being arrived at, but they were beginning to feel that they were becoming a people, and that they could stand up against white people.

This is what Dr. King in a unique way made possible. This is his contribution: the confrontations which he created enabled us to see white people as they really are. All the dreams and myths that we had picked up in our churches, in our Sunday School literature, and at our mothers knees, disappeared, because in these confrontations we began to see white people unmasked. This was the beginning. You can't fight an enemy that you don't even recognize as an enemy. You can't fight an enemy that you believe is your friend, dedicated to your welfare and your best interests. But as you confront him day after day, you begin to understand how he really is. And this Dr. King made possible. Every time the cattle-prod was used, every time the fire hose was used, every time a black person was beaten, we saw the bestiality to which the white man has degenerated in a racist society. And so we began to see that we had an enemy and to understand his nature.

Dr. King made this possible. White people will never admit it, but they financed the movement which emancipated our minds. They will never admit it, but now they are beginning to know that it is true. In just the last few days we have seen the difference. Black people have been killed by the hundreds in the past and there was no spontaneous national response. But now, thirteen years after Montgomery, Dr. King is killed, not at the peak of his career, but at the bottom of his career, and black people all over America rose up together to retaliate. A whole new black world has come into being, a Black Nation now exists. And Dr. King had a large part in helping to shape it, in creating the very people that Uncle Toms on radio and television now criticize. In Washington, in Chicago, and throughout the country, the people who marched, who fought, who broke windows, who retaliated, are disciples of Dr. Martin Luther King. His wife may not like it and his followers in the Southern Christian Leadership Conference may not like it, but Dr. King played a bigger part in creating this situation than any man in America. The people who marched, the people who looted, and the people who burned were in a deep sense, his disciples.

Much of this looting is a mystical kind of thing. People loot stuff they don't even want. You saw the picture of the black man in Washington, sitting there trying on a pair of old work shoes. He had money enough to buy work shoes, he didn't need to steal them, but there was a sense of defiance in the very nature of the retaliation.

In Washington they walked up to police officers standing there with shot guns and rifles, taunting them, "Kill me, kill me." One man pushed two police officers with rifles and shotguns aside, climbed into a store, got what he wanted, and came back out again. They may not realize it but this was exactly the same thing that Dr. King did in Birmingham, Greenwood and Albany—non-violent protest; they didn't even have a gun. And this was going on all over Washington, D.C. Black people are a majority of the population there, and the whites don't know exactly what to do with them. They would walk up and do whatever they were going to do, and the white officers would just stand there and look at them. That's the power of defiance, of not caring. "I've taken all I can, kill me if you want to." That's what they were saying. Black people said the same things in Birmingham and Selma.

Dr. King turned out some strange disciples—just ordinary people getting a whole lot of clothes out of the stores, and sitting on a bench and trying them on right in front of the police, picking out what they wanted and throwing the rest away, taunting white folks, telling them, "I'm going to be free. If you don't like what I'm doing, try to stop me."

It has been a long journey from where we were to where we now are. A whole lot has happened to bring us this far, and today we are a different people. I don't say that we have come all the way. We still don't know too much about what we are doing, but we are getting an attitude. I know that a lot of people want a planned protest. "Let's march downtown or something." But I really do not feel that planned protest could really express our anger and indignation. White people would probably take it over any way. I have profound trust in the masses of black people. I don't trust black leadership too much, but in a crisis, black people tend to react correctly. They do what has to be done, and the best thing that leadership can do is go off and wait until they get through. When they get through, black leadership can say, "Let's see if white folks have learned anything. Let's see if we can do a little programming now." And if white folks haven't learned anything, it will happen again and we will have to go through the same thing again.

Dr. King made a genuine contribution, and black militants ought to be willing to admit it. I mean we ought to be big enough to admit it, at least after he's dead. From Montgomery to nation-wide retaliation for the murder of Dr. King is a long journey, but it took just thirteen years. Let us honestly and sincerely pray to God that we can develop a leadership that can take us as far in the next thirteen years.

"The people wept for Moses on the plains of Mohab for thirty days. Then the days of weeping and mourning for Moses were ended."

16/Not Peace but a Sword

"Do not think that I have come to bring peace on earth; I have not come to bring peace, but a sword. For I have come to set a man against his father, and a daughter against her mother, and a daughter-in-law against her mother-in-law; and a man's foes will be those of his own household." (*Matthew* 10:34-36).

I would like to talk about a very simple subject—conflict. I have taken a text from the Gospel of Matthew, the 11th chapter, the 34th verse, "Do not think that I have come to bring peace on earth; I have not come to bring peace, but a sword." Jesus is no doubt answering critics who feel that he is preaching hate and creating conflict. He answers directly and does not seek to evade the question, "I do not come to bring peace on earth, but a sword." Jesus came to an oppressed black people who were in bondage to the white Gentiles, exploited by the Roman government and policed by the Roman army. As a Black Messiah, he came to offer black people a way of organizing against their oppression, of coming together, and again becoming a Black Nation.

So Jesus was essentially a troublemaker. He was a threat to Rome, not in the sense that he was organizing an army, but in the sense that he brought people to the place where they were willing to struggle, where they were willing to enter into conflict, where they were willing to face the enemy. All through the synoptic Gospels, Matthew, Mark, and Luke, we see indications of the kind

mands for the removal of white administrators recognized the administrator's importance as white power symbols, as well as their general inefficiency and inability to restructure inner city schools to meet the needs of black children. Black parents were forced into a position where they had to decide. Would they support their children or would they support the oppressor?

The answer at this point is quite clear. Parents in a number of schools have decided that they do not like conflict and that they will support the oppressor. This is understandable at the Post Junior High School. It is located in a rather affluent black community, in which black people tend to identify with the white power structure. There were few parents there who were accustomed to open conflict, and they were poorly prepared to support it. When representatives of the white administration came out to deal with the parents, friendly and smiling, shaking hands, serving coffee and tea and cookies, it was very difficult for these black parents to know how to cope with the situation. The white administrators said, "Well, there may be a few things wrong here, and I think that the best thing we can do is to set up a committee to investigate." The parents said, "Yes, that's what we need, investigation."

Our schools have been investigated to death for the past fifteen or twenty years. Every year we have had a blue ribbon investigating committee. We very rarely hear anything about the implementation of reports, but we hear much about the setting up of the committees. When the superintendent and his assistants suggested an investigating committee, it sounded reasonable to these black parents. The black children in the school had shown a different conception of struggle. They protested, they forced the issue, they made demands, and they followed up their demands with action. They created a conflict situation and the parents did not understand conflict.

There are certain basic things which we must understand. The acceptance of oppression, exploitation, and injustice insure peace. If you want peace, and you are an oppressed and exploited person who suffers injustice from an oppressor, you have only to continue to accept injustice, oppression and exploitation. It's an axiom: if you want peace, then accept what exists. Rebellion and revolution occur when people rise up to destroy the existing status quo in order that they may find escape from oppression, exploitation and injustice. If you want peace, you do not rebel, you do not spark a revolution, you do not engage in conflict. Any time you point out an injustice and seek a confrontation, peace has become impossible.

If you are mistreated wherever you work, you can have peace or conflict. You can be a doctor in a hospital, a worker in a factory, an employee in a store or an office, or a social worker for the county, and you can be mistreated because you are black. If you decide that you want to do something about the injustice, you will have to force a confrontation. You will have to go to someone in power and say, "I'm not going to stand for it any more." Then you stand there and the white man stands there. You have said that you are not going to stand for it any more. That's confrontation, and nothing can result but conflict unless he says, "Well, I have been wrong, I shouldn't have been treating you like a dog the way I've been doing, and I'm not going to do it anymore. I'm sorry." If he says that, there's no conflict. You had your confrontation, and the issue was resolved by the removal of injustice.

But if he stands there and says, "I'm the boss here and I'm going to treat you just the way I've been treating you, and if you don't like it, get out," then you have another situation. You can say, "I'm sorry I brought it up, don't think any more about it. I'm happy here, I'll go back to my job." Then you have resolved the conflict by accepting injustice. The oppressor must either change the situation or you must accept the injustice—or, there is conflict.

When you first went up to him, you should have known that there was going to be conflict and you should have been prepared for it. You should have known because never in history has anyone given up his right to oppress and exploit, and the status and privilege that injustice makes possible, without struggle. So when you walked up to him and said, "Im not going to stand it any more," you should have been prepared for the inevitable conflict. If you had selected your moment well, and you had him at a momentary disadvantage, he might have played for time and pretended to capitulate, but this would merely have given the initial stage of the conflict a different character. Most of us know this automatically, but we don't bring it into consciousness. We try to repress it. When you demand rights, conflict is inescapable. Confrontation leads inevitably to conflict, and conflict can only be resolved for the oppressed by death, surrender, or the end of oppression.

In a number of instances in the schools, the parents sought to resolve the conflict which their black children had initiated. They became engaged in a series of meetings, discussions and negotiations. The children had initiated conflict by saying, "We don't want this, we are not going to stand for it." The children said this before the parents came upon the scene. The parents, acting for their children, had a choice. Either they could resolve the conflict by doing away with the injustice, or they could resolve the conflict by accepting the injustice. There were no other choices.

But most parents did not understand this. They were convinced that the conflict itself was bad. They were disturbed by children breaking windows, by children sitting down in the halls. This is what disturbed the parents, the struggle and the conflict. Black children were disturbed by injustice and oppression but black parents were disturbed by the existence of conflict. This meant that the parents and the children could not communicate. The children were demanding, "We don't want this, and we don't want that," and the parents were saying, "Let's resolve this conflict quickly. Let's get these children back in school. Let's get some kind of working relationship with the administration."

They were sincere. They wanted to resolve the conflict because they thought that conflict was the problem. They didn't understand one basic fact. Conflict is never the problem. Conflict is a method by which problems are solved. Not understanding this, most parents thought that they were doing a noble thing by resolving the conflict. It did not occur to them that they should support their children's struggle against injustice.

So in most of the schools an uneasy temporary kind of peace has been restored by the acceptance of oppression and injustice. The children have been forced back into school. The same pattern of action has been followed by parents in most inner-city schools. Investigating committees have been set up and the oppression of black children goes on as usual.

At the Winterhalter Elementary School, the parents met around the clock for three or four days and then the superintendent came out, bringing his black assistant, brief cases, secretaries, experts, and all the paraphernalia of power and knowledge. They came in, affable and friendly. "Let's sit down and have a little cup of tea here, first, and just sort of get acquainted with each other."

The parents had come to definite conclusions as to changes that must be made. They had talked to the teachers who had been trying to get a change of administration for months. Everything wrong with the school could be traced directly to the administration. The white principal had failed in the basic task of educating black children. The parents knew it and yet when they met with the superintendent they were afraid to sharpen the confrontation. A number of them had been saying even before the superintendent arrived, "Can't we settle this thing some way?" Let's send a small hand-picked committee down to see them. Let's not bring them out here." They were trying to avoid the confrontation, wish it out of existence if possible.

When they heard that the superintendent was coming out, everybody was scared. "Who wants to be on the committee?" Everyone started looking at the ceiling and out of the window. Their children were involved, but they didn't want to be on the committee. They were afraid of confrontation, they were afraid of conflict. When they finally got a committee, they were still worried. "When they come out, they are going to know a whole lot. We better do some studying to get ready for the meeting." These people downtown have been abusing and mistreating our children for years. They haven't educated a black child in the past twenty-five years, but black parents are still afraid of them. What kind of studying does a black parent need to get ready to confront the superintendent of schools about the education of black children? Why not just tell it like it is. "Black children are not being educated in the city of Detroit, and we will never get black children educated until we get rid of white administrators."

How much studying do you need for that? He has the studies downtown. He has the achievement records. Black children are three and four grades below grade level in achievement in every inner-city school. He knows that, he has the records. He has the tests. When you tell him that we don't want white administrators in our schools anymore because they have already failed, what can he say? He knows they have failed in every school and that their failure gets worse every year. Our children are lower in achievement this year than they were last year, and they are going to be lower next year than they are this year. The administrators have failed. I don't care how great they seem to be in terms of academic degrees. They have failed to educate black children in inner-city schools. So we want them out. We have only one thing to say, "Take these white administrators and put them in your own white schools."

Why is that so difficult for black parents to do? Why? Because they are not sure that black children are equal. That is the crime, they are not sure. When a white man comes and sits down and opens his brief case and acts like he has something in it, they are not sure that their black children have the ability to learn. When he looks at them, they are not sure. That is the problem. All of these black parents sitting around the table have, in the back of their own minds, this reservation, "Maybe black children are stupid." They wonder about themselves, "Maybe I'm stupid, and if I'm stupid, maybe my children are stupid." So when you watch some of these parents wringing and twisting, they are wringing and twisting with a real psychological problem. They may try to act important and talk a lot about being black, but they are not sure of themselves.

This the white man has done to us. They are looking and wondering, and when the white man implies, "It's your fault," they think, "That's right, that's right." They are ready to agree because deep down inside they feel that the man must be right. They can't really believe that the white man is mistreating their children. After four hundred years of oppression and more than five thousand documented lynchings in a hundred years, and all the discrimination and oppression that we face every day, many black people still can't believe it. You say, "The white man wouldn't do that." But he is doing it. He's doing it every day. Everything in the school system is designed not to educate black children. They send old beat-up, broken down white administrators to black schools. I'm not saying there are not some good, dedicated black teachers in all of these schools, but how can a dedicated black teacher educate when she has to fight the administration every day—all day?

They have a dedicated black counselor at Winterhalter, and everything in the school is designed to get rid of him. The principal of the school, inefficient, inept, stupid as he is, is afraid of this black counselor. So everything in the school is designed to make this black counselor a scapegoat for the principal's inefficiency. You ask, "How can a white man act like that?" He's been doing it for four hundred years.

But I don't worry about white administrators. I don't worry about anything a white man does because I know what he's going to do before he does it. What worries me is what's happening to black parents. In this day and age when black children are trying in every way possible to change the schools so that they can get a decent education in this city and in cities throughout America, black parents are not supporting them. Black parents are not fighting with them. Black parents are afraid because they do not understand the nature of conflict.

Conflict is a method by which problems are solved. We will never secure quality education for black children in our schools

until we create enough conflict to force basic changes in the administration of these schools. You may think that you can sit down
and drink tea and eat crumpets with the Board of Education and
talk them into making changes. Try it, and your great grandchildren will have poorer schools than your children, if they survive.
The kids who kick out the windows and set fires in the buildings
are closer to a solution to the problem than you are. They at least
understand that they are in a conflict situation and that they are
fighting for survival. They understand that they must use any
means necessary to highlight the conflict and to make it impossible
for the administration to escape the issue with some easy kind of
fake solution like an investigating committee. Children understand
and parents don't. In every instance, the parents have accepted
some kind of flukey settlement when they should have notified the
Board of Education and the Superintendent, "Either that white
principal goes by Monday morning or we are going to close this
school down." Then the battle lines would have been drawn.

But parents have peculiar concerns, "What will our children do
out of school?" Your child might miss three or four days or a week.
It wouldn't make any difference if he missed a whole semester. He's
not learning anything anyway. If you don't believe it, go up there
and look around or test him on what he is supposed to know. He's
not learning anything unless you're teaching him at home. But
then, still trying to avoid conflict, parents will say, "Let them at
least get the little bit they're getting." No, because you're teaching
your children to be slaves. That's the little bit that they're getting.
They're fighting, they're involved in conflict, they're learning how
to be men. They're learning more in the conflict than they would
sitting there in school.

And they would learn a whole lot more if they knew their parents
were standing with them. Parents are afraid to struggle because
they're all tied up in this idea that there is something evil about
conflict. They really believe it. The parents at Winterhalter had
agreed to walk out of the meeting if the administration didn't accept
their demands. But do you know what one black man said? "I

can't walk out; that would be impolite." They're killing his child, but for him to walk out of a meeting would be impolite. The white man ought to love us to death. We are so easy to get along with. We don't even want to be impolite and hurt his feelings!

The question is a very simple one. If we are afraid of conflict, then anyone who is not afraid of conflict is our master. If you present an ultimatum and the enemy declares that he will not settle on your terms, then he is prepared to accept conflict. But if you humbly acknowledge defeat rather than risk conflict, the battle is lost before it has begun. It's the same thing if we're afraid of violence. Anyone who is willing to use violence can make anyone who is afraid of violence his slave.

Growing numbers of black people are no longer afraid of conflict. The revolt at Howard University in Washington, D. C., was significant. The students won! Perhaps because there weren't any parents around to mess it up. Howard University is not a black university. White folks run it with a Negro president. Classes teaching music, art, literature and drama teach white music, white art, white literature, and white drama to black students. The administration frowns upon Black Power and last year Dr. Nathan Hare, faculty advisor for Black Power student groups, was fired and Black Power student leaders were expelled. Student efforts to get rid of the President and to make the University relevant to the needs of the black community continued. Climaxing a number of student-administration confrontations, the students took control of the Administration Building and demanded the right to negotiate directly with the Trustees.

The President threatened to send in troops, and ordered the University closed. No meals were served and the students were ordered out of the dormitories. People from the community brought them food. No one left despite reports that the marshalls, the police and federal troops were on the way. The administration backed down. The President, in spite of his bluster, was more afraid of conflict than were the students.

Finally, the trustees came to the campus and met secretly with the students, accepting their demands. They agreed that from now on they would deal directly with the students; that any punishment meted out to students would be handled by the student government; that a student-faculty committee would be set up to modernize the curriculum in terms of the needs of black students. The students won their demand because they were not afraid of conflict. They knew what had happened in Orangeburg. They knew that students had been shot and killed there because they were protesting. They knew that it could also happen at Howard, but they were not afraid of conflict. They refused to back down, as the Detroit parents did. This was constructive conflict because it ended injustice and oppression.

Black folks are no longer running away from confrontation; we are seeking confrontation. We want to confront the white man on every issue. We know that we are going to have conflict whenever we have confrontation. That's what a revolution is all about. It isn't all fighting in the streets. Many times, it is easier to fight in the streets than it is to look at the enemy and tell him what you're going to do, and what you're not going to do.

The problem of education in inner city schools raises basic psychological problems for many black parents because they are not yet convinced of the intellectual equality of either themselves or their children. There can be no other explanation for the black communities' acceptance of the fact that black children are approximately three years below grade level nationally. Most black parents would fight if someone walked up and slapped them. But mistreat their children by denying them a decent education and human dignity, and they won't fight. They are too uncertain of their own value to question the methods which the white man is using. The low achievement of their children does not raise questions as to the ability and intentions of white educators, but only serves to reinforce their own sense of inferiority and self hate. For this reason, conflict in the area of education is most important.

There are certain things that are not negotiable. We can't negotiate justice, we can't negotiate freedom, we can't negotiate equality. Those things belong to us. We are going to take them, one after the other, as fast as we can. We must believe in our children and support them in any conflict designed to establish their intellectual equality. We must bring the achievement level of our children up to national grade level. Even if this involves national conflict and fighting in the streets, we cannot accept any justification for the white man's failure to educate our children.

If your child comes home and says that he is not being educated, believe him. Go to your school with him. Support him. Organize other parents. Fight and keep fighting. Don't let a little bunch of handkerchief-heads settle an issue that's not settled. The issue will not be settled until every black child in America is achieving at grade level and above. Do not be ashamed of conflict. Black parents cannot settle the issue in any other way. It is *not* better for your child to be in an inferior school where he is being destroyed, than out in the street protesting. In the inferior school he is learning to be a slave. Protesting in the street, he's learning to be a black man. We cannot resolve conflict by accepting injustice and oppression. We must fight on!

Jesus said, "Do not think that I have come to bring peace on earth; I have not come to bring peace, but a sword." I want you to keep that in mind in all of these situations. You go on thinking that you are on the right side by advocating peace; you're on the wrong side. You cannot accept indignity and injustice, you must fight against it, and when you fight against it, you are fighting with Jesus at your side. That's why we are followers of the Black Messiah.

Heavenly Father, we thank thee for the opportunity of coming together in thy house, for the many opportunities which we share of walking in thy footsteps and doing the things which thou hast commanded us to do. Give us the courage, the conviction, to be truly thy disciples in the world, in this time. Be with us to strengthen use when we are weak. Give us courage and knowledge when we are confused. Be with us to help us in conflict. This we ask in the name of the Black Messiah. Amen

17/Black Church, White School

"When the day of Pentecost had come, they were all together in one place. And suddenly a sound came from heaven like the rush of a mighty wind, and it filled all the house where they were sitting. And there appeared to them tongues as of fire, distributed and resting on each one of them. And they were all filled with the Holy Spirit and began to speak in other tongues, as the Spirit gave them utterance . . . At this sound, the multitude came together, and they were bewildered because each one heard them speaking in his own language" (*Acts* 2:1-4,6).

The Black Teachers Workshop and a group of ministers sponsored a conference at the University of Detroit, dealing with the role of black churches in the overall problem of the miseducation of black children. It was an interesting conference and a milestone, in that some three hundred people attended. There were more black teachers present than there were black preachers, although the problem being considered was essentially the role that black churches should play. Not very many black ministers were concerned enough about the education of black children to attend. This is symptomatic of a very important fact in our society. Black churches, for the most part, do not play any significant constructive role in the education of black children. In fact, they play a destructive one.

I was asked to address the conference, and I remarked that it was interesting to have an opportunity to speak to representatives of the two institutions most responsible for the destruction of black children: the church and the school. In American society, the black church and the white school (which our black children must attend) perpetuate, and hand down from generation to generation, the white man's interpretation of the world, of history, of religion, of God, of everything. Schools are an instrument for handing down to black children the white man's conception of the world. You send your little children to school, you clean them up, you feed them, you tell them to study hard, and almost everything they are taught is wrong.

There are some objective skills that they ought to learn in school. They ought to learn how to read because this is a tool for searching out the truth wherever it may be. They ought to learn something about numbers if they are to function in this twentieth century. And the way white folks are getting the world all ready to turn over to computers, they ought to learn what they call the New Math so they can communicate with the computer. Black children must learn in school, so you can't say, "The schools are vicious, therefore I am not going to take my child to school." But you must know that the schools are vicious. They are a destructive influence on our children because they are teaching them white supremacy, for the most part, through the curriculum, the classes, the teachers, the books, the very power symbols, like the preponderance of white teachers and administrators in inner-city schools.

I know that there are a lot of white teachers in inner-city schools who say, "Oh, we love little Negro children. We drive way in from the suburbs to work with them. We would rather be teaching here." Let's say, just for the sake of the discussion, "O.K., you love little black children, you drive clear in from the suburbs to teach them, you are going to do everything possible for them. But still, it would be better if you stayed out in the suburbs, because that little black child you love needs black power symbols, not white."

A black child cannot help wondering, "Why is it that everywhere I look I see nothing but white people running everything? Why is it that my teacher is white, my principal is white?" And when the administrator comes in, he's white. This is the situation that a black child faces.

In the school library, for instance, the books are going to be white supremacy books. Maybe they have put newer pictures of savages in them than they used to have. In the older text books, we used to have bones in our noses. That would be the only black person pictured in the book. Now they've shortened the bone, but essentially the book is still advancing the point of view that the white man has done everything in the world that is important, and that black people have been nothing but hewers of wood and drawers of water. So your children, our children, are being destroyed by the schools.

I had a feeling that the teachers there were overly optimistic about black parents. They seemed to feel that black parents are getting fed up and are going to rise up and change the schools. I am not convinced that black parents are fed up. Because if they were, we could change it all. We could stop the whole thing and make them revamp the entire educational system, if we really wanted it changed. If all black people really felt that the education of black children was important, we would stop sending our children to school until the entire system was changed. We would make the schools over the way we want them. We would demand community control of schools so that we could supervise the education of black children. Do you think they would put us in jail? They don't have enough jails. They would change the schools, because they wouldn't have any alternative. They wouldn't just sit there with seven hundred thousand black folks keeping their children out of school. They would change them. We can change the schools any time we decide that black children are important enough.

Either we don't believe that they are important enough, or we believe something that's even worse: we believe that white folks know best how to educate black children. I know many black parents who really do believe that. When they begin to get black teachers in their schools, they get all upset. I'm talking about black people now. They look around and say, "This school is entirely too black." That's pitiful, isn't it? But it's true. It isn't as true as it was five years ago, but it's still true. And if a school gets "too black," many black parents begin to look for some place to move where they can get their child in some school that isn't quite so black.

The problem of educating black children is essentially ours. You cannot expect white folks to be very much concerned about it. I don't expect them to be. I don't get at all upset when I find out that white teachers are not really trying to teach black children. When they tell me that white folks run a school system, and that in that school system black children have an achievement level that's 3, 4, or 5 grades below the national grade level, I am not surprised. I know how white people operate in every other area of life. Why would they act any different in running a school?

For instance, you know how they treat you on the job. You can know all there is to know about your job, but you are going to stay right on the bottom. You know that they are going to have you training white boys for promotion. When you sell your property, and look for a better house, what do they do? A house is up for sale for fifteen thousand dollars, but when you ask about it, it suddenly costs nineteen thousand. Why would they treat you like that on the job or when you are trying to buy a house, and then get all honest and good when it comes to teaching black children? When your child goes to school, the white teachers and administrators look at him and say, "We just can't teach these people anything." They are not pretending, they believe it.

I am not surprised that white people do not educate our children, but I *am* surprised that it is taking us so long to get concerned enough to do something about it. The white man's actions are normal human actions. If I had charge of education, I would give black children the best, and give white children what was left. I am not concerned about white folks, but I am concerned about black folks, because we are not doing the things which must be done. We are letting a whole lot of things slide that we ought to change, just because we are indifferent, because we are still operating as individuals. We are still our little individualistic selves, taking care of our own business, and letting other black folks take care of their business. But all of us are being destroyed together because we are black. There is nothing individualistic about our destruction.

You say, "It doesn't make too much difference. Our children are not so bad." Don't sit there and say our children are not so bad! Black children right now, out there on the street, will knock you on the head in a minute for fifteen cents. They have been destroyed. Explain it away, say, "Those are just bad kids." Those aren't just bad kids, those are black kids in a white man's civilization who don't feel that anybody is interested in them or concerned about them, and who don't have any sense of identification with anything. They are bad all right. Anyone would be bad under the same circumstances.

Do you know what saved you when you were growing up? You had a dream. Your mother told you, "If you study hard, you can be better than the rest of those niggers." That's what she told you. "Don't you go out there and act like them. You study hard, you wash your face, you stand up and walk proud. You don't have to be like them." And you spent all your time trying not to be like "them." And when you looked around and everyone black was "them," and you were trying not to be like "them," what were you trying to be? You were trying to be like white folks! As asinine, ridiculous, and absurd as it is, that is what saved you. You had some kind of a dream, a fool dream, but a dream. And don't blame your parents for giving you a fool dream because that's all they had. We didn't believe in ourselves. We didn't believe in each other. We hated ourselves, so all we could do was try to escape from ourselves.

Our whole life, everything in our community, was built on escaping from ourselves. We worked at it twenty-four hours a day, and we went to Church on Sunday and tried to shout our way out of our black skins and become white like snow. That was us. But we had something. We were still hanging on to a foolish dream that some day things were going to be different—everything was going to change. "I got a dream. I'm not going to be on the bottom all the time. One of these days, everyone is going to be alike, and when I look in the mirror I won't even know that I am black." We really believed in all that integration foolishness, and it kept us going. It destroyed our minds, but it kept us moving. We hated ourselves, but we worked hard to become like the enemy who destroyed us. Even a nightmare was better than no dream.

Now what does your child have to keep him going? He knows that integration is done, finished, dead. The white man doesn't want us, and we don't want him. But all of our problems remain. Your child knows that everything he has is second class. Upon what basis can he expect a better tomorrow? With which ingredients is he to build a new dream?

Those of us here in the Nation not only reject something but we have the ingredients out of which your child can build a new dream. We not only reject integration and accept voluntary separation, we work to control our own community. We are building something black that we can be proud of. We are not ashamed of being black. We are developing a positive image to take the place of the old distorted dream that is dead. It takes time to build a new dream. You can start hating white folks, and decide that everything that they stand for is vicious, that they are enemies, but that doesn't necessarily put anything in its place. You hate yourself because you haven't gotten over the old identification with white folks yet, and now you hate white folks, too. So you hate everybody!

That is a stage through which we pass. A lot of black people out there hate everybody, including themselves. This is especially true of a lot of our children because they don't have anything to build on. When they suddenly realized that white people are really enemies, they had nothing at all. They looked at the world through new eyes and they saw only hostility. They got this idea just like they got everything else, from T.V. They saw white violence and hatred, the cattle-prods, the firehoses, the police dogs, the mobs, the unmasked hatred of ordinary white people, and suddenly they understood that they were alone. An entire generation of black children was changed and they had no place to turn for security and identification.

Look around in the black community now. What does a black child have to attach himself to? He can go to some Uncle Tom Church, but he will find only the image and power of the enemy. If he picks up a Sunday School quarterly, he will find only white folks all the way through it. He will find stained glass windows and pictures of white people all around the Church. Even the smallest Church will have a picture of a white Jesus up front. There is nothing in an Uncle Tom black Church for an alienated black child. When he rejected white folks, he rejected all of them. He is not going to come to Church and make any exceptions for a little white Jesus. He can only say, "If that's what they are putting down in there, forget it." So he doesn't go to Church. And Uncle Tom Churches are crowded—with old folks.

Alienated black children still go to school because they must. But the Church is a voluntary institution and there is nothing there to encourage a black child to seek it out. What institutions do we have in the community to which a black child can attach himself to find a new black identity, when he has renounced identification with white people? Only the Shrine of the Black Madonna and the emerging Black Nation. When you see him running up and down the street, strong-arming people, grabbing old black ladies, dragging them into alleys, raping them, and stealing fifty cents out of their pocketbooks, you say, "He's horrible." Yes, he's horrible, and that's the way anyone becomes when he no longer has an identity, anyone.

When you don't belong to anything, when you don't have any hope, you are in the process of degenerating into a monster. What else is there? When you don't have any attachment, any identification, you ask yourself, "Who am I?" I don't belong to a people, I'm not a part of this country, I'm not a part of anything. What can I do? The answer is simple and clear and inescapable. "Get by the best I can, take care of myself."

So we are developing a generation of monsters, little vicious individualists concerned only about themselves. You can idealize them, you can say, "They are the vanguard of the revolution." But they are the vanguard of no revolution. They are the vanguard of chaos. They are mad, they are evil, and they are lonesome. They are by themselves, and nobody offers them anything to believe in and to become a part of. This, then, is a basic task of the Black Nation. The only thing that can save black children is a Black Nation that they can come into. Nothing else! Many adults come into the Black Nation because they believe in its program and they believe in the Black Messiah. For a child, it is much more important. For him, it can be the difference between life and death.

I know black mothers who won't let their children join the Nation. A girl sent me the most pitiful letter just last week. She joined Church, the weekly letter came to her home, and her mother said, "What in the world is this? You joined Rev. Cleage's Church? Well you tell him you're not coming there any more. You're not going to get tied up in all that black stuff." Can you picture that mother standing there just as black as she could be, telling her black daughter and the rest of her black children, "Don't go to Rev. Cleage's Church and get tied up with all that black stuff." She made the girl write a letter of resignation. In it, the girl said, "As soon as I'm of age, I will join again." For a black child, this Church is the only place where he can find a sense of identity, and to take a child out could very easily be the destruction of the child. To be out there on the street with nothing to believe in is psychological death for a black child.

We must build institutions that can save our children. We can't wait until we take over the schools. We must use what we have at hand, the Church, the Black Nation. We must do more to save black children. We can't leave them out there hating everybody. They are losing their minds from loneliness. They don't believe in anything, and somebody has got to stop them long enough to tell them that that isn't the way. Don't try to give them some Uncle Tom story, just tell them, "You're black and you don't have to be ashamed of it. There are many things that you can do that are meaningful. You must come into the Black Nation and work and sacrifice, to help us build something for black people." We must do this. They can't do it by themselves. You can't expect them to get together out there on a corner and make a Nation for themselves. We must bring them into it and make them feel a part of it.

The Scripture lesson I quoted at the outset was chosen deliberately because it points out a kind of mystical thing that people tend to get away from. Our text, the beginning of the second chapter of the Acts of the Apostles, deals with the day of Pentecost. Pentecost is a religious holiday. The Jews had it first. It comes fifty days after their Passover, which means it is fifty days after Easter for us. The Jewish religion celebrates the day when Moses received the Ten Commandments on Mount Sinai. For Christians, it commemorates the day when something mysterious happened to a group of people, and that's why it is important for us. "When the Day of Pentecost had come, they were all together in one place. And suddenly a sound came from heaven like the rush of a mighty wind, and it filled all the house where they were sitting. And there appeared to them tongues as of fire, distributed and resting on each one of them. And they were all filled with the Holy Spirit and began to speak in other tongues, as the Spirit gave them utterance. At this sound, the multitudes came together and they were bewildered because each one heard them speaking in his own language."

Now you may say this is just one of those Bible stories, and it is. But the people who lived it are trying to put into words an extraordinary experience which they shared. Many times we have a hard time communicating an experience which we have shared. When they talk about tongues of fire, and the rush of mighty winds, they are trying to put into words something they felt. That is hard to do. Much had happened to the disciples and followers of Jesus after the crucifixion.

First, they were completely disillusioned. Their leadership had failed. Everything they had tried to build had fallen to pieces. They went back to their fishing boats and other occupations, trying to live as they had before they had been persuaded to follow the Black Messiah. But they couldn't, because people can't go back to something that they used to be, when their very mind has changed. When your ideas begin to change, you can't step back and say, "I am going to act as though I never had that thought," because when you think a thought, you are different. They tried to live as they had lived, but they were irresistibly drawn back together. They just sat around and talked, trying to remember the things Jesus had said and the things he taught.

Now these were black people who were oppressed. Their oppression was almost as bad as ours. The white Gentiles, the Romans, were oppressing and exploiting them in every way possible. Jesus had tried to bring them together to give them hope, to build a Black Nation, but he had not succeeded. The only thing he left, according to the Book of Acts, was about one hundred and twenty people who set up a synagogue in Jerusalem. They were still Jews, black Jews. But this little group of one hundred and twenty believed that Jesus was the Black Messiah. In all the other synagogues where Jews were worshiping (and there were synagogues not only in Israel, but in Egypt and all across Africa), Jews were still waiting for the Messiah to come.

Peter was a revolutionary, a Zealot, an extremist, the leader of this synagogue, and they talked and tried to figure out what they ought to do. And at Pentecost, fifty days after Easter, something happened to them. They had been a group of people meeting. No doubt there had been arguments and differences of opinion. You know how it is when you try to figure something out—"I think it ought to be done this way." "No, it will fail if you do it that way." "No, this way is best." "No, it will fail if you do it that way." Personalities always enter into it. "You are just saying that because you want to run it, if it goes that way."

The disciples of Jesus were just ordinary people. We tend to read the Bible as if God were doing the whole thing, but the Bible deals with people just like us. You know how many problems *we* would have to figure out before we could decide what to do? It would have taken us more than fifty days to come to the place where we were together, where we understood and could agree on certain things. But in fifty days they had an experience. This hundred and twenty people who had been meeting together, celebrating the sacrament of Holy Communion, in that they were eating and drinking in fellowship together, suddenly had a strange experience. It seemed as though the room was filled with a mighty wind, and fire was over each head. Suddenly, at Pentecost, they were welded into a group and the Black Nation had power.

The Nation that Jesus had tried to build had suddenly come into being, miraculously, mysteriously, mystically. Suddenly this little group of people who had argued and differed as they tried to understand with only the vague remnants of a faith, were welded together and felt like a people. This was Pentecost. There was no way that they could have predicted the day before that it was going to happen. There was no way someone could have written a book and said, "Do these things step by step, and one day it will happen." And when it happened, they still didn't quite understand what it was. They were changed. They had suddenly come together and they were a group. The Nation Jesus had tried to build had come into being.

You know how the disciples had acted while Jesus was with them, fighting about who was going to be first in the kingdom. But at Pentecost, suddenly they became a people. Turning a group of individuals into a people was the most important thing God did for men, both in the Old Testament and in the New. One hundred and twenty individuals became a people. A new kind of unity had come to them. Remember for a moment the experiences of Israel which led to this climactic moment. They had wandered all over the ancient world, all over Africa. They had intermarried with people from the various countries of Africa. They had endured slavery for four hundred years and finally escaped. They mysteriously, miraculously, crossed the Red Sea. They had wandered in the wilderness for forty years because of their faithlessness. They had fought their way into the Promised Land.

In the Promised Land, they had degenerated into individualism. They exploited each other. They had lost the sense of being a people. Each one was taking care of his own little business, buying and selling his black brothers and sisters into slavery, just as we see some black businessmen today exploiting their own exploited brothers and sisters. Then Jesus appeared, trying to talk to a divided people and bring them back together, but his ministry apparently ended in failure when he was crucified.

All of this was background for the miraculous rebirth of the Black Nation at Pentecost. There is always something mystical about the process by which a people become a group or a Nation. We start out as individuals, and it is very difficult to escape from individualism. We need a Pentecost here and now. We need something miraculous and mysterious to bring us together in a way in which we have not yet been brought together. We are calling area group meetings. Each area group has somehow to go through a Pentecost. You can't just call a meeting, I don't care who your chairman is, and expect it to happen. You call forty families and they sit there and say, "We are going to be a group in the Nation. We are going to work for the Nation, we are going to be missionaries for the Nation, we are going to do projects for the Nation." They are just a group of folks sitting there, looking at one another, and nothing is happening.

Something has to happen to people, and it's not going to happen with you home looking at television. The one hundred and twenty followers of Jesus met with Peter daily. The Bible says, "They were together in one place." They came together day after day. They wanted something to happen, they wanted to become a group, they wanted to become a Nation, they wanted to become a people. They were conscious of the fact that they were surrounded by enemies. They realized that they had to figure out something that they could do. At Pentecost, a hundred and twenty people suddenly had a new conception of themselves and their power. They went out into the street to persuade other people.

On that occasion there were black Jews in Jerusalem, from Egypt and from all the other countries, and they too began to feel a part of this new thing—whatever it was. This is the reverse of the story told in Genesis, of how they were building a tower into heaven, trying to make a name for themselves, and how God confused their tongues and separated them. They couldn't understand each other and they were scattered all over the earth. But here, on the first Pentecost, they came back together. They were able to understand each other, to communicate. They were in the process of becoming a group, putting down individualism, becoming a people, becoming a Nation.

This is important for us to understand because we are in the process of rebuilding the Black Nation. Somehow we, too, must go through this mystical experience. We will know when it happens. It hasn't happened yet. We have a lot of people, we have a lot of things we are trying to do, but we haven't yet had the kind of experience that gives power to a group. Some of you will say, "I don't believe in all that religious stuff." If you don't believe in it, that's just *one* of the things that hasn't happened yet! Because that is one of the basic elements of whatever it is that's going to happen.

You can't explain the universe, you can't explain why you are here, you can't explain where you are going. There are things in the world that you can't explain. You don't have to be ashamed and say that is white folks' mysticism. Mysticism belongs to black people. We had it before white people knew what it was. We must somehow recapture that mystical faith in ourselves and our destiny. We can't hand it down to our children unless we have it. We must have a mystical faith that the future belongs to us and this mystical faith will give us power. All of those alienated black children out in the streets, from the smallest one up to the high school dropout, all need a mystical faith that black people are God's chosen people and that we can do anything that needs to be done, together.

Here in this fellowship we must come to the place where it seems that the room is filled with the rush of a mighty wind and a tongue of fire over every head, and suddenly we are welded into one. Then we can go down from this place with power and change the world. When sometimes it seems hard and you feel that many demands are being made upon you, think of our black children out in the streets, and how much they need what we are trying to put together here. If *we* don't put it together, nobody else will, and our children are going to be destroyed. And if they are destroyed, we will be destroyed with them . . . perhaps by them.

18/What Can We Give Our Youth?

"And the devil took him up, and showed him all the kingdoms of the world in a moment of time, and said to him, 'To you I will give all this authority and their glory; for it has been delivered to me, and I give it to whom I will. If you, then, will worship me, it shall all be yours'" (*Luke* 4:5-7).

What can we give young people that's worth handing down from one generation to the next? If we have anything to hand down, it is the concept and the growing belief in a Black Nation, "a Nation within a Nation." This is one thing we can give our children today which we could not have given them a few short years ago. We couldn't have given it to them because we were not conscious of ourselves as separate and apart. We *were* separate and apart; we lived in the midst of a white nation from which we were, in fact, excluded. We lived in an alien land in which we were abused and mistreated every hour of every day. Yet we did not feel that we were a Black Nation. We identified with the enemy.

It is peculiar now to look back and wonder how we could have had so much hope in the possibility of our becoming integrated into this nation, how we could not have seen ourselves in our separateness, how we could not have longed for the day when this separateness could take on value and meaning for us. It is difficult even today for many people to understand what we mean when we talk about a Black Nation. I heard Brother Milton Henry on TV trying to explain to some white folks about the Nation, but I don't think they understood what he was talking about. They said, "We're alienated, too. We don't believe in this civilization. We don't accept all the things that are being done in the United States. We don't believe in war. We don't believe in racial prejudice." They were trying to say, "We're just as alienated as you black people are." It wasn't true, but they really felt that they were just as alienated as we are. If a white man could just live one day as a black man in America, he could begin to understand what alienation is.

Perhaps the greatest thing that we can give our young people is a place to go out of this white man's decadent society, a Black Nation to which he can give loyalty and devotion. This we are building, and this is the one important thing that we possess. In the Old Testament, we find again and again the sense of commitment to a nation. This is the very heart and soul of the Nation Israel— God's chosen people, set apart from the world, in whom God has a special interest and concern, a people for whom God was willing to break the very laws of the universe.

Let us go back in the Old Testament to Joseph. Hated by his brothers because of his precociousness and his arrogance, Joseph was sold into slavery. As a slave, he was taken into Egypt, and was looked upon with favor by Pharaoh. He rose to become second in power only to Pharaoh himself. When famine struck, Joseph's brothers came to Egypt seeking food. Joseph recognized them, and brought Israel into Egypt that they might share his good fortune and the blessings of Pharaoh. Even though Joseph had been sold into bondage by his brothers, he maintained his sense of identity with the Nation Israel. It was as though God had used the hatred of his brothers to save Israel.

So it went until there came a Pharaoh who knew not Joseph, and then the treatment of the Nation Israel changed. The new Pharaoh was afraid of the children of Israel because they were increasing in number. Pharaoh said, "What if an enemy attacks? What will these 'enemies' in our midst do?" So the Israelites became slaves in Egypt, and were oppressed. They were alienated from Egypt.

Next, we come to the story of Moses. From childhood he had been raised in the palace as the son of Pharaoh's daughter. He knew all of the people in power, yet he realized that he had kinship with the enslaved people of Israel. The story is told that he was walking one day and saw an Egyptian strike a Jew. He turned and killed the Egyptian, because the Jew was his brother, and the Egyptian was his enemy. Here is this inner sense of kinship and Nation. There was not a moment's hesitation. Moses didn't have to think about it, to build philosophical arguments. His brother was being mistreated, and he reacted spontaneously.

This sense of Nation ties the Bible together, both the Old Testament and the Gospels of Jesus. After killing the Egyptian, Moses fled to Midion, the land of black people. There he married a black woman. The Nation Israel was a Black Nation intermingled with all the black peoples of Africa. So there was nothing strange about Moses marrying a black woman. His father-in-law was a priest of Midion, and Moses tended his flocks. In the quietness of the hillside, Moses would think of the condition of his people in bondage back in Egypt, and he wondered what he could do.

In the Bible, the internal anguish and sufferings of men are symbolized by an external act or event. When Moses was in Egypt and struck down the Egyptian, he did it in a moment of emotionalism. There wasn't a whole lot of thinking about the Nation and his responsibility to the other Jews. But as he sat and watched his father-in-law's flocks, he thought of the meaning of the situation in Egypt. He began to realize that there was no possibility of freedom for his people merely because individual Jews might strike individual Egyptians. He had come a long way from the impetuous anger of youth.

Most young people strike out in anger, frustration, indignation, and emotionalism against the things that antagonize and oppress them. Moses had done just this. But as he grew older, it became clearer and clearer to him that if Egypt was to be met in confrontation, if the Jews were to stand against Egypt, then it must be a united people who stood against Egypt. A single Jew could not do it. He could kill one Egyptian or a hundred Egyptians, but the system of oppression would go on. If the children of Israel were to be free, they would have to develop the kind of unity which would make it possible for a united people to stand against the system of oppression.

Then he began to wonder, "How do you unite a people? How do people who have suffered from oppression and bondage come together?" He knew that the people of Israel didn't trust each other. He remembered that the day after he had killed the Egyptian, he was walking on the street and he had seen two Jews arguing with each other. He stopped and said to them, "You shouldn't be arguing, you're brothers." And one of the Jews stepped back and said, "Who made you judge over us?" Knowing that this Jew would soon betray him, Moses fled to Midion. He knew that his people were filled with self-hate and mutual mistrust, as a result of their oppression.

So as he sat and watched his flocks, he developed the idea of building a Nation, a people who would understand and love each other, who would unite and stand together. Gradually the idea came to fill his mind. Then, one day, he was tending the flocks and he saw a bush. The Bible says that the bush suddenly burst into flame, but it was not consumed. He was curious, he stopped and moved closer to watch. A voice spoke out of the burning bush, "Take your shoes from off your feet, for the ground upon which you stand is holy ground." God spoke to him from the burning bush, adding, "I'm sending you back into Egypt to set my people free. I'll give you all the knowledge that is necessary. I'll put words in your mouth; don't worry about what to say." Moses argued. He felt inadequate for the task. But God said, "Tell Israel that God sent you for their deliverance."

This is the key to uniting an oppressed people. The people must have a sense that God has sent their deliverance. You can say, "That sounds like old time religion. That's what the slaves used to say." That's right, that's exactly what the slaves used to say. And if you think back, God delivered them.

So Moses went back into Egypt, and he did all the things that were necessary, with the guidance of God. And eventually, the Jews were delivered from bondage. But every step of the way, the people fought against it. They were afraid and divided. There were Jews who had more than others and were afraid that they might lose their position. And there were those who were just afraid. There were those who believed that the Egyptians were superior because they had superior power. All of these things Moses had to deal with, but eventually he led Israel out of bondage. Even as they escaped, the people argued with Moses because they were still afraid.

"Were there not enough graves in Egypt that you brought us out here in the wilderness to die? Were there not enough graves in Egypt that you brought us here to the Promised Land to fight with these superior people who are more powerful than we are? Were there not enough graves?" Always the people were afraid to do the thing that had to be done. But always Moses was struggling to hold them together, to make a nation out of these fragmented, frightened people.

This is the foundation for the New Testament, this gradual welding together of a people, creating a Nation out of individuals who had been destroyed by oppression. We can remember the words of Isaiah, "The Nation Israel is in danger." Isaiah was a young man. He had lived in the palace as a courtier. Then the king had died, and the Nation was threatened. Everywhere there were selfish individuals trying to take power. Isaiah went into the Temple and suddenly it seemed that the Temple was filled with the rush of a mighty wind. Remember, in the Bible, external events represent what is going on in the minds and hearts of people.

Isaiah was sitting in the Temple wrestling with himself about what he should do, and it seemed that he could hear the voice of God. He knew that the Nation needed committed leaders, yet he hesitated to make that commitment for himself. He knew that the

Nation was to be torn asunder, that selfish interests were fighting for individual power. He heard the voice of God say, "I need a man to lead the Nation. Who will go?" Isaiah replied, "I am unfit; I am unclean." And the Bible says that an angel took a coal from off the altar, touched his lips and said, "Now you're clean." Isaiah stood up and said, "I will go."

Now you can get hung up on the literal descriptions of the Bible, and say, "I never saw an angel, and I don't believe that an angel can touch a man's lips with a hot coal and make him clean." And even as you say that, you can't believe it, you know that that is not what the story is saying. You know that each individual who is going to serve a Nation has to achieve this kind of inner conviction. What you're saying is the same thing that Isaiah said, "I'm afraid to make the commitment that I know I ought to make." It's not the angel that bothers you; it's your own weakness. I have heard young people sit down for hours and pick out description after description in the Bible saying, "Oh, I can't take that, I can't believe that." And they knew all the time they were talking that these descriptions of inner feelings were not what really bothered them about the Bible. The Bible's literary description of an individual's inner turmoil, anyone can understand. You can read a poem and know what the poet's talking about. You don't get hung up on his language. Why, then, does the Bible bother you so?

You have the same decision to make that Moses had to make when he saw the burning bush. You can say, "There are no burning bushes around here." But not too long ago I saw a whole *row* of burning bushes on Twelfth Street, and I heard the voice of God. Only you can decide whether or not you are going to commit your life to a people or whether you are going to turn and walk away. Like Moses, you can say, "These are my people. They are only at the beginning of a long hard fight, but I don't care how long it takes or what sacrifice is demanded. I will fight with them until we all are free."

Young black people today, from coast to coast, must face the same kind of decision that Isaiah had to face. There are no easy days ahead. Isaiah went into the Temple because he knew there were days of testing for the Nation ahead. He knew that there were selfish people everywhere who would use the situation for personal gain. He went into the Temple to see what he should do. Young black people today are doing the same thing. They may not conceive of it as religious in nature when they sit around on college campuses and try to decide "Where is my allegiance? Is my basic loyalty to the Black Nation, or am I going to continue to be a black individualist concerned only about myself?"

It is surprising, the number who are deciding that their allegiance is to the Black Nation. It is even amazing, and we can't explain it any more than we can explain Isaiah. Why didn't all the other young men jam into the Temple to make a decision? On every black college campus and every white campus where there are black students, black young people are making this decision every day. It is an entirely new world for black young people, and they know it better than we do. They are making the decision. Some of them are going to make the wrong decision. You saw the article in *Time* magazine about a young black man who said, "I'm honkie-oriented, and I like big cars and fine clothes." But he *knew,* and that's a long way from a few years ago when everybody was oriented in the wrong direction but nobody would admit it. Now many young people are saying, "I know I want these things—but they are less important to me than my people." This, then, becomes a heritage for our people, a Black Nation to which they can give complete and absolute loyalty.

I went up to the University of Michigan for a big get-together. I've been going up there on and off for years, and black students at the University of Michigan have always been invisible. They walked around one by one. They wouldn't get together because they figured that was segregation. They wouldn't even talk to each other. But last week there were black students everywhere. They were in the halls wearing jackets with Black Power written all over them—right in front of the white folks! They were handing out leaflets to the brothers and sisters in front of the meeting, and when white folks asked for one, they ignored them. You know, that's hard to do because these were the same white kids that they go to class with and live with in the dormitories.

On every college campus Black Caucuses are springing up. You may say that these are excesses. But how wonderful it is that our black students are coming to the place where they feel a part of the Nation, and that what they're going to school for is to learn how to serve the Nation. How wonderful to hear them say, "While we're here, we can't lose touch with our own people. We've got to let them know that we're with them so that when we get out of school, we'll be in a position to serve them. That's why we're here: to learn how to serve our people more fully and more adequately."

What can we give our young people? We can give them a Nation. For many of us that's a difficult thing to do because we've got a whole lot of hills to climb ourselves in our own minds. In our scripture lesson this morning we read about the temptations of Jesus. Jesus was a young man when he went out into the wilderness to think about what he was going to do. That's what you have to do if you're a young person. You have to go apart into some kind of wilderness and think about what you're going to do. You older people must also figure out what you're going to do. If you decide that what is really important is getting ahead yourself, then you're no good to the Black Nation.

We can't worry too much about the Federal government giving us a lot of things like OEO money and public housing. We don't like the rats, but we can get rid of them. We can live in tents if we must, if we are together, if we believe in something. Think back to the Indians living in tents. They weren't less happy than we are just because they did not live in big houses made out of brick. The thing is not what we have, but what we *are*. Our young people must understand that. And every day some of us keep trying to destroy our young people because we try to hand down to them those old individualistic values. Even if you have a little bit of the Nation in you, you are still messing up your children. You say, "I want more for my children than I had myself." The only "more" you can give your children is commitment to the Nation.

You have to decide how important *things* are going to be. You know, the SNCC kids went down South and put a Movement together working for almost nothing. They weren't unhappy because they were doing something they believed in. That's the decision that Jesus had to make. The Devil said, "See all the kingdoms of the world. You just bow down and worship me and I'll give them to you, every one. Don't worry 'bout a thing." He says that to you every day, on your job, everywhere. You might say, "It's a mighty little kingdom that he's asking me to bow down for." But if you bow down to the Devil, you can get ahead, even if it's just a little bit ahead, if that's what you want. You can sell out your brother, and get a little bit ahead. "This has all been given unto me," that's what the Devil said. And he wasn't lying; it has all been given unto him.

Jesus had to decide. He could have said what a lot of us say, "If I get ahead, if I get power and prestige, then people will listen to me, and I can build a Nation." But he would have known that he was lying. You can't bow down to the Devil, and then turn around and liberate your people, because in the process of bowing down you destroy yourself. You can't get in a position to help your people by letting the white man use you. You can't say, "I'm going to let him use me until I get what I want, then I'm going to turn on him!" The first time you let him use you and you don't say anything about it, that's it!

Then the Devil said to Jesus, "Jump off the Temple, don't worry about a thing. Angels will hold you up, and then the people will follow you. They'll see that you're doing spectacular things." We have a lot of that too. We have young people who get wound up and say, "I want freedom for my people right now! I'll do anything for my people. I'm going to blow up . . ." That's foolish talk! Because if they were really going to blow up anything, they wouldn't be running up and down the street, telling us all about it. More important, that's trying to find an easy way to do it without really knowing what you're doing. Like a young man said at the University of Michigan, "We've got to get our thing together." That doesn't mean getting something spectacular together. Any five of you could get together some explosives and blow up something, but that wouldn't free us. There's no spectacular way to build a Nation. It's done bit by bit, person by person, until everybody believes and everybody is a brother. It doesn't consist of jumping off the Temple. It consists of little things like learning to get along with each other. We have got to love each other, even when we're acting a fool. And there'll be many times when we all act a fool because this is all new to us. We're going to make all kinds of mistakes. But we're building a Nation, and that's the only thing that's important to any of us: to build this Black Nation and hand it down to our children. And it will be easier for them, because the idea won't be as new to them as it was to us.

In today's world our young people have a tremendously difficult task. You can look back to the beginning of the struggle, to the stage of the struggle that began with the Supreme Court decision and the bus boycott in Montgomery. Then the building of SNCC, with black students from all over the country coming down South to fight for freedom. They had commitment. They were willing to live on almost nothing and they were willing to risk their lives. Their parents were arguing and urging them, "Please go back to school; you're going to get killed down there in Mississippi." But they went on, day after day after day, and they kept a Movement in existence when those of us up here would never have done it. We never would have built this Movement without these young people, and we have to recognize their contribution to its beginnings and to keeping it together. But we also have to realize that they still have a whole lot to learn.

It is ridiculous for you to just go along and say, "It's the young folks' thing; they've got to do it." This "thing" belongs to all of us. They're making mistakes, and you could help some of them if you weren't too chicken to try. You sit around and look at them like they're something special that you can't even talk to. They don't have to do what you say, but they will listen because they aren't as confident as they would like to pretend. And we have the responsibility, whether they listen or not, of telling them what we think.

One of the most important things we have to do in building this Black Nation is to maintain honest dialogue between young people who are doing most of the work and old people who must finance it and give what help and advice they can give. It's amazing what SNCC has accomplished with a very few people. They started out with Robert Moses as their leader. He went into retirement for a reason which would seem ridiculous to most of us. He said, "I don't want to become just a personality cult, I want this to be a group." And so he just disappeared. That was one of the first leaders that the Movement produced, and one of the greatest. He left on purely philosophical grounds. He left the Movement that had begun to jell around him, left it loose. But they believed. As they said, at that time they were "Freedom high." They didn't want anything to curtail freedom. You don't build a Movement or a Nation with everybody trying to be individually free. That was a mistake. It was a natural mistake because they had been brow-beaten and oppressed so long that their first natural impulse was to build a Nation in which everyone could do as he pleased. It was understandable, but it was wrong. A Nation requires organization and discipline.

Then I remember John Lewis who came in as the next leader of SNCC. I heard him give his first major speech at the University of Michigan before he went to the March in Washington. There wasn't anything very special about his speech, but when he got to Washington, the white folks tried to change it. They said he couldn't say this and he couldn't say that. They made him an important black leader just by trying to change what he was going to say. People who wouldn't have listened to him became incensed because white folks were trying to decide what one of our leaders was going to say. It was a good speech, but not tremendously important, until white folks started trying to mess with it. John Lewis was sincere in a very special way, and he made a significant contribution.

And then came Stokely Carmichael. You know Stokely. He was wonderful all the way. You could see in the changing SNCC leadership, the increasing alienation of our young people from white society. When they were sitting in at Woolworth's, they weren't alienated; they were trying to redeem good white people. They really believed in redemptive suffering. But gradually, the white man alienated them, bit by bit. Only gradually did they come to see the white man as he really is. When Stokely Carmichael was national leader, white folks said, "There can't be anything worse than this." And he was talking about love most of the time, "We've got to love our black brothers and sisters." Stokely wasn't totally alienated; he still had a faint semblance of hope.

And then H. Rap Brown appeared. Stokely had said, "You all think I'm something, you just wait till this man starts talking." And Stokely went abroad to relate the Black Movement to the black world.

This is the process which all of our young people are going through; even young people who don't realize it are sliding down the scale of alienation. More and more of our young people are saying everyday, "I just don't believe that the white man has sense enough to do the things that must be done. I believe that the white man is so brutal that he's going to take the way of genocide, and try to do what Hitler did in Germany."

You older people, if you're going to try to help young people, you have to peg it at some point by making white people do some of the things that must be done. If you run around, echoing the white people, saying that H. Rap Brown is terrible, you are only adding to the process of alienation. You ought to be telling white people, "Yes, I know what H. Rap Brown is talking about. I understand it completely. And his analysis is accurate. He's looking at white people exactly as they have been revealed by history." Tell the white man the truth, "All of us have a whole lot of H. Rap Brown in us." Then maybe he'll do some of the things that H. Rap Brown says must be done.

We are a Black Nation, and if we are going to be destroyed by genocide, we are all going to be destroyed together. Don't think he's going to pick you out and spare you. Whatever happens to us is going to happen to you. Understand the urgency because time is short. Talk right wherever you are. Tell the truth because you don't have time to lie!

What can we give our young people? A Nation, in which we are all together—young and old, rich and poor, learned and unlearned. Let us do all that we can to support our young people in every way possible. Sacrifice, so that as many as possible can go to college. Make the public schools educate our children. Fight for them, and even when they're wrong, love them.

We're building a Black Nation. And no matter what the white man does, it's my faith that we'll be here. We're going to survive because we're God's chosen people. A thousand years from today we'll be here, no matter what he does. We believe in the Nation that we're building—and we find in Christianity a new direction and new truth. A Black Messiah and a Black Madonna. The Bible becomes something new when you understand that it is talking about a black people and a Black Messiah. This faith in our future we give our youth.

Heavenly Father, we thank thee for our young people, for their energy, for their enthusiasm, for their willingness to sacrifice, for their devotion and commitment to the Black Nation. We thank thee for the great ferment which is seething everywhere and is bringing our young people back into the Nation. Make each of us truly a part of the Nation, giving to the Nation those things which we can give, especially leadership in learning to love. Be with us, help us, strengthen us, guide us, so that all that we do may redound to the building of thy Black Nation. Give us a sense of certainty that we do thy will. We thank thee for the gift of thy Son, the Black Messiah, Jesus Christ. Give us his faith, and let us worship here with the sure and certain conviction that we labor with thy power. We cannot fail because we are thy children. These things we ask in his name. Amen.

19/The Promised Land

"Then all the congregation raised a loud
cry; and the people wept that night. And all
the people of Israel murmured against Moses
and Aaron; the whole congregation said to
them, 'Would that we had died in the land
of Egypt! Or would that we had died in the
wilderness! Why does the Lord bring us into
this land, to fall by the sword? Our wives
and our little ones will become a prey; would
it not be better for us to go back to Egypt?' "
(*Numbers* 14:1-3).

Our Scripture lesson is taken from the Book of Numbers. It describes the moment when Israel first reached the Promised Land,
which God had given to them. God had made it possible for them
to escape from bondage in Egypt. Almost against their will they
had escaped. God saved them time after time. And in almost every
crisis they were without faith. Finally the wilderness was behind
them, and they could see the Promised Land. They looked at it,
and they were afraid. Representatives of the twelve tribes went in
to spy out the land. They came back and reported that the land
flowed with milk and honey, but the inhabitants were like giants.
"We were as grasshoppers in their sight, and so we seemed to ourselves." The people were discouraged. Only Joshua and Caleb
wanted to take the land which God had given them. So they stood
at the very gateway to the Promised Land, trying to decide whether
or not to go in. And "all the congregation raised a loud cry and
the people wept."

It is always a hard decision when a people tries to make up its mind to risk the sacrifice involved in fighting its way into the Promised Land. They can think about it for four hundred years, but when the time comes, they aren't sure. "Maybe we had better think a while longer."

We can understand Israel's reluctance. There were personal dangers involved. And so they hesitated and all the congregation raised a loud cry. Any time you hear folks making a whole lot of noise, they are not certain about what they're going to do. And then "the people wept that night," because they had to decide.

One of the most difficult things for any people to do is to make a clear-cut decision. We can talk about it. We can say, "Wouldn't it be nice if . . . ?" Or "Maybe some day . . . maybe our children will." "Too bad our fathers didn't." But when you have to make a decision yourself, you cry out, and you weep all night. The people wept that night, and in the morning they murmured against Moses. That is understandable too, because Moses was their leader.

Moses had brought them out of Egypt, brought them across the wilderness to the Promised Land. Now he was the one who posed the decision for them. He said, "Are we going in?" They cried, they wept, and they murmured against Moses. If you have to make a decision, you look around and you ask yourself, "Who put me in this fix? I was going along pretty good, and now I've got to decide something." Suppose you are getting ready to buy a house. Your wife has been telling you for months, "We ought to own our own home. I'm tired of paying rent." Finally, you go out to look at a house. She drags you out. You sit there, and you try to decide, "Am I going to buy this house?" You don't know whether or not you can afford it. You figure things are liable to get worse. And first thing you know, you're just as mad at your wife as you can be. Not because she has done anything wrong, but because she has posed a question and you are forced to make a decision. It's uncomfortable trying to decide anything, because you know that you can always make the wrong decision, and if you do you will have to suffer the consequences.

So they murmured against Moses because they had to blame someone. The whole congregation said, "Would that we had died in the land of Egypt!" And that is understandable, too. They didn't really mean it. But looking back, it seemed like anything was better than this! It hadn't been all that bad back in Egypt, compared with trying to decide whether or not they were going to risk getting killed. You can understand that, can't you? It's hard. That's what they were talking about. Would that anything had happened so that they wouldn't have to stand here in this spot at this time, and try to decide what they were going to do! Anything! And then they go on, "Why did the Lord bring us into this Land?" Now they are going even beyond Moses. "Our wives and our little ones will become a prey."

That's what people always say. "I have plenty of courage myself, but I have to think about my wife and my children." When you say that, you're just trying to find some excuse for not doing anything! Your wife and children aren't proud of that big coward lying around your house. There's no real truth in your cry, "I would do something if it weren't for my wife and children. Turn me loose, wife and children, turn me loose." The Israelites knew that they had wives and little ones when they left Egypt. All the way across the wilderness, they knew they had wives and little ones. But all of a sudden, it had become a great big concern!

And then comes the thought, "Would it not be better for us to go back to Egypt?" The human mind is a weird thing. You know, every generation says the same thing. Every generation goes so far, and then they begin to hesitate and worry about their wives and their children. "Let's go back into Egypt. We don't have to go forward! Let's stay here." We say, "Let's cement our gains. Let's stabilize our positions. It would be unwise to move forward at this time!" "OK, let's go back into Egypt. Let's go back into slavery." That's what it means. It's better to be a slave than to risk the dangers of being free.

And in many ways, that's true—if you have a slave mentality. It's better because you won't have to make any decisions. You won't have to worry about anything. You'll have your little garbage to eat three times a day. The white man will put some kind of rags on your back. He'll tell you what to do, how long to work, when to quit. He'll tell you how many children to have. You won't have a thing to worry about. So, in a sense, it was better back in Egypt. In a sense, it's always better to be a slave.

You get off from work on Friday night and you're half drunk before the sun goes down. Nothing to worry about. The place can burn down before Monday morning. What do you care? You get back to the job by Tuesday or Wednesday, and ask the man next to you who was with you Friday night, "Did I have a good time last weekend?" He has to tell you what happened, where you went, and what you did! Those are the comforts and conveniences of slavery; nothing to worry about, no decisions, no responsibilities, and no obligations.

If worst comes to worst, get on the welfare, because the white man is going to have to take care of you anyhow. And he's not going to give you too much, whether you're working or on relief. It's only a matter of a few cents difference, and you're a slave either way. I know a lot of people who find it a very comfortable existence. Some of them call me up in the middle of the night. "A white policeman just tried to kill me. He dragged me into an alley and whipped me half to death." I ask, "What did you do?" "Didn't do nothin." "Do you have money enough for a lawyer," I ask. "No." "How much money do you have?" "I ain't got nothing." "Don't you work?" "Yeah, I work every day, but I ain't got nothing."

It used to be like that on the plantation. But if you are going to be a man, if you are going to be free, there are certain obligations that come with it. And these are not easy.

I was talking to a little child who just came into the Nation, and he was very worried because he said that I'm always saying in sermons that we aren't organizing to die but we may have to. And he said, "I'm too young to die." He is really too young, he's only a child. But that's what we all say. We never get so old that we figure we're old enough to die. He's young enough to say it out loud. But all of you sitting out there think the same thing. "I'm too young to die. After a while maybe, but right now I'm too young to die." He was honest and sincere about it; he was asking why, if we fight for our freedom, why may we have to die in the streets? And why keep saying it? The only reason I say it is because it's true. I'm sorry if that upsets little children at night, but it's true. We'll do everything possible to keep you alive because you have to carry on the Nation when we're gone. And everything we are doing is for you. We don't want to give you nightmares, but you can't live like a plantation child because we have seen the Promised Land.

We asked ourselves "Shall we go back to Egypt?" and we said "No," and for all you little children, that makes a difference. Because we are trying to take you into the Promised Land. It would have been easier for you if we had decided to stay out there because then you wouldn't have to worry about fighting in the streets and getting killed. We might lose fighting in the street, but we're going on in, anyway. And so to the little children I say, "I'm sorry that you have to worry about it. But I'm not sorry that we are trying to take you in. And I hope that, as time goes on, you will get to the place where you, too, are glad that we decided to go in."

That's what we hope. Little black children are important to us. We want them to understand. That's why it is beautiful Saturday afternoons to see children coming to the Afro-American history classes. It is important that they find out where Africa is and what it is, and the very simple little things that begin to change their attitude and give them pride in their culture and their past. As black parents, you don't do enough of that at home. You should have seen them coming into class. It wasn't like it is when you visit a public school where they are running around and screaming. They were sitting down and trying to learn something.

We hope that they'll learn enough to feel proud that we didn't go back into Egypt. And when we fall by the way, we hope they'll go on. We hope that they won't stop and say, "My family's gone, my friends are gone. Maybe we ought to turn around and go back into Egypt." We want them to go on and on and on.

That's what you must bring your children to understand. I don't care how little they are, you must be teaching them. Don't just sit around thinking it's beautiful in the Nation (and it is). We come here as desert wanderers seek an oasis, but we cannot forget the world out there. You must prepare your children to struggle in a hostile world which will seek to enslave them or destroy them. Children who find it disturbing must understand that we are trying to fight our way into the Promised Land, trying to take the land that God promised us. And we are trying to get it for them and their children.

I was talking recently on television about the $100,000 that we gave back to the white folks. You know, I never knew that money was so important. We called the press about four o'clock and announced a press conference for five, to explain why we were rejecting the hundred thousand dollars offered by the New Detroit Committee. Normally you call them a day ahead and they are never sure that they can make it. But by five o'clock the lounge was just full; everybody was there. They came to find out if it was really true that black folks were turning down $100,000. And that night they had my picture on TV explaining. Wilma Vaughn asked her little daughter "What is Rev. Cleage saying?" And Sybil said, "He's talking about Black Power." Now Sybil hasn't even started school but she knew that if I was talking about anything I was talking about Black Power. Even if she couldn't understand the words, she understood the message.

It is amazing how important money is. You know, The Federation for Self-Determination was supposed to be a leadership thing with the heads of organizations coming together to work for Self-Determination. We put together a little proposal. It wasn't too much, not too fancy or anything. We were just going to try to coordinate the work of organizations working in the black community by providing them certain essential services which their present budgets will not permit. We submitted the proposal to the

New Detroit Committee which is engaged in "building a new Detroit." They considered it and said that it was a "beautiful proposal." "We'll give you the money to do this because this certainly needs to be done. This is the kind of thing we had in mind; we're glad somebody submitted it." Then some of the black brothers who are ready to go back into Egypt got together and said, "Don't give it to them because they're not going back into Egypt. Give it to us, and we'll use it to lead everybody back into Egypt."

So the New Detroit Committee started thinking about it and concluded that maybe there was something to that. If I had been a white person, I would have thought that, too. "Look, now we got two groups here. This one group, they don't represent anybody, but they say they're going to take this money and lead all black folks back into Egypt. And this other group, we don't know where they're going to lead black people, but we know that it isn't back into Egypt." So they kept trying to decide.

And, you know, when white folks get disturbed and upset and don't know what they're going to do, they go through so many aimless motions. Maybe you think white folks are running the world and never have to worry about anything because when you see them, they're walking along like they know what they're doing. But in reality they are the most confused people in the world. They make more mistakes, talk more double-talk, and take back what they say even faster than we do. They're just walking fast because they don't want you to know how confused they are. If they stopped walking fast, they'd have to sit down and cry, because they've lost all contact with reality.

It was pitiful. All week long they were trying to get this thing worked out so that all of us black folks could march back into Egypt together and everybody would be satisfied. And they figured they had the lever because they had the money. We wanted to organize, we wanted to enter the Promised Land, we knew where we were trying to go. But they had the money. And all down through the years, money has been the answer.

You remember when A. Phillip Randolph was trying to organize the Pullman porters; it was the first time black workers had tried to organize. All the Pullman Company had to do was to send a man around the country and give all the black preachers fifty dollars. Fifty dollars! We were really selling ourselves cheap then. All the white man wanted them to do was to preach against the union. Most of you young people here can't remember when the CIO was trying to organize the automobile industry here in the city of Detroit. The companies bought up everybody. You could hardly hear a voice in the black community saying that unions were good for black people.

The white man has always been able to buy up the black community with money, so he has a lot of faith in its power. Once again, they were calling back and forth, but they knew that they had the ace, because finally the money was going to be the deciding factor. Then Joseph L. Hudson, the head of the New Detroit Committee, came out and announced that he was giving us the money. He was going to give us a hundred thousand dollars, with two or three hundred thousand more on the way, if we acted right. But he was going to put "an overseer" over us to make sure everything was done properly. That was a mighty poor choice of words, but that's what he said. It was to be a black overseer but an overseer, nonetheless. Even in slavery days some of the overseers were black. So the white folks were going to put an overseer over us, and they were going to tell us how we must relate to other black organizations. They were going to give a hundred thousand dollars to us and another hundred thousand to the other group, and they were going to tell us what to do, how to do it, and how to relate to other organizations!

The Federation had a meeting. We were just an ordinary group of black people. Everybody said, "We don't want money like that." And they meant it. We spent an hour discussing the matter and all we talked about was "How do we say it?" There was no argument about rejecting the money. The only disagreement was, do we say it bluntly or do we say it nicely? There wasn't a living soul there who wanted to go back into Egypt! And there were at least two hundred people there. There wasn't any difference of opinion. We all knew that that kind of slavery was over.

Since then I've had at least twenty-five phone calls from out raged white people. It's amazing. They are outraged because we wouldn't take the money. They call up and ask, "What's the matter, why do you hate white people? Isn't that why you didn't take the money?" It's just like that integration thing. When we stopped trying to integrate, white people concluded that we must hate white people. And now they have concluded, "You won't take our money—you must hate us!" Do you know why they're so upset? It's not the money. They could have given five organizations a million dollars apiece. It's not the money. It's just the idea that black people have finally decided that they are really going to be free. That's all it is. That's what disturbs them.

We say we want "Self-Determination." And they say, "Well, that's just a word; that doesn't bother us." But when we say that Self-Determination means that we are going to control things ourselves, then they begin to look worried. We tell them, "Don't try to tell us how to run our community. If you want to help by providing funds, that's good. But don't come by telling us what to do with it. Because that wouldn't be Self-Determination now, would it?" If he's going to give us money and tell us how to spend it, then we're working for him. But he can't understand that. He says, "Yes, I go along with Self-Determination. Now, here's some money, and this is what I want you all to do with it." We say, "Listen, we're talking about Self-Determination!" He says, "Well there's nothing wrong with these natural restrictions, is there?"

The idea that black people are going to be free is a whole new idea for white people. And it's just beginning to seep into their minds that we are serious about it, that when we say Self-Determination, we mean we're going to run the thing ourselves. He doesn't understand that the Promised Land is not any definite place. It's the way you are. Now he may not know it yet, but we're there already. Because we have made up our minds. We have decided. We are in the Promised Land. There isn't any way that he can persuade us to go back into Egypt, because we have made up our minds. And when we decided, that was it.

You know that the white man can't set up any conditions that will make you accept the kind of oppression that you accepted a few years ago. The reality within which he has to function now is a different one. In a way, we are already in the Promised Land. We may have to fight to stay there, and we may all get killed in there. But we're there because we decided not to go back into Egypt. There's nothing he can do; no amount of money can change that. He can raise that hundred thousand to a million, and it doesn't make any difference. If there are strings on it, we don't want it. I tried to explain it to them, but they couldn't understand. I just upset them.

It was a beautiful thing, in many ways. It was worth almost a hundred thousand dollars just to throw it back at them. And good black brothers and sisters from all over the country have been calling just to say thank you. Just glad. That's the feeling of a Black Nation that we have now. People I had never seen called from Chicago to say, "It's beautiful what you all did." I said, "Thank you, brother."

Self-Determination is a wonderful thing. And this too-young-to-die worry that bothers a lot of us, we have got to put out of our minds because we follow a Black Messiah who was willing to die. That's why we have the sacrament of Holy Communion. That's exactly what it means, the wine, the broken bread, the body and blood. Jesus was just thirty when he started his ministry, and almost immediately he was forced to take over leadership of the revolutionary movement which had been headed by John the Baptist. Just thirty, and he hardly lasted for three years before they killed him. That's usually the way they do. You don't expect to fight for freedom too long. But he didn't say, "I'm too young to die."

Following his baptism, he went off in the wilderness, and he thought about it. That's what the temptations were, trying to figure it out. Was he going to stay with this thing? He knew what the problems were. The forty days in the wilderness constituted his preparation of himself for what he had to do. He had to decide, just like we all have to decide. "Am I going to be a man and take the risks that are involved?" He was just thirty. That's usually "too young to die." Let some old man do it. But if you try to figure it out, how old is an old man? About your age? But Jesus was willing to take the risk. And that's why two thousand years later we still have the sacrament of Holy Communion. When we have Holy Communion here in the Black Nation, we recommit ourselves to that kind of dedication. We remember the Black Messiah who was willing to give his life that his black brothers and sisters might be free, who spent his life fighting against white oppression, and who was finally destroyed by the white oppressors who called him "King of the Jews."

We have open communion. Any Christian who commits himself to the freedom struggle, to the Black Revolution, and to the Black Messiah, is invited to share it with us. We need to remind ourselves constantly of who we are, of what we are fighting for. We need to recommit ourselves. You may think, "Oh, I don't need any recommitment." But you do. If you think back, there were times last week when you didn't do what you ought to have done. I don't want you to stand up and tell me about it. You know. There were times when you were either too busy, or you were afraid, or something came between you and the Nation. If you can get through a whole month without any weakness, any flaw, if everything you do is for the enhancement of the Black Nation, for your black brothers and sisters, then you come up here on any first Sunday and say "I don't need to take communion this Sunday because I have been perfect for thirty days." And if God doesn't strike you dead for lying, we'll let it pass.

Holy Communion is a sacrament which we take as people who are together, who are dedicated and committed. We recommit ourselves, that is, we ask forgiveness of each other for the weaknesses which we have displayed during the past month. If you know anything I've done that hurt our cause or hurt any brother or sister, then forgive me for it. I didn't mean it; I was weak. I am rededicating myself, and in the future I will try to be stronger that I may walk in the footsteps of the Black Messiah.

Heavenly Father, we thank thee for this opportunity for being in thy house, feeling ourselves a part of thy Nation. Help us in our commitment to each other. Help and build the growing unity which binds us together, the willingness to sacrifice ourselves in the struggle of which we are a part. Give us a sense of thy presence here and now in our midst as we partake of the sacrament of Holy Communion. Be with us, that this sacrament may bind us together, may recommit each of us to his black brothers and sisters everywhere. Help us, strengthen us, forgive us. These things we ask in the name of the Black Messiah. Amen.

20/Coming In Out of the Wilderness

"And your children shall be shepherds in the wilderness . . . and shall suffer for your faithlessness . . ." (*Numbers* 14:33).

Our text is from the Book of Numbers, the 14th chapter, 33rd verse. We are dealing with a critical period in the life of the Nation Israel. Having fled from captivity in Egypt, the Nation Israel was trying to enter the Promised Land. They believed that the land had been promised to them by God. God had led them out of captivity and bondage in Egypt and across the desert wilderness. Now they had to decide whether or not they dared enter the land which had been given to them by God. Last week we dealt with the text, "Let us go back ino Egypt," and the fear of the people and their reluctance to make the necessary sacrifices.

Our text reads, "And your children shall be shepherds in the wilderness . . . and shall suffer for your faithlessness." This has to do with the relations which each generation has with the generations which have gone before. It is said again in the Bible in different words, "The fathers have eaten sour grapes and the children's teeth are set on edge." We hand down intangible things as well as property to our children. Here in the Book of Numbers, the Nation Israel has demonstrated its fear. They have murmured against God, they have murmured against Moses. They have lacked the courage to do the things necessary to secure their freedom. And so their children are to be punished for their faithlessness. Their children are to be shepherds in the wilderness.

If we were to describe the black man's life in America today, we could certainly call ourselves shepherds in the wilderness, property-less, wandering nomads, going from place to place, dependent upon chance, upon circumstance, without a real place to call home. Shepherds in the wilderness.

To be a shepherd in a rich and fertile land is one thing, but to be a shepherd in a wilderness is quite another. And so God is saying to Israel, "You haven't measured up to the demands that were placed upon you. You were created in the image of God. You were supposed to stand up and be a man. You didn't have the courage, and now you are to be punished. I am sending you back into the wilderness because you lack the courage to do the things necessary to enter into the Promised Land. And your children will suffer for your faithlessness. You could have fought your way in, if you had had the courage. But you were faithless. And so your children will be shepherds in the wilderness." And God told them that everyone over the age of twenty would have to die before Israel could enter into the Promised Land, because they bore the mark of slavery. Fear, self-hatred, and self contempt had been built into them, and they were too old to root it out. So God sent them off to wander in the wilderness for another forty years. Only when those who bore the mark of slavery had died could their children have another chance to fight their way into the Promised Land.

It is easy for us to take this as just a Bible story recounting the faithlessness of Israel, the fears of Israel, the lack of courage of Israel, and God's punishment. But it is not so easy to recognize the faithlessness of black people here in this country for the past four hundred years, and how God could say to us today, in the same way, that our children will be shepherds in the wilderness and will suffer because of our lack of courage. You can ask "When were we ever faithless? We've been oppressed, we've been downtrodden. We've been deprived." And that is true. But the people who accept oppression, who permit themselves to be downtrodden, those people are faithless because God did not make men to be oppressed and to be downtrodden. And many times a man faces the choice between living as a slave and dying as a man. And when we choose to live as slaves, we are faithless and our children will be shepherds in the wilderness.

Sometimes we forget our history. I have a little book which I read from time to time. It is called *One Hundred Years of Lynchings.** Everywhere in America today we hear talk of the necessity for firm government action to end violence in the streets. White lawmakers tell us that it may be necessary to suspend the Constitution to permit police officers to stop and search anybody. Legislators are greatly upset because of crime in the inner cities and the constant danger of riots, and they suggest that mayors be given the power to declare martial law. Combine the right of any mayor to call martial law with the sophisticated weapons that city police are now purchasing, and we have a very dangerous situation which will permit a mayor to call martial law and have police gun down defenseless black citizens with deadly Stoner rifles. White folks say that this is necessary to fight crime in the streets.

I would like to suggest that crime in the streets didn't just start in Watts two years ago. Crime in the streets is not something new in these United States. Crime in the streets is part of the American tradition. It is part of the American way of life. Why, all of a sudden, are people concerned about crime in the street? I give you *One Hundred Years of Lynchings* with the detailed account of 5,000 lynchings in the U.S. Not every lynching is included, certainly, because most lynchings were not even reported. Another black man just disappeared. These were just the ones that were written up in the newspapers. You can see the names in the back of the book, page after page after page.

The names of black men and women who were lynched in the United States—you can hardly read them because the print is so small, but you can read the stories which have been reprinted from newspaper accounts. Crime in the streets all over these United States, year after year, in every community! This is a part of American life. This is our history. This is our tradition. This is

* R. Ginzberg, Lancer Books, Inc., (New York, 1962).

what we have lived with. The book opens with a recent account. Houston, Texas. "Four masked youths hung a Negro man from a tree by his heels last night and carved two series of KKK's into his chest and stomach after beating him with chains, allegedly in reprisal for recent city demonstrations by Negro students at Texas Southern University." And that wasn't so long ago. Well, that was just one. Maybe you think, "Must have been something wrong with him or they wouldn't have done it."

Here's another one way back in 1880. First Negro at West Point knifed by fellow cadets. Fellow cadets. They are getting ready to be officers in our armies. "West Point, New York, April 15, James Webster Smith, the first colored cadet in the history of West Point was recently taken from his bed, gagged, bound and severely beaten, and then his ears were slit. He said that he cannot identify his assailants, and the other cadets claimed that he did it himself." Crime in the streets. November 22, 1895, Texans Lynch Wrong Negro. It didn't make any difference, they went out and got "the right one" and lynched him too. Crime in the streets.

You bear with me just a minute. "Sam Hock Burned at the Stake. Negro who was thought to have murdered Alfred Cranford's wife was burned at the stake one mile and a quarter from Newland, Sunday afternoon, July 23, at 2:30 o'clock. Fully two thousand people surrounded a small sapling to which he was fastened and watched the flames eat away his flesh, saw his body mutilated by knives and witnessed the contortions of his body in his extreme agony." This was a black man. Could have been related to any one of you. Two counties, Campbell and Cowitta, were directly involved in the crime. White people throughout the entire state "waited with impatience for the moment when the Negro would pay the penalty for his sinister deed. Everybody waited for the moment when they were going to lynch him. Such suffering had seldom been witnessed. And through it all the Negro uttered hardly a cry. Those who witnessed the affair saw the Negro meet his death and saw him tortured before the flames with unfeigned satisfaction." Crime in the street.

Two thousand people from two counties came together, and publicly lynched this black man. No masks, no concealments. Crime in the streets. For sickening sights, harrowing details, and blood curdling incidents, the burning of Hock is unsurpassed by any occurrence ever heard of in the history of Georgia. He was never identified as the person who participated in the crime. "Negro Burned Alive in Florida. Second Negro Then Hanged." Crime in the streets. You go through the book and it makes you sick to the stomach. You begin to wonder what kind of people these white people are. You don't know anything about crime in the streets until you go back and read what white folks have done to black people in this country. You have to bear all of this in mind just to keep "crime in the streets" in its proper perspective.

The thing that is amazing to us now is that we permitted it to be done. We were there. We could have defended these black men who were being tortured and lynched. But each one of us was an individual. We were taking care of our precious black skins. There is one story that is enough to make you cry. A white mob was chasing this very young black boy who had nothing to do with a crime. He ran to his father's house. And his father ordered him away. "Go away. I can't help you. If I do, they'll get me too." Can you think of anything more symbolic of individualism? His own son. "Get away from my house. Hide out there in the woods and swamps until the dogs find you. I don't want them to get me, too."

"Your children shall be shepherds in the wilderness and shall suffer for your faithlessness." For more than one hundred years we permitted this kind of thing to happen. That was our faithlessness. We let it happen! They could go into the middle of a black community and take a black man out and lynch him. They would often round up black people from miles around, and make them watch. That was our faithlessness. And that is what God is talking about. Our children shall be shepherds in the wilderness *and shall suffer for our faithlessness.*

Now we look around and ask "How did black folks ever get like this?" Why are we always fighting one another? Why don't we trust each other? Why aren't we organized? Just think back, for more than a hundred years we betrayed each other daily because we were afraid. We let the white man kill and rape our brothers and sisters. It is a wonder that we have enough sanity left in this generation to begin the building of the Black Nation. We have so much to forget. It is a wonder that even today we can say, "Fear is gone."

Some of you say, "If God is just he ought to make it possible for us to go into the Promised Land right away. We have suffered enough." God cannot wipe out our weakness and faithlessness to each other. We must make amends for more than one hundred years. For every moment of cowardice, when our grandfathers hid under their beds while black men died, there has to be a moment of courage before we can dare think about entering a Promised Land. For every moment when our sons came to us and we turned aside because we were afraid, we must now go out to meet them wherever they are. For every moment of cowardice there must be a moment of courage. For every moment of individualism, there must be a moment of togetherness. We can't enter the Promised Land like this. There's too much blood on us. We still carry the mark of slavery. Each time we stood and watched and did nothing, it wasn't just the black man being lynched who died. The manhood and soul of every black man who could have resisted and didn't, died at the same time.

Until we make amends, we are not fit for a Promised Land. Don't ask, "When is the Kingdom coming?" Ask, "What can I do to wipe out one hundred years of self-hatred, cowardice and betrayal? What can I do now in my lifetime to wipe out those years of which I am ashamed, those years in which I was afraid to defend my brothers and sisters? What can I do?" Don't ask, "Is the Promised Land at hand, and do they have the red carpet out for us to march in?" The red carpet is already there. It is the blood of our mothers, our fathers, and our grandfathers.

Our children shall be shepherds in the wilderness and shall suffer for our faithlessness. Our faithlessness has been our individualism, our fear, our self-hatred, the years when we did nothing. One hun-

dred years of lynchings. It is a horrible recital. And remember that
for every case recounted, there must be a hundred or even a thousand whose stories were never told. But we were there.

Shepherds in the wilderness, not ready for the Promised Land.
What do we do as we wander in the wilderness? That is the problem that confronts us today. What do we do today as we wander in
the wilderness to which we have been condemned by our own faithlessness? How do we prepare ourselves and our children to end our
exile? Today our basic task consists of bringing together a Nation,
bringing together black men, women and children with courage,
who believe in themselves and who love each other. This means
that we must conquer individualism. We must realize that our
strength, our power, our hope, everything that we dream of, lies in
our coming together. We will wander in the wilderness until we find
a way to unite as one people.

We must build a program. It is not enough just to come together,
however delightful that may be, or to say "black is beautiful" however wonderful that may be. However warm the feeling may be,
upon the basis of that feeling we must build a program. It is easy to
take the first steps, to begin to understand that you are somebody,
that the white man has been lying to you for four hundred years, to
look back at history and to understand what the black man has
gone through, to rediscover the black man's culture, his glorious
heritage, and to realize that we must unite if we are to change conditions by escaping from our powerlessness. But even then we
don't really know what to do. How do we build "a Nation within a
nation," a Black Nation in the middle of the white man's world?
That is the basic problem which must be solved. How do we build
a Black Nation, with economic power, with political power, and
with control over our educational institutions, and our police department? How do we take that kind of power? That is the problem. And we will wander in the wilderness until we solve it. We
will wander in the wilderness until we learn who we are, how to
unite and rise above individualism, and how to program for
power.

No one is going to do it for us. There is no blueprint in the white man's book to tell black people how to struggle for power. Most of the things that you read in his books are designed to keep you from discovering how to struggle for either power, freedom, or justice. We must do it for ourselves. But we are easily confused. We say unity must be the main thing because we have been separated so long. We know that all these things couldn't have happened to us if we had been together. We look about us and we realize that almost everything that has happened to us couldn't have happened if we had been together. If we were together, we could very easily control the city of Detroit. If we were together, we could own businesses everywhere. We wouldn't be trying to get one little co-op super market open, we would be opening them in every section of the city.

But unity is not enough if that unity must be secured by sacrificing the things we believe. This is going to be one of our big problems. Everybody is going to be demanding unity on any basis. "Why don't we get together?" And white folks are going to use it to embarrass us whenever possible, screaming "Why don't you black folks get together?", until we begin to feel self-conscious about not agreeing with every black halfwit who makes a suggestion. You know how it is everytime you go somewhere now, you get into an argument. I don't care whether you go out to dinner, or on a date, or to a club meeting or a card party, or even on the job. Wherever you go, you find yourself the center of controversy. Perhaps you'd like to suggest that if we could just soften what we're talking a little bit, we could get unity faster. That's a great temptation.

But that lowest-common-denominator kind of unity is not the kind we're looking for. We want to bring all black people together because all black people believe in something together. Until we share a common faith we can't have unity. It's not enough to say "Well, come on in. You don't believe in anything but we'd like to have you anyway just because you're black." We have more than a thousand members in the Shrine of the Black Madonna. We have more than a thousand members who believe in the Nation. Suppose we brought in fifteen hundred more who didn't believe in anything. They'd just look around and say, "That's a booming thing over there. Let's join." And so fifteen hundred more would come in and pretty soon we wouldn't have a Black Nation any more but just a whole mass of black people who don't believe in anything.

True, we would then have twenty-five hundred members, but would we be any stronger? No, we would be weaker. Because then on every issue we would have to deal with individualistic black people who don't believe in anything, who are not committed to anything. At every step we would be held back by people who do not have any idea of the Movement, of what we are trying to do. They could not participate in a Black Revolution which they do not understand. Our strength lies in bringing people into the Nation who understand and believe, and in training and developing ourselves as quickly and as completely as possible. We do not want people who still bear the mark of slavery in the organizations of which we are a part. We are growing in strength because we are together in a sense that black people are not together anywhere else in the world.

Now we are moving into the complex and difficult area of building Black Power through carefully designed programs of struggle and development. If we were not together in understanding and commitment, programming would be impossible. We would have a meeting, we'd start talking about what we're going to do, and we would have a million different ideas. Agreement would be impossible. There would be people arguing "Let's not do anything controversial. Let's not make the white man mad. Let's not get out on a limb. Let's not take any chances." Then we wouldn't be a Black Nation with discipline, program, and leadership anymore. We would be just another black church trying to get by from Sunday to Sunday. We believe in the doctrine of Black Power as a religious concept revealed to us, as God's Chosen People, in the Old Testament and in the teachings of Jesus.

We are trying to build a black unity that stems from a concept of self-determination for black people. We have a basic analysis of the world in which we live. Black people must have black pride. Then they must come together in terms of black unity, and black consciousness, because this is the basis of Black Power. And only Black Power can make possible self-determination because all of life is a power struggle. If you don't believe that, then you are not ready for the Black Nation. You belong out in the wilderness. We can't go into a Promised Land with people who don't accept the doctrine of self-determination—a doctrine which we deduce from the fact that we were created in the image of God.

We also believe in the doctrine of accountability, which reflects the teachings of Jesus regarding the responsibilities of love within the Nation. Every black man, woman, and child must feel that he or she is accountable to the Black Nation. Even in school a child must feel accountable to the Black Nation. If a teacher trying to teach a class is acting a fool (and a whole lot of them are), a black child must feel the same sense of responsibility that you would feel on your job if someone was doing something harmful to the Black Nation. That black child must tell the teacher, "I am sorry but we can't have that in this room."

I am not asking black children to be impertinent. The child must say we can't have that, and when the teacher asks why, the child must be ready to tell the teacher why. "We can't have that in this room for a variety of reasons. First, you are teaching us self-contempt and we are through with that. We do not care to have you giving us symbols of white supremacy and white superiority." He must be able to explain it to the teacher because most teachers do not understand and many of our children do understand. They must be able to defend what they believe in terms of self-determination. And if it becomes necessary, they must be ready to go to the principal and explain "I have a backward teacher who is using the wrong books, saying the wrong things and I don't like it." Then the principal will call the parents. And if you are an old handkerchief-head parent, you will go to school and say, "Johnny, I told you to do what the teacher said. Why are you up here causing trouble?" But if you have any sense and you are in the Nation, you'll go to school and tell the teacher that "What Johnny said is absolutely correct. I support Johnny 100%. Are you going to take care of it here or must we go elsewhere?"

Sometimes we don't think that our children ought to get involved, but they must. That's where they learn. And when your child is talking to other children, your child has to know how to argue just like you argue with old folks. Because if we are going to be a Nation, we must understand what we're doing, and your children must understand. All day long out in the street they are being indoctrinated to accept the American dictum, "a nigger ain't nothing." Your child must be able to refute that position, because we have a lot of black kids who think that that is a smart analysis of the racial situation. And if your child can't answer it, he will believe it.

We have to come to the place where building a Black Nation takes on real meaning in our daily lives, where we know what we stand for, where we can defend it, speak for it, and fight for it if need be. And so, as we go about building the Nation, we must understand the kind of unity we're trying to build. We're trying to educate black people everywhere. Perhaps that is an arrogant thing to say. But that's what we are trying to do. And don't think that because a man has a Ph.D., he doesn't need you to educate him. You can go to a learned meeting where only professional black people are holding forth, and most black high school age young people could educate them because all of their basic assumptions are wrong. The same thing is even more true of educated white people.

We're trying to educate black people and we're trying to bring them into the Black Nation. We're trying to create a black unity that's built on understanding and commitment. I know many black people who understand but are not willing to be committed. Because it's in their self-interest not to be committed. They can make more money not committed than they can committed. Sometimes you wonder how you can argue with a person day after day and always come out where he has lost the argument, only to find him

the next day with the same stupid arguments all built up again. He
has a reason. His problem is not one of logic, but of self-interest.
Look at his total situation. Maybe he's bucking for a promotion.
He has some little thing that is separating him from the unity of
the Black Nation.

You have to teach people so that they will understand, but you
have to realize also that many black people are not ready because
they have commitments on the other side. They're working for the
white man. The man is paying them well. A black man told me recently, "I can't afford to get in things. I live good; I've got all I
want. And the man takes care of me. I can't afford a Black revolution." Then he added, "When you all get the revolution over and
you can afford me, then you come get me." I told him, "Don't
worry, we'll come and get you all right."

Our basic task is bringing black people together and building a
Nation. This church is the hub of the emerging Black Nation. From
it we go out in all directions to educate, to set up action centers, to
do the things that must be done. I know some of you who have
joined during the last few months are impatient to be doing something. You are going through a period of really trying to understand
what the Nation is all about. During the next three months you will
be assigned. We are opening centers all over the city and we are
going to need people working in each center. We can't expect everybody in the black community to come in here on Sunday morning.
So we are planning centers for the East side, the Northwest side,
Southwest Detroit, Inkster, Royal Oak Township and Pontiac. In
each one we will need fifteen to twenty people working. I know that
the transition from listening and talking to working is a difficult
one, and some of you all would much rather say "Amen" than be
assigned to some district to work with people you never have seen
before. But they are our black brothers and sisters and someone
must talk to them. We are going to build one black community, one
Black Nation, all stemming from the hub which is at the Shrine of
the Black Madonna. That's the only way we can come in out of
the wilderness. We are preparing for tomorrow. If we cannot enter

into the Promised Land, we can at least build the institutions that are necessary so that our children can enter in, with courage and knowledge. Our children will not be shepherds in the wilderness because of our faithlessness!

Heavenly Father, we thank thee for strength as we undertake to build a Nation, to educate our people, to build black consciousness, black pride, black unity, and Black Power, that we may obtain self-determination. We thank thee and we understand that these tasks which we undertake for ourselves are thy will. We do these things in thy name, and in the name of thy Son, the Black Messiah, Jesus. Help us and bind us together. Give us the commitment necessary to do the things which must be done. All this we ask in his name. Amen.

Best Selections/AWP Series of Books

OPERATION TIMBER: Pages From the Savimbi Dossier
edited with an introduction by William Minter
ISBN: 0-86543-103-5   Cloth $19.95
      0-86543-104-3   Paper $ 6.95

AFROCENTRICITY *by Molefi Kete Asante*
ISBN: 0-86543-067-5   Paper $9.95

PROPHETIC FRAGMENTS *by Cornel West*
ISBN: 0-86543-085-3   Cloth $17.95

**THE TIES THAT BIND:African-American Consciousness of
Africa** *by Bernard Magubane*
ISBN: 0-86543-036-5   Cloth $32.00
      0-86543-037-3   Paper $ 9.95

WHITHER SOUTH AFRICA? *edited by Bernard Magubane
& Ibbo Mandaza*
ISBN: 0-86543-048-9   Cloth $29.95
      0-86543-049-7   Paper $ 9.95

**FRANCOPHONE AFRICAN FICTION: Reading a Literary
Tradition** *by Jonathan Ngate*
ISBN: 0-86543-087-X   Cloth $32.00
      0-86543-088-8   Paper $ 9.95

**FULCRUMS OF CHANGE: Origins of Racism in the Americas
and other essays** *by Jan Carew*
ISBN: 0-86543-032-2   Cloth $29.95
      0-86543-033-0   Paper $ 9.95

**CONSCIENCE ON TRIAL/WHY I WAS DETAINED: Notes
of a Political Prisoner in Kenya** *by Koigi wa Wamwere*
ISBN: 0-86543-063-2   Cloth $25.95
      0-86543-064-0   Paper $8.95

ENDGAME IN SOUTH AFRICA? *by Robin Cohen*
ISBN: 0-86543-090-X   Cloth $24.95
      0-86543-091-8   Paper $ 7.95

**DUMBA NENGUE: RUN FOR YOUR LIFE/Peasant Tales of
Tragedy in Mozambique** *by Lina Magaia*
ISBN: 0-86543-073-X Cloth $14.95
   0-86543-074-8 Paper $ 6.95

UNDER A SOPRANO SKY *by Sonia Sanchez*
ISBN: 0-86543-052-7 Cloth $16.95
   0-86543-053-5 Paper $ 6.95

**AID & DEVELOPMENT IN SOUTHERN AFRICA:
Evaluating a Participatory Learning Process** *edited by Denny
Kalyalya, Khethiwe Mhlanga, Ann Seidman, Joseph Semboja*
ISBN: 0-86543-046-2 Cloth $25.95
   0-86543-047-0 Paper $7.95

**BLACK AFRICA: The Economic and Cultural Basis for a
Federated State** *by Cheikh Anta Diop*
ISBN: 0-86543-058-6 Paper $7.95

PRECOLONIAL BLACK AFRICA *by Cheikh Anta Diop*
ISBN: 0-86543-070-5 Paper $8.95

MARCUS GARVEY: Anti-Colonial Champion *by Rupert Lewis*
ISBN: 0-86543-061-6 Cloth $29.95
   0-86543-062-4 Paper $11.95

**THE COLONIAL LEGACY IN CARIBBEAN
LITERATURE** *by Amon Saba Saakana*
ISBN: 0-86543-059-4 Cloth $24.95
   0-86543-060-8 Paper $ 7.95

WOMEN IN AFRICAN LITERATURE TODAY *edited by
Eldred Durosimi Jones, Eustace Palmer, Marjorie Jones*
ISBN: 0-86543-056-X Cloth $29.95
   0-86543-057-8 Paper $ 8.95

IF THIS IS TREASON, I AM GUILTY *by Allan A. Boesak*
ISBN: 0-86543-055-1 Paper $7.95

**ON TRANSFORMING AFRICA: Discourse with Africa's
Leaders** *by Kofi Buenor Hadjor*
ISBN: 0-86543-044-6 Cloth $25.95
   0-86543-045-4 Paper $ 7.95

RASTA AND RESISTANCE *by Horace Campbell*
ISBN: 0-86543-034-9 Cloth $32.95
   0-86543-035-7 Paper $10.95

HAMMERING SWORDS INTO PLOUGHSHARES: Essays in Honor of Archbishop Mpilo Desmond Tutu *edited by Buti Tlhagale & Itumeleng Mosala*
ISBN: 0-86543-054-3   Paper $12.95

SOWETO: The Fruit of Fear *by Peter Magubane*
ISBN: 0-86543-041-1   Cloth $29.95
　　　 0-86543-040-3   Paper $14.95

THE SOUTH AFRICAN DISEASE: Apartheid Health and Health Services *by Cedric de Beer*
ISBN: 0-86543-038-1   Cloth $19.95
　　　 0-86543-039-X   Paper $ 7.95

STRANGERS IN THEIR OWN COUNTRY: A Curriculum Guide on South Africa *by William Bigelow*
ISBN: 0-86543-010-1   Paper $12.95

BARREL OF A PEN: Resistance to Repression in Neo-Colonial Kenya *by Ngugi wa Thiong'o*
ISBN: 0-86543-001-2   Cloth $15.95
　　　 0-86543-002-0   Paper $ 6.95

AFRICA AND THE MODERN WORLD
by Immanuel Wallerstein
ISBN: 0-86543-021-7   Cloth $32.00
　　　 0-86543-022-5   Paper $10.95

NGAMBIKA: Studies of Women in African Literature *edited by Carole Boyce Davies & Anne Adams Graves*
ISBN: 0-86543-017-9   Cloth $35.00
　　　 0-86543-018-7   Paper $11.95

MARXISM AND AFRICAN LITERATURE *edited by Georg M. Gugelberger*
ISBN: 0-86543-030-6   Cloth $29.95
　　　 0-86543-031-4   Paper $ 9.95

THE ROOTS OF CRISIS IN SOUTHERN AFRICA
by Ann Seidman
ISBN: 0-86543-025-X   Cloth $19.95
　　　 0-86543-026-8   Paper $ 8.95

ROBBEN ISLAND HELL-HOLE: Reminiscences of a Political Prisoner in South Africa *by Moses Dlamini*
ISBN: 0-86543-008-X   Cloth $25.95
　　　 0-86543-009-8   Paper $ 8.95

THE CRISIS IN ZAIRE: Myths and Realities *edited by*
Nzongola-Ntalaja
ISBN: 0-86543-023-3   Cloth $32.00
   0-86543-024-1   Paper $11.95

**UGANDA: AN HISTORICAL ACCIDENT? Class, Nation,
State Formation** *by Ramkrishna Mukherjee*
ISBN: 0-86543-015-2   Cloth $35.00
   0-86543-016-0   Paper $14.95

**AFRICAN REFUGEES: Reflections on the African Refugee
Problem** *by Gaim Kibreab*
ISBN: 0-86543-006-3   Cloth $25.00
   0-86543-007-1   Paper $ 7.95

BEIRUT: Frontline Story *Selim Nassib with Caroline Tisdall*
ISBN: 0-86543-000-4   Paper $6.95

AGRIBUSINESS IN AFRICA *by Barbara Dinham
& Colin Hines*
ISBN: 0-86543-028-4   Cloth $29.95
   0-86543-029-2   Paper $ 9.95

IMPERIALISM AND FASCISM IN UGANDA
by Mahmood Mamdani
ISBN: 0-86543-003-9   Cloth $15.95
   0-86543-004-7   Paper $ 6.95

**CHALLENGING RURAL POVERTY: Experiences in
Institution-Building and Popular Participation for Rural
Development in Eastern Africa** *edited by Fassil G. Kiros*
ISBN: 0-86543-019-5   Cloth $29.95
   0-86543-020-9   Paper $ 9.95

**To order by mail send $1.50 for the first book and 50¢ for each
additional title for postage.**

Africa World Press, Inc.

P.O. Box 1892
Trenton, New Jersey 08607
(609) 695-3766

African Diaspora Research Project
Urban Affairs Programs
Michigan State University
East Lansing, MI 48824 -- USA